EMOTION

Other Books by Ashish Dalela:

The Science of God
Time and Consciousness
Conceiving the Inconceivable
The Balanced Organization
The Yellow Pill
Cosmic Theogony
Mystic Universe
Moral Materialism
Signs of Life
Uncommon Wisdom
Gödel's Mistake
Quantum Meaning
Sāṅkhya and Science
Is the Apple Really Red?
Six Causes

EMOTION

A Soul-Based Theory of Its Origins and Mechanisms

Ashish Dalela

Emotion—A Soul-Based Theory of Its Origins and Mechanisms
by Ashish Dalela
www.shabda.co

Published by Shabda Press
www.press.shabda.co
ISBN 978-93-85384-09-7
v1.5(04/2021)

SHABDA
PRESS

Dedicated to His Divine Grace A. C. Bhaktivedānta Swami Prabhupāda. His teachings on Bhakti or emotional love of God as the only way for permanent happiness, contrast the de-emotionalized and depersonalized influences of modern materialism. In a world haunted by emotional disturbances and illnesses, frustration and anger, true salvation lies in a scientific understanding of emotion, its true origins, its rejuvenation and gratification.

Contents

List of Figures

List of Tables

Preface

Emotion. That dim and obfuscated realm we are all shy to talk about. That which hides in plain sight. The mechanism—of how reason can control emotion, and why often emotion rules over reason—we don't understand. The reality lurking in the recesses of our minds, but whose existence we are afraid to acknowledge, to avoid showing "weakness". It makes us angry or lusty, greedy or fearful. It is the most important basis of our health—mental and physical—and yet so little is understood about how emotional disturbances affect our body. Art, music, literature, sport, and humor would be impossible without emotion. There would be no love without emotion. We would not talk about happiness or sadness, and without these there would be no guiding force in life. How systematically have we ignored such a prominent and obvious aspect of our life? Pause and think about that for a moment. Have we been too busy looking for happiness to even ask what exactly happiness is? Of course, we know happiness, claims the molecular biologist: it is chemical reactions caused by serotonin, dopamine, and norepinephrine. But questions about the relation between molecules and emotion remain, e.g., are these molecules themselves emotions or accompaniments of emotions?

If happiness and sadness are molecules, why do we prefer happiness over sadness? What is so profound about chemistry and physics that makes some molecules desirable and others undesirable? In fact, how can some molecule become desires, anger, pride, and feelings when others are just physical states? Why would some molecule be an object, and another molecule be the *desire* or *hatred* of that object? How can a molecule be a disposition towards another molecule? What brings intentionality in molecules?

The questions surrounding emotion are very difficult. Nevertheless, given that the quest for happiness is the only quest in all forms of life, they are also the most important questions. This book hopes to shed some light on them. It covers issues ranging from philosophical and moral questions of happiness to the physical and chemical bases of feeling, desire, and pleasure. In the middle of these extremes is the question of the interaction between thought and emotion. The scope is vast, and to attack a wide-ranging problem, we need to anchor ourselves in some indispensable concepts.

I will anchor this book in the Vedic notion of the soul[1] as comprised of three aspects—called *sat* or awareness, *chit* or concepts, and *ananda* or feeling. The idea is as follows: we first connect to parts of the world through awareness, then we gain a conceptual and functional knowledge of the chosen parts, which then leads to feelings. Conversely, we have innate feelings such as desires, which lead to conceptual imagination and functional planning, which connect us to worldly objects in new ways. There is, hence, an outside-in path from worldly connection to cognitive understanding to feelings such as happiness. There is also an inside-out path from the desire for happiness which is then converted into specific ideas and plans, which are then implemented through a worldly interaction. Feelings follow the worldly interaction on the outside-in path, while feelings cause imagination and planning resulting in world changes on the inside-out path. Describing emotion on only one of the paths—outside-in or inside-out—is a prevalent folly in many modern theories of emotion. A complete theory must incorporate both.

Emotions are both causes and effects. They are the cause on the inside-out path, and they are the effect on the outside-in path. This dual role combines to create a loop in which the external world creates emotions in us, which then become the agents of new decisions by which changes are effected. Life is lived in the circular causality from outside to inside to outside.

The Vedic model of the soul is not just a description of a transcendent non-material entity, as it is treated in most religions—e.g. Christianity— where the soul and matter are fundamentally different. In the Vedic model, both soul and matter have the same three capabilities although they are expressed in different ways. The soul has the capacity for relationships, concepts, and happiness, and matter is the possibility of relationship, concept, and feeling. In an experience, the capacity for relation, emotion, and cognition combines with the possibilities of the same. The study of the soul is distinct from matter as subject and object, but, beyond this distinction, there is similarity in the nature of the soul and matter. For that reason, an understanding of the soul can be employed in the description of the nature of matter.

Preface

The awareness of the soul comprises a relationship between a knower and a known, and while matter doesn't have the capacity for awareness, it incorporates relationships when two or more specific objects are subject to an interaction. The relationship is objective, but the awareness is subjective. Similarly, the soul has the capacity to know concepts and act, and the world is described materially as concepts and actions. Finally, the soul has the capacity to enjoy and feel, but pleasures and feelings are themselves material.

Thus, the abilities of the soul to form a relationship, know the world conceptually in a relation, act in those relationships, and enjoy because of that knowledge and action are expressed or "reflected" in matter as relationships, concepts, and emotions. In our present context, the emotions we call love, desire, happiness, anger, etc. are material. However, they exist as reflections of the native ability in the soul to feel and enjoy. The soul and matter are mirror images of each other: the world exists for the soul's needs.

Emotion arises because there is *purpose*. While we form relationships and obtain a cognitive understanding of the world, and act on that cognition, there is no reason why we should do so. Relationships and concepts are facts, but our acquaintance with these facts hinges upon a purpose. Why do we want to know the world and interact with it? The answer is that we desire to enjoy, be happy and fulfilled, and knowledge through relationships serves that purpose. The origin of our experience lies in our desires, and by desire, I mean the quest for happiness. The basic desire—happiness—never changes, although there are varieties of other desires which manifest from the basic desire. Emotion is identical to desire and its various modifications.

Once a desire has been established, its fulfillment leads to happiness, pride, and greed, while its frustration leads to anger, depression, and frustration. All emotions stem from the original desire. The study of emotion, therefore, is identical to the study of desire, and the consequences of its fulfillment or frustration. The feelings of frustration and anger are offshoots from a tree's root, just as happiness and greed are possible branches emanating from the tree's root. This is because we become angry or greedy only in relation to an original desire. There is hence a hierarchy of emotions, and when one branch is cut off, the root remains to spawn off new desires. The spiritual component of this viewpoint is that the root of desires is eternal and can never be cut off: the root of desire is the soul's tendency for pleasure[2] or *ananda*. However, there are different kinds of desires, some of which are natural, and others are unnatural, some are achievable, and others are not. While we study the

iii

mechanism of desire, it is also important to note its origin, because only in relation to that origin can we identify which desires are natural.

The world can be described in terms of three categories—relationships, concepts, and desires. Of these three, modern science only recognizes *concepts*: the world is concepts such as particles and waves, which possess conceptual properties such as position and mass, and which are governed by conceptual laws and mathematical formulae. Relationships—and by that, I mean the *choice* of which two objects interact with each other—were never part of classical physics because the natural forces caused *all* objects to interact with each other simultaneously. The scenario has now changed in atomic theory where even forces are quantized as particles, which means that only a pair of objects interact at any time, but quantum theory cannot predict which objects will interact. In effect, we cannot say which two objects in the universe will exist in a relationship at any given time. We have progressed from eliminating relationships to not being able to explain relationships.

The awareness of the soul (by which it becomes aware of selected parts of the world at any time) is expressed in matter as a selective encounter between our bodies and other bodies, and that selection has a counterpart in material causality by which an object interacts with select objects at any time. Science foregoes such relationships—and thus awareness and choice—when it postulates that all objects interact with one another simultaneously. Awareness or consciousness becomes a difficult concept because the natural forces of causality are defined to act *universally* rather than *contextually*. If this contextuality were incorporated in matter, consciousness would have scientific implications. Specifically, we could talk about choice deciding which specific objects will interact, whereupon the mechanisms and outcomes of that interaction would be completely natural and lawful. What we call "soul" and "matter" would then not be contradictory ideas. They would be complementary. Quite specifically, the tendency in the soul to become aware would have a natural counterpart in the existence of material relationships. Similarly, the ability in the soul to know the world would have a natural counterpart in matter as the existence of concepts. Finally, the ability in the soul to enjoy and be happy would have a material counterpart as purposes in nature.

This background about the nature of the soul and how it complements matter is the preliminary step to understanding emotions. Once this complementarity is recognized, it becomes easier to see how there can be material feelings—such as lust, anger, greed, or pride—as the counterpart of the soul's desires for happiness in matter. The soul accepts or rejects the knowledge produced from an interaction, and that acceptance or rejection is the feeling of happiness or distress. Guilt and unhappiness manifest as feelings when the knowledge is rejected, while happiness is produced when the knowledge is accepted. Since this guilt or happiness is overlaid on other feelings such as lust, greed, or anger, there are different grades or levels of feelings.

Guilt and happiness are deeper emotions, relative to lust, anger, or greed, which are even deeper than sensual pleasure. The soul experiences the entire hierarchy from sensual pleasure and pain to mental lust and anger to moral guilt or happiness. The hierarchy of feelings is an essential fact and some of these feelings are deep while others are shallow. Unless we recognize that emotions themselves have a hierarchy, we would be hard-pressed to explain how they are *prioritized*, how a person is often overwhelmed by one emotion, and how one can emerge from unwanted emotional depredation.

I will describe how the hierarchy of feelings can be organized as a *tree*—the deepest emotions being the root, the shallower feelings being the branches, and the sensual pleasures being the leaves and fruits of the tree. The tree constitutes a description of the emotional world, but it is incomplete.

The emotional tree also interacts with two other trees—cognitive and relational. Our concepts and relations are also hierarchical. There are deep or abstract concepts while there are shallow or contingent concepts. We can perceive the physical properties by our senses, the object concepts and beliefs by the mind and intellect, while intention and morals are perceived by even deeper faculties like the ego and the moral sense. Similarly, there are superficial relationships of the senses, somewhat deeper relationships of the mind and intellect, and even deeper relationships which cause the interaction (and the harmony or clash) of intentions and morals. Emotion thus is not divorced from cognition or relationships, and the three always co-exist. Sometimes the emotions are caused by cognition produced from relationships. At other times relationships and cognition are produced due to emotion. Therefore, to understand emotion we have to understand both cognition and relationships, and the voyage is, therefore, not limited to emotion alone.

The human body materially comprises emotions. The emotions are not just in the mind, but even in the body, and emotional disturbance, therefore, leads to bodily changes. However, the matter which causes emotions is fundamentally different from that which constitutes things and thoughts.

The parts of the material body—e.g. hands and legs, their subdivisions and so forth—are what we commonly call "matter" in modern times; it is the cognitive component of the soul reflected in matter. These parts contact other objects, putting each part into a *role* or relation to the other parts. For example, the legs are used to run, and the hands are used to hold. The part and the role played by the part are distinct because a part can play different roles, and the same role can be performed by other parts. Similarly, each function has an associated purpose—that leads to feeling. The same purpose can be achieved by different parts and functions, and the same part and function can be the instrument of different purposes. Therefore, purposes are different from parts and functions. The matter that we call emotions exists in the body as the *purpose* of the body and its parts—we live to enjoy via the body.

Modern science models the parts of the body as *objects* and the interactions between these parts as mediated through *forces*. But there is nothing in modern science that describes *purposes*. The reason is that the purpose exists in the *future* and guides changes towards that future. How can we perceive something that exists in the future? The answer is that even the things that exist in the future are material, but they are designated as *purposes*. For example, I might desire tasty food; the food is material; it exists sensually in some cases, and conceptually in others. The desire for that food is the purpose, but it is separate from the object of the desire—food in this case.

If we keep studying the material object—e.g. food—and neglect the desire (which exists in the observer), then our scientific ontology is limited to objects and forces. The ontology must be broadened to include purposes when we induct observers, and this ontology will be useful in explaining the behavior of living beings with emotions, not required in the explanation of non-living things devoid of emotions. In other words, non-living things can be modeled without purposes and emotions, but living things necessitate purposes and emotions. There is, hence, an additional kind of matter in the living body, absent in non-living things. That variety of matter has to be modeled differently as goals and purposes rather than as objects or forces.

This problem requires the use of two kinds of forces: one which causes objects to interact and creates effects and consequences (which science aims to study at present) and the other that causes the objects to interact without effects and consequences, although it pushes them towards or away from an interaction that has effects and consequences. This kind of distinction doesn't exist in modern science because we always think of forces as those that not only create effects and consequences but also that there is no *choice* such that the current interaction cannot be changed towards a future goal. Thus, emerges the classical conflict between free will and determinism because we are not allowed to have goals that can change the current material interactions. To understand emotions, we must modify our picture of causality in which our emotional stance—e.g. a desire—modifies current interactions.

In the new causal picture, physical interaction is not deterministic. Rather, the interacting objects are *abilities* brought in contact through *opportunities*, and the combination of ability and opportunity can be converted into a reality provided there is a *choice* to use the abilities and the opportunities. Such choice appears as the purpose by which we choose to combine abilities and opportunities. For example, the body has the ability to eat and the opportunity to eat is presented by the environment, but there is also a choice by which the ability is combined with the opportunity. Abilities and opportunities are therefore two kinds of possibilities converted into a reality by choice. This description of natural causality can also be scientific, but it describes material objects as abilities, the relationship between such objects as opportunities, and the conversion of this opportunity into reality as the purpose.

There is causality in each of the three—abilities, opportunities, and purposes. We could have a purpose but no ability and opportunity; we could have the opportunity but no ability and purpose; and we could have the abilities but no opportunities and purpose. In such cases, each of the three ingredients remains sterile. It is only their combination that creates experiences and all three must be combined to produce conscious experiences.

The significance of this causal model is that material objects must be described as *abilities* rather than things. The ability is objective, but it is not an object. Rather, the ability must be converted into an object. Similarly, the interaction between different abilities is not predetermined. Rather, different abilities are brought into interaction producing what we call *opportunities*. Again, the fact that there is an opportunity doesn't entail a reality. Rather, the opportunity must be converted into a reality through a choice that exploits the opportunity through the ability. The choice is mediated by our purposes—which we call our desires, feelings, emotions, pleasure, enjoyment, etc.

The understanding of emotion is a part of a larger problem of explaining our experience of the world. The explanation must account for the role emotions play in decision making, how these decisions produce outcomes, and how those outcomes change the course of our lives. This is possible when emotion is given a central role in the scientific causal model, unlike the simplistic object-and-force view of causation prevalent in modern science. However, the revision of the causal model also involves shifts in the very notion of objects and forces as noted above. We must now think of objects not as fixed things but rather as abilities waiting to be converted into reality. We must also think of forces not deterministically but as opportunities available to abilities. And we must think of emotions as something that mediates the conversion of abilities and opportunities into reality. In short, the revision needs an overhaul of our material ideology regarding matter and causation.

We cannot understand emotion within the current physical theories of motion because emotion has no causal role in changing that motion. In that sense, no matter how far we seem to progress in correlating emotion to molecules, the *human* causal explanation of behavior as being caused by emotion and choice would remain incompatible with the *physical* explanation of behavior as force. The presence of emotion causes us to act, and, similarly, emotional changes cause bodily changes. In that sense, there is *empirical* evidence for emotion. But emotion is not identical to that empirical evidence.

Just as matter and force are fundamental categories in science today, there is a need for purpose in the scientific ontology. Purpose, however, exists only in living beings and in that sense, biology is not reducible to matter and force. The body involves matter and force, but they are sterile without a purpose. As the purposefulness is modified, the body also changes. Therefore, matter and force are tools in the hand of purpose. We can study the tools, but we cannot explain the outcome unless we also study the purpose.

The fact that we don't see purpose in matter should not surprise us because we don't see force either. Nobody can perceive, for example, electromagnetic or gravitational forces, although we perceive the *effects* of forces. These forces are modeled as "fields" and science does not measure the field but only its effects. Similarly, purpose is a field which cannot be perceived although its effects can be perceived. Purpose, therefore, need not be any more esoteric than force. However, it does require a fundamental shift from modern evolutionist pictures of nature in which living forms evolve without any purpose to one in which life adapts and evolves due to a purpose.

The purpose is also material, just as matter and force. My aim in this book is not to reduce or supervene purpose on matter and force. The aim is also not to advocate purposefulness in contradiction with the ideas of matter and force. The aim is to show that matter and force together are *incomplete* without purpose and an additional category is needed to explain behavior. What modern science calls "force" is called *karma* in Vedic philosophy. It brings us in contact with parts of the world thus creating opportunities for interaction. Conversely, what we call purpose is called *guna* in Vedic philosophy. It creates our disposition toward the world which manifests as emotions like desire, hatred, guilt, fear, apprehension, happiness, etc. *Guna* and *karma* are the two "forces" that drag the soul through the succession of bodily changes. The body is what we call "matter" but the soul's connection to this body is the "forces" of *guna* and *karma*. Modern science studies these "forces" in a very limited manner—limited to physical interactions with other objects—neglecting the internal forces that create purpose in our lives.

The ideology inherent in the Vedic notion of the soul can be brought to bear upon the questions of scientific causation, and how emotion plays a role in this causation. The scientific counterpart of this issue is the need to postulate a new kind of "field" that remains invisible quite like the modern force fields (such as gravitation or electromagnetism) but is *perceived* only through its effects. This is commensurate with the fact that *guna* and *karma* are the hidden causes of our life changes—we cannot perceive them, but we can perceive their effects. In order to explain the effects, we must postulate the hidden causes, and, in that sense, the issue of emotion is not confined to how you and I feel about our lives, but to a much broader scientific question.

I cast the question of emotion upon the philosophical backdrop of the above concepts—*sat, chit, ananda, guna*, and *karma*—not because it would be impossible to have this discussion without these words. Rather, by assimilating these words we open the doors to an ancient way of thinking, which, if understood, can shape science in new ways. Thus, I intersperse the English words with those mentioned above, while providing their English equivalents along with intuitions that can aid their assimilation into our thinking.

The key idea—if there were only one idea to take away from the book—is that we are suspended in two "force fields". We cannot perceive them as objects, but we can *experience* them as emotion and relationship. Relationship is not a material object, because it is *in between* two or more objects. Similarly, emotion is not a material object because it is a disposition *toward* that object. The surprise—if there is one—is that our experience is not limited to object perception. We also perceive things that are "in between" objects and "towards" those objects, and yet not those objects. We don't have to facilely assume that if something is not a material object it must simply not exist, because we indeed experience relations and purposes *empirically*.

We just don't have, at present, a scientific vocabulary to describe what lies "in between" and "towards" something because science has focused its attention upon objects, excluding the other constituents of causality which can be experienced. My ask of the reader is, therefore, to open their minds to alternative forms of empiricism, abounding in our experience, but absconding from the scientific vocabulary of modern time. If the mind has been thus opened, the rest of the journey promises to be exciting and rewarding.

1

Emotion and Materialism

Human science fragments everything in order to understand it, kills everything in order to examine it.

—*Leo Tolstoy*

Emotions and Atomic Theory

That emotional arousal causes physiological changes is well known. If you are angry or excited, your heart will race faster. If you are scared, you might have sweaty palms. And if you are unhappy, your lips might curl downward, and your hands and legs might be crossed instead of open. Body language and physiological states—such as blood pressure, sweating, or heartbeat—are well-known determinants of psychological state, including emotions. The connection is so common that doctors employ them to diagnose mental illnesses and forensic investigators use lie detection tests relying on such factors. But it is also clear that sweating, faster heartbeat, or body language is itself not the mental state. At best, they are *indicators* of that state, like a book is the expression of an idea, not the idea itself. Nevertheless, when scientists employ measurements to deduce a cause—such as emotional stress from a racing heartbeat—they tend to confuse the cause with the effect.

They are likely to believe that if the heart is racing faster, there must be a chemical trigger for it, which would mean that what we call "emotion" must be the chemical. This claim is never empirically confirmed because you cannot equate sweat, blood, or bodily contortions to emotions: the physical state is observable by everyone while the emotions are only felt by the subject experiencing it. That emotions have chemical triggers is presently justified

1

based on two reasons—one empirical and the other theoretical. Empirically, we can observe a statistical difference in the chemical composition followed by physiological and somatic changes. Theoretically, we are conditioned to think that a chemical change must only be caused by other chemicals.

The materialistic theory of emotions—in which we equate emotions with molecules—suffers not just from empirical problems (you cannot observe emotions in a third-person manner) but also from problems in the theory of chemicals itself, namely that the state of atoms according to atomic theory is uncertain and something must be added to this state in order to produce a definite object. In other words, the fact that we observe some chemicals is currently unexplainable because the state of atoms is described as possibilities from which a *selection* must be made. The selecting agency is not known, although "conscious choice" is speculated to be one cause[1].

Unless this choice is applied, the atomic state remains a possibility, not a reality. When the molecular state is uncertain, there is no need to reduce emotions to molecules. These emotions can also be produced from a purpose, which selects one from among many possible alternative states, essentially focusing the material change towards a goal. As such, they would be the counterparts of what quantum theory considers "choice"[2], although they can be regarded as a new type of matter. What we call "matter" today would correspond to the *cognitive* component of perception, but the new "matter" would be the *emotive* component of experience. The cognitive component can be observed, but the emotive cause remains internal and unobservable.

The fact that we see emotions accompanying molecules need not mean that emotions are indeed the chemicals that we observe empirically. It can as well mean that emotions are agencies that drive the selection of an alternative from among multiple possibilities, which then *manifests* a molecule for observation from the infinite possibilities of such molecular states. All emotions can now be characterized by the presence of molecular differentiators—because each such emotion implies a specific choice of molecules from among the possible molecules—and yet emotions won't be molecules.

Such an approach opens a new way of thinking about experience as the combination of cognitive and emotive contents such that the cognitive component can be observed in a third-person manner but the emotive ingredient that creates the cognitive state would only be accessible in a first-person manner. This is consistent with observation but also with a theoretical result in atomic theory—Bell's Theorem[3]—which demonstrates that (a) atomic theory is incomplete, and (b) we cannot find empirically measurable "hidden variables" to complete it. If we reduce materialism to all that can be observed in a third-person manner then atomic theory, and hence the theory of emotions (which equates emotions to molecules) would forever remain incomplete. If instead, we think of materialism as ingredients that correspond to our emotive and cognitive experiences then it is possible to remain consistent with present empirical observations and theoretical results, while finding a new path on which atomic theory can be completed and that completion creates a new fundamental role for emotions even in the study of molecules.

Emotions, however, would not be reduced to molecules, although they would be material—a new kind of matter that we don't understand today. I will use this book to discuss what that new kind of matter is, drawing from philosophy, psychology, art, linguistics, social sciences, and religion. All these areas are empirical, although the inquiry is not reducible to the cognitive experience, or the inquiry remains incomplete without an emotional component. The scope of the problem is very vast, but the proposed solution to the problem promises to be quite enriching because it can bring together heretofore unrelated ideas pertaining to disparate areas of modern thinking.

Can the Future Change the Present?

The relation between cognition and emotion can be compared to a similar—although not identical—problem concerning the relation between word and meaning. The meaning that exists in our mind manifests externally as words, and by the existence of the word we can deduce the meaning. But the words are not the meaning. Rather, the meaning acts as a choice in the selection of possible sentences in a language. Emotion, similarly, has chemical manifestations, but emotions are not those chemicals. Rather, when chemicals exist as possibilities, then emotions can be conceived as choices that pick one from many alternatives. This analogy can be useful to demystify the theoretical problem concerning emotions because they can now be described as that agency which reduces the infinite possibilities to a single reality.

Choices, so far, have been related to a non-material consciousness. That might not be entirely false; we can suppose that consciousness has the capacity for free will. However, this doesn't imply that to study choice we must step outside matter, if we permit the inclusion of a different kind of matter that creates emotions instead of cognition. This approach removes problems in our inquiry because we are all intimately familiar with emotions, and their existence cannot be denied. We also know from atomic theory that the cognitive component of experience cannot be described completely[4]. Therefore, we have both the push and the pull to move to a new theoretical stance. The push is that we require an additional causal agent to even explain cognition. The pull is that the experience of emotions can't be explained chemically.

When objects are defined as *possibilities* of many alternatives, then the choice of what that possibility becomes can be encoded as the *purpose* for which the object is used. We could say that the material objects are possibilities but a selection by a purpose or goal converts them into a reality. Just as we study matter as possibilities, we would now need a new type of matter that constitutes *purpose*. The purpose exists in the present but its *effects* manifest in the future. Therefore, if science is defined as the empirical observation of effects, which are then used to deduce the causes, then purposes don't fit the bill. The purpose can only be observed when it creates an effect—e.g. by selecting—but otherwise, it remains unobservable to the senses.

Classical physics is defined as the measurement of particles and waves, which cause changes to other particles and waves. Both the cause and the effect are empirically observable, and one can correlate the properties of the cause to the properties of the effect creating laws of motion. Purposes are different because they refer to a future state which selects one from among many alternatives in the present. Since the purpose exists now, this causality involves something that exists now affecting something that exists in the future. However, since the purpose refers to something in the future, this causality involves something that exists in the future affecting the present.

It is the latter form of causality (future changing the present) that presents ominous issues in current notions of causality driven from the present to the future, upon which the idea of scientific determinism rests. In classical physics, for example, determinism arises because the present completely determines the future. When determinism collapses—e.g. in atomic theory—we open the doors to the idea that the present doesn't fully determine the future. Rather, the present is only a set of possibilities from which a purpose—indicating a future state—selects. While all of us are intimately familiar with the existence of purposes, we have a theoretical problem in postulating a cause that comes from the future to change the present. And yet, this problem is only an outcome of a flawed picture of matter as definite particles and waves.

If reality at present is uncertain, then the causation from the future is not just theoretically necessary but also conceptually uncomplicated, because we are all driven by goals and purposes to make choices in the present.

What we called "choice" earlier can now be equated to a purpose which exists in the present and yet points to the future. It cannot be observed by the senses although it can be seen in first-person experience. The sensual experience, in fact, is the byproduct of combining the possibility with the purpose. The possibilities are the past, and the purpose is the future. Their combination creates the present, which we call our experience. This is a radical conception of causality in which the past and the future interact materially because both exist right now materially. This is not how we think of causality in science. There are, however, intuitions in modern science that can assist us.

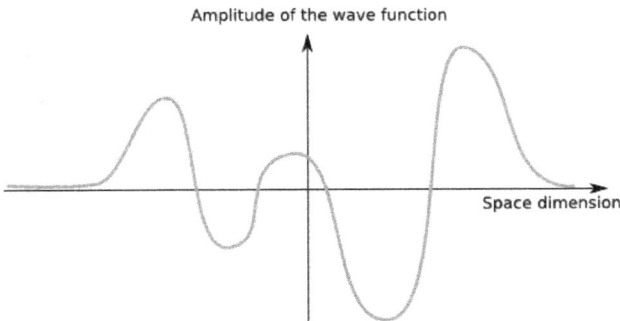

Figure-1 Probability Distribution in a Wavefunction

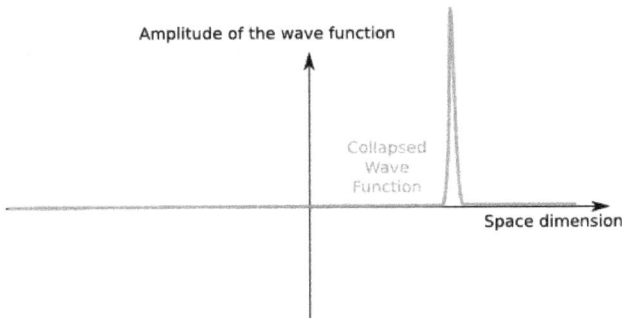

Figure-2 Probability Collapse in a Wavefunction

In atomic theory, when a measurement is performed, the possibility is reduced to a certainty. A few moments thereafter the certainty again becomes a possibility. This is described in atomic theory by Schrodinger's Equation[1] in which a spread of possibilities expands after a sudden contraction caused by a measurement. Figure-1 illustrates a probability distribution prior to measurement, which is called a 'wavefunction'. Figure-2 depicts the 'collapsed wavefunction' upon a measurement. The wavefunction returns to a state of spread after the collapse. The irony is that we can never measure the spread of possibilities because the spread reduces to a single alternative upon measurement. Nevertheless, since our equation predicts this spread and the prediction is consistent with the randomness in the future observations, we presume that the possibilities indeed spread after a measurement.

This spread of possibility represents the immediate past; it cannot be observed because it is in the past. Likewise, the purpose that selects from the possibility represents the immediate future; it cannot be observed because it exists in the future. We can only experience the present created by combining the past and the future—i.e. the collapsed state of the wavefunction.

Towards a New Conception of Matter

We must now distinguish the matter that constitutes possibilities from that which constitutes purpose from the observation that combines possibility and purpose. Both possibility and purpose can be *objective* although they are not *objects*. Rather, objects are byproducts of the combination of possibility and purpose and can be observed. Possibility and purpose cannot be sensually perceived because they are yet to be realized into a concrete object. Nevertheless, they are *conceptual entities* that must be invoked in the explanation of observation because the classical physical notion of definite objects with possessed properties has now irrevocably collapsed in science.

The collapse of deterministic causality in classical physics doesn't necessarily entail a collapse of causality itself. Rather, it requires us to revise the notion of causality from the properties of classical material particles which exist in the present, and can therefore be observed, to one that involves possibility and purpose, which are in the past and in the future, respectively. The observation is in the present, but its explanation lies in the past and in the future. We can call the observable present the *manifest* reality, and the past and the future which cause the present, the *unmanifest* reality, such that the unmanifest produces the manifest by the combination of the past and the future. Somewhat paradoxically, the past and the future exist in the present and yet *refer* to something that cannot be observed within the present.

The nature of this reference is the key unsolved problem in science because all objects in classical physics existed in and of themselves and did not refer to anything. This idea about material objects was the cornerstone of classical physics but it must be revised now. The revision involves two ideas pertaining to the nature of the reference to the past and the future.

The first idea we need to grasp is that when we select an alternative from a set of possibilities, the observable is the selected alternative, but the other alternatives are present in that selection (although not observable) because the selected alternative is only *defined in relation* to the other discarded alternatives. For example, when you toss a coin or throw a dice, one of the faces turns up and becomes observable. But you cannot explain the outcomes without considering the other alternatives because the face that you see is defined in relation to the other faces. This is empirically seen on repeated tosses where heads or tails will have a 50% chance of being observed on an unbiased coin while one of the six faces of a dice will have a $1/6^{th}$ probability of being observed. By observation we confirm that other possibilities exist, but we cannot perceive them in each observation. This is represented in atomic theory using *orthogonal* functions[2], which are orthogonal because you cannot see them at once. You see one of the alternatives but the alternative you see is defined by taking the *whole* uncertainty and *dividing* it into mutually exclusive options. The dice or the coin is uncertain, but that uncertainty can be divided into mutually orthogonal or exclusive alternatives. When you see one of the alternatives, the others exist but are hidden from our vision. The observation is thus defined in relation to what remains hidden. This is the first sense in which the observation refers to the unobservable.

The second sense of reference is easier to understand because it emerges as purpose; the purpose exists in the present, but it refers to the future. This is quite intuitive because we use our goals to do things to attain goals. The goal selects what I do in the present based on the available opportunities. The selection of present activities is not random if we know the goal. But if we don't know the goal, then the selection from alternatives appears random to us. We can think of this in terms of the coin toss or dice casting as the ability to somehow *will* the correct alternative that helps achieve a goal.

Einstein had issues with atomic theory, which is paraphrased as "God does not play dice"[3] because he did not foresee a role for will in deciding the outcome and without it, the outcome is indeed random. Einstein's problem also stemmed from the fact that if we allowed the future to determine the present, that would violate the principles of relativity in which only the past influences the present, and that too after a delay (measured by the speed of light). The error in Einstein's view was that purposes exist in the present although they *refer* to the future. By their existence in the present, the problems of reverse causality in relativity are avoided. And by their reference to the future, the problems of indeterminism in atomic theory can be overcome.

The key to the solution is the idea of *reference* in matter by which an object becomes a *symbol* of another object. The meaning of a symbol—e.g. that one face of the coin represents 'head' while another face represents 'tail'—is defined in relation to other symbols. In effect, symbols exist individually but their meaning is always given in relation to other symbols. To understand references, we must now think of material objects as symbols, which have two characteristics—a physical existence and a meaning. Similarly, the existence of a goal is also a reference to something that exists in the future. The things in the future can only exist as conceptual possibilities, not as real objects. But we should now have no problem with possibilities since all of quantum theory is only about the description of matter as possibility! The difference now will require us to estimate some possibilities as existing in the past (which quantum theory calls possibility), while others will exist in the future (which we can now call the *purpose* underlying an action). The importance of this idea to science is that causal predictions can no longer be done simply by considering the material existence of a symbol. Rather, the prediction requires inducting the meaning and reference of the symbol as well.

The meaning and reference are two distinct ideas. The former is seen when 'head' is defined in relation to 'tail', while the latter is seen when a symbol denotes something other than itself—e.g. pointing to the future. At the bare minimum, the study of possibility necessitates the use of meaning, and the description of purpose requires the use of reference. However, once we see that these two are required, we can actually broaden our use by incorporating additional intuitions. For instance, a symbol need not necessarily refer to something in the future; it can also refer to something that exists right now. Our experiences—e.g. that the apple is red—involve such references because the apple is perceived to be distinct from the observer. Similarly, a symbol need not necessarily be defined in relation to all the alternatives that exist at present; it can also be defined in relation to things that exist in the present or the past. Our ordinary notions of time—e.g. morning, afternoon, evening, and night—are described relationally to other instances in time that don't exist simultaneously. The generic problem to address now is that there are two kinds of symbols—called possibility and purpose—each of which has two kinds of properties which we call *meaning* and *reference*.

The existence of possibility constitutes the notion of *sematic space* in which symbols are defined in relation to each other and refer to other symbols, but all those symbols are possible at once although they exist at different locations in space. The existence of purpose constitutes the notion of *semantic time* in which symbols are again defined in relation to each other and potentially refer to other symbols, but all those symbols are possible at the same place although they must exist at different locations in time. The four properties mentioned above—possibility, purpose, meaning, and reference—therefore quite simply reduce to a new notion of *semantic* space and time in which locations are mutually defined and can refer to each other.

The study of emotion pertains to what exists as purpose materially and it creates the forward movement of time. Instead of studying time as some objective arrow of forward movement, we can also describe time as an *effect* produced by *purpose*. If we did not have purpose, there would be no forward movement, and hence no time. With a changing sense of purpose, we can move faster or slower, and time can appear to be slower or faster. Similarly, instead of studying space as some infinite expanse, we can also describe space as an *effect* produced by *possibility*. If we did not have the need to realize alternative possibilities for ourselves there would be no need for the diversity of space. We would remain inwardly focused, aware of just ourselves. With a changing sense of possibility, the space can expand or contract.

Thus, the so-called relativity of space and time, where time goes faster or slower[4], and space expands or contracts[5], are embedded in our ordinary notions of possibility and purpose. Space when described as possibility expands with the increase in possibilities and shrinks with the decrease in alternatives. Time when described as purpose goes faster with the increase in purpose and slower with the lack of purpose. As a result, our experience shrinks and expands, moves faster or slower, which we describe as the consequences of observer relativity. This idea has enormous advantages from a scientific standpoint because with a new way of thinking about space and time we can overcome the current contradictions between atomic theory and relativity which have baffled physicists for over a century now[6]. The notion of space and time when revised to possibility and purpose fits naturally with the tenets of both atomic theory and general relativity in an intuitive manner.

The shift in thinking involves discarding the ideas of space and time as objective realities and replacing them with possibility and purpose as subjective realities from which space and time are produced as *effects*. The novelty is that time is produced by purpose, and space is created by possibility. If we don't seek possibility, then the space of alternatives shrinks to just our own existence. As we seek more possibilities, the space of alternatives expands from our existence. If we don't seek a purpose, then the evolution shrinks to just our present state which remains eternally unchanged. As we acquire more purpose, the time of evolution expands to new states in the future. Space and time can therefore be constructed from possibility and purpose, which can then be viewed as completely subjective realities. In a sense, the world expands from the innate needs of the observer, inside-out.

Semantic Space and Time

I call this notion of space and time *semantic* because it incorporates meanings and references. We can also call it *subjective* because it emanates from the necessities of the observer—purpose and possibility. The essence of the shift is that we don't treat the experience of distance and duration—from which modern notions of space and time are derived—as *realities*; instead, we treat the experience of distance and duration as *phenomena* that are produced from some reality that remains unobservable. While the reality (possibility and purpose with meanings and references) is not observable, the phenomenal effects—as distance and duration—are perceived. What we call space and time as the "container" of physical objects, is in fact not a container at all. It is rather a phenomenal experience produced from a noumenal reality. The noumenal reality is logically prior to the phenomena and causes it. But the noumenal reality is also "closer" to the observer than the phenomenal experience, rather than being farther from the observer's experience.

In modern science, we believe there is an observer and an external reality, and the phenomena are *in between* the observer and the reality when the observer comes in contact with it. In the new conception outlined above, the reality that causes the phenomena lies *in between* the observer and the phenomena. This reality "covers" the observer, and as a result *projects* a space and time of objects outward. To know this reality, we don't have to go further outward from our experience, presuming that there is something "outside" which is the real cause of our perception. We must rather go inward, presuming that there is something closer to us from which the outward phenomena are produced through *projection*. In current science, there are objects outside which cast an image on our senses. In the new scientific model, the observer is a movie projector who projects a picture from within. To explain that picture in modern science, we seek to understand what lies outside our senses. But the same picture has to be now explained by understanding what lies deep within from which sense experience is projected outward.

The materialistic view is grounded in the idea that space and time are materially objective realities, but the semantic view is based on the notion that space and time are phenomena. The reality is deep within, not further outside. This has considerable benefits philosophically and empirically.

The empirical benefit addresses the issue that if reality is outside the senses then we are permanently barred from knowing that reality empirically. We must now speculate on its nature and all such speculations are tentative and prone to revision in the future as more data is collected. Owing to this fact, Karl Popper[7] defined science as knowledge that can be falsified but never confirmed[8]. No matter how many times our speculation is proven correct, we have no way to guarantee that it is *true* because we may well have not found that data which falsifies the speculation. However, when reality is deep within then it is possible to directly experience that reality without speculation although it requires perceptual advancement. To explain our experiences, we must know ourselves much better because that experience is projected inside-out rather than outside-in. This changes the *method* of science, not in terms of reason and experience, but in terms of outward vs. inward observation. The inward observation is both rational and empirical. It is, however, different from the method espoused by modern science.

The philosophical benefit is that true knowledge is no longer the prisoner of a few academic professionals who study nature through machines. It is rather the prerogative and responsibility of each individual to know themselves in order to explain their experience. The phenomena and its explanation are in control of each observer, although some might grab that opportunity to know while others might neglect it. There is no need for people to drive consensus on that reality because each person has direct access to it via observation. There is however a need to define the *process* for perceptual advancement by which something that lies hidden can be revealed.

The theory of this internal reality is necessary to drive consensus about the method of perception of this reality. Theory and experiment go hand in hand; when we know the theory of nature, we devise specific experiments to measure it. If we had no clue about what reality *could be,* we would have no way to confirm if reality is indeed what we think it is. In that sense, formulating the scientific theory of this internal reality is a stepping stone toward its direct experience. It sets up the motivation both for the exploration of that reality as well as justifying why specific methods will be fruitful.

Insights from modern science can be reinterpreted considering the basic idea that reality is semantic, observer-centric, and projected inside-out. I have done this in my previous books, reinterpreting quantum theory as pertaining to symbols with meaning and reference, possibility and purpose[9]. I have also discussed the relationship between atomic theory and relativity and how their contradiction can be solved in the context of physics[10]. I will refer the interested reader to those works. This book will take the insights developed earlier and rely mostly on the description of possibility and purpose, meaning and reference, and their relationship to space and time briefly highlighted above. These are not substituting for technical rigor, but that rigor is not the primary aim of this particular book. Therefore, I would just point the reader interested in that rigor to my previous writings.

Reason vs. Emotion

It is important to see how the question of emotion is entwined with the other questions of modern science, including those in particle and cosmological physics because without such insights this book would be no different than those that rely on psychometric studies, chemical imbalances, and cultural or anthropological investigations to formulate theories on emotion. I am going to argue that emotion is as fundamental to material causality as it is to human decisions. Emotion is not just a human fact that we leave to be investigated based on a non-emotional theory of atomism, space, and time. Rather, we must find a new synthesis between emotion and reason for a fuller grasp of the nature of reality because modern science relies exclusively on reason and experiment and rejects any role for emotions, feelings, and goals.

The problems we face today in studying emotion date back to the time when emotion was evicted from physics because it was believed to interfere with the objective study of nature, and nature itself is not influenced by our emotions, will, perception, or beliefs. Our psychological reality was relegated to a "mind" different from the "body" in order to describe the body objectively. A lot has changed since then. Now we know that emotion, will, perception, and belief do change our body. The effects are well-known in biology and medicine. Mental depression is often the cause of physical ailments such as pains and aches, and emotional satisfaction creates a slew of hormones that cure diseases, up until the point of medically being called "placebos".

The separation of reason and emotion in physical sciences doesn't work in life sciences; although we abhor the idea of our scientific data being interfered with by emotion, we frequently employ emotion in the explanation of biology. The reduction of emotions to chemicals also doesn't work because all these chemicals are simply possibilities from the standpoint of modern physics. We can say that there are infinitely many possible states of molecules and infinite possible molecules. Therefore, nobody can insist that there is indeed a fixed set of chemicals that make up the body unless we induct a direct role for emotion as a separate category that chooses from the alternatives. The explanation of emotion based on chemicals closes the only door we presently have open to finding answers to serious problems in modern physics. I would therefore like to keep this door open and argue that emotion and reason are indeed separate categories; reason deals with the possibilities and emotion with choice; together they combine to create our sense experience.

This means reason is inadequate. It tells us of the options we have but doesn't tell us what we want to do. The choice of a goal, which results in the selection of one among the many alternatives, is made by emotion. Thus, the awareness of all the alternatives is a rational function, but the choice of a goal or where we would like to be in the future is an emotional function. Scientific determinism reduced choices to reason by formulating mathematical laws that deterministically predict the future given the present state. Emotion, choice, and goals were not relevant for science because reason sufficed. With the failure of scientific determinism based on reason, we can resurrect a role for emotion, not just in the human mind, but also in scientific causation.

This is a far more profound role for emotion than envisioned in any scientific theory which aims to reduce emotion to chemicals, chemicals to physics, physics to mathematics, and ultimately everything to reason. The breaking news is not just that determinism has failed, but that reason itself has failed as a tool for predictions. Science is incomplete because reason is incomplete , since it precludes choices that manifest in goal formation. The goal formation is mediated by an emotional response to facts obtained from the external world or an internal desire for premeditated goals, and therefore reason must be complemented by emotion. Now, we must reinvent reason itself—not as something contrary to emotion as it was envisioned during Western Enlightenment and Renaissance—but one that includes emotion through the process of goal formation, choice making, and purposefulness.

Emotion is also rational, just not the rationality of objects. The rationality of emotion manifests in our choices of goals, which are derived from our sense of good and bad. In contrast, reason (as presently conceived in science) only deals with the question of true or false. For example, when science studies material objects we only deal with questions of whether some claims about objects are true or false. We don't question the ethics or morality of action, nor do we question whether someone would desire or crave for these objects. The rationality of emotion mediates a different kind of judgment (good and bad) than the rationality of scientific reason (true and false).

There is hence no basis in the conclusion that emotion cannot be studied scientifically, but it does mean that we must bring the questions of good vs. bad within the ambit of rational scientific inquiry. This is not possible unless we broaden our concept of matter from things to which the judgment of true and false can be applied to things to which other kinds of judgments can be applied. Thus, when I say that there are alternative kinds of material reality, I mean that they involve alternative forms of judgment. The judgment of possibility involves the question of true or false: *if* you take your medicine your disease will be cured, *if* you exercise your body will be energized, *if* you read this book you will know. All these statements are *conditional,* and their truth verification depends on someone performing those activities. The scientific truth is therefore not universal because it depends on someone setting up an experiment by following a procedure and making the measurements as per the specified methods. Beyond this truth is the question of *whether* someone actually *wants* to do something—e.g. taking, exercising, or reading.

If we reduce emotions to molecules, then we would have to reduce the judgments of good and bad to the judgments of true and false. That reduction entails that to have different desires, emotions, likes, preferences, and goals, we must be chemically different. Ultimately it entails a denial of choice. The separation of the judgments of good and bad from that of true and false however reinstates free will because the same facts (true or false) can be chosen or rejected by desires (good or bad). The process is still rational although it is based on a different type of rationality than we presently envision.

Another contention between reason and emotion pertains to the idea that reason applies to the external world while emotions are in the mind. We can afford to be emotional about our choices, but we must be rational and objective about the external world. This separation between emotion and reason came from the idea that external reality creates perception in us. When the reality that creates perception is as internal as that which creates emotion—through the reversal of the perceptual model we noted above—then the separation of emotion vs. reason based on internal vs. external has no basis. The psychological distinctions between reason and emotion can now be made by instituting different kinds of judgments in the observer.

The study of emotion constitutes a different domain demarcated by a new kind of rationality based on the judgment of good and bad. This rationality should be applied to a different reality from that to which the judgment of true and false is applied. The interaction between these two realities—possibility and purpose—now presents not the mind-body problem of the past, but a logical question that the judgment of true and false does not complete the nature of reality because that judgment only pertains to a possibility. Reality cannot, therefore, be equated to all that exists right now and happens to be true. It also cannot be equated to all that is possible in the future. Reality must be broader than all that exists right now and all that is possible in the future—it must include the choices by which future truths (facts and possibilities) are created. Now we can see that the conception of reality equated to truth becomes incomplete and we must broaden the concept of reality to include not just what is true, but also what we consider is good.

What we call 'reason' includes only the quest for truth, and it is incomplete because of other judgments. The problems of incompleteness in modern science—of which the quantum problem is just one—are indicative of this wider malaise in which we have tried to reduce reality to all that is true when we should have included the question of right and good because those judgments produce what is true. If we remove the questions of right and good, then we cannot explain what will be true—i.e. scientific predictions—based on what is true. Science becomes incomplete when it is unable to predict the truth. Determinism supposes that truth is enough to predict truth, but we now know that this is not the case. To address the problem, we can broaden the conception of causality and enlarge the conception of reality and rationality. The demise of determinism is symptomatic of the fact that reality includes right and good beyond truth, and only by enlarging the conception of reality can we solve its incompleteness problems. That in turn indicates new kinds of matter which are described by alternative forms of rationality.

A Mathematical Description of Purpose

All living entities are goal-oriented. We are here right now, but we want to be somewhere else in the future. The goal exists as something that *points* to the future. Science employs mathematical entities called *vectors* to represent entities that point elsewhere. However, so far, we have only had vectors in space. Momentum and angular momentum, for example, are spatial vectors. A goal, on the other hand, is a temporal vector. It points to something that lies in the future, but the current notion of vectors is inadequate to fully describe what a goal is. Here is the key reason why it is inadequate.

Consider the statement "the sun is yellow" in which the word "sun" is used as a *name* that *refers* to the real world. If we encoded this statement into physical states, some state would have to encode a *name* (the sun) while another state would encode a *concept* (yellow). When the name and concept are combined, we obtain a description of the world— "the sun is yellow". This description *points* to the real sun, but not like a vector, since vectors only have a *direction* but no *destination*. The momentum vector for example can point in +z direction but it is not referring to a destination. Ordinary propositions involve *names*, which are used to encode object destinations.

One might argue that if we described the destination, we would not need the direction. For example, we could call out the sun in our proposition "the sun is yellow" and it would identify the intended object without the need for a direction. This is true in many cases, but not all cases. If the proposition is "the president is tall", you can't be sure that "the president" singles out the leader of a nation, of a football club, or the apartment where you live in. The names used in language are often contextual, which means they are in relation to the person speaking the sentence. Given the context—e.g. a nation, a football club, or the apartment complex—the meaning of "the president" is unique. Thus, we need two things—the name of the entity being identified, and the name of the person who identifies the entity and hence the context.

The names in ordinary language are used contextually because we imbibe the speaker into language. Modern scientific claims, however, preempt the speaker because nature is described not from the *perspective* of a specific *person* but universally. We don't say that a scientific claim is true for a person, and therefore we must use observer-independent conventions, and that implies that just a destination would suffice. The destination in the vector mentioned above, therefore, identifies the referred object contextually. The direction, on the other hand, pertains to the observer who identifies the object.

A goal, similarly, is a temporal vector with both destination and direction. The destination identifies a state in the future (or past) while the direction is relative to the observer who makes that identification. In other words, when we identify a goal, we identify ourselves in relation to that goal. The goal is personal and objective, although not an object. I might be hungry and have the goal of eating. I might be poor and aim to become rich. Or I might be at home and aim to get to work. We start with goals—vectors with destination and direction. Once the source and destination have been identified by a name, then there are further *properties* of these objects encoded by *concepts*. In the statement "the sun is yellow", the "sun" is a name, while "yellow" is a concept, which identifies the properties of the "sun". In modern physics, we similarly distinguish between particles and their properties. The particle is the name and its properties (energy or momentum) are concepts[11].

This might seem unique in modern physics because we are used to vectors with a direction and quantification, but it need not be unique if we converted the quantification into a *name* that referred to the "location" of the object we *intend* through the goal or description. For example, when we say that the "sun is yellow" the word "sun" is a vector that refers to an object. The direction of the vector would now be used to refer to the person who speaks that sentence. Now, the "sun is yellow" is a vector but not an *objective* property independent of observers. It is rather describing the *subjective* experience of a person, who is embedded in that description because the experience is from a specific person's viewpoint. The description is still mathematical, but it is subjective and contextual, rather than objective and universal.

With this redefinition of vectors, we can understand *intention* as a vector. I will call the redefined idea of a vector an intentional vector or *ivector* to distinguish it from a physical vector. Knowledge involves intentions—e.g. when we refer to the sun. Goals also involve intentions when we refer to something that lies in the future or the past. Knowledge and goals are different as spatial and temporal *ivectors*. The notion of spatial intentions comes from the empirical knowledge of the world while the notion of temporal intentions comes to us from the experience of goals to which we are headed. The knowledge and goal exist here and now, but they *refer* to something elsewhere or elsewhen. It is also possible to combine the knowledge and the intention and make claims about things that are elsewhere and elsewhen. That would be an *ivector* with both spatial and temporal components.

This digression helps us see how goals need not be esoteric objects outside science. We can conceive of them mathematically like we describe physical properties. That by itself doesn't entail the reality of purposes, but I don't believe that the existence of goals and purposes is itself in question here. Given that we are seeking to describe goals, we are already well-versed with the phenomenon. The challenge for us lies in demystifying the phenomenon *theoretically* by employing concepts that could be imbibed in a predictive theory. The challenge also lies in integrating the new kind of property—purpose—with other existing facets of reality called matter and force. If we can address these challenges, we would be well on our way to a new science in which the notion of matter is broadened to include emotion and purpose, which don't supervene matter and force, but act in conjunction with them.

First-Person vs. Third-Person Observation

Purposes exist here and now but they refer to the future. Since they exist here and now, they can interact with other things—such as the possibilities of reality—which also exist here and now. However, just because they exist here and now doesn't entail that what they *mean* exists here and now. The meaning is the thing that the vector points to, different from the existence of the vector itself. The state intended by the vector can be elsewhere and elsewhen, while the vector exists here and now. In that sense, there can be a goal that refers to a state in the future, but the goal itself exists in the present.

The interaction between a possibility and a purpose would convert the possibility into a reality compatible with the goal. But what we observe—e.g. an object or state—did not exist prior to the observation because the observation is the byproduct of combining purpose and possibility neither of which could be observed individually until they are combined. The possibility and the purpose must therefore remain theoretical constructs employed to explain the observation, which are not observable in a third-person manner. We could, however, observe these constructs in a *first-person* manner.

This first-person observation involves the mind. Through the senses we can see what the world *is* but through the mind we can see what the world *can be*. When the world exists as a possibility, it cannot be perceived by the senses, which is why modern physics struggles to re-create the classical world from atomic theory. The problem is that in classical physics the world was objectively definite—i.e. perceivable through the senses—even prior to observation. What if the world is not classically certain prior to sense perception? What if the world exists as a possibility of alternatives which can be observed by the mind (in first-person manner) but not perceivable by the senses (in third-person manner)? How will science differ in this scenario?

The difference between sensual and mental observation can be characterized as the distinction between seeing a definite state of objects and seeing the indefinite state of what the world can be. Clearly, the definite state perception involves the senses, but the indefinite state requires mental intuition. When the world exists—prior to observation—as possibility and purpose, then it is not less empirical, although we must expand the definition of empiricism to include the mind. The mind can see possibility and purpose, but the senses cannot. In a simple sense, the cognitive faculty in the mind perceives all the alternatives while the emotional state recognizes the goals.

The combination of cognition and emotion produces a definite state when the goal or purpose is employed to select one among the many possible alternatives. What atomic theory calls the "wavefunction" is the cognitive component of our perception where the mind perceives all the possibilities. Similarly, what atomic theory calls "collapse" of the "wavefunction" (in which the possibilities are "reduced" to a reality) is the emotive component of our perception where the mind formulates a goal to choose an alternative from the available options. Possibility and choice combine to create reality.

The first-person observation of possibility and purpose is now more important than the third-person observation of facts that emerge from the combination of possibility and purpose. It is only in the first-person perspective that we see *all* the alternatives and *all* the goals. The reality produced from their combination is a subset of all that is possible and desirable. In that sense, the first-person observation by the mind is broader than the reality perceived by the senses. The world that the mind sees as possibility and purpose is the precursor to the world that the senses perceive. Cognition and emotion in the mind pertain to the logically-preceding possibility and purpose while the sensation and pleasure of the senses are created by their combination. Therefore, if we were able to broaden empiricism to include the mental observation of possibility and purpose, beyond the sensual observations, then we would no longer consider atomic indeterminism a serious theoretical problem; the world would now be *mentally* definite, but *sensually* indefinite. You could say that the sensual reality is produced from a mental reality when the different components—which the mind can perceive individually—are combined to produce the experience of the senses. The senses cannot see them individually, but the mind can; therefore, the reality prior to sense perception can only be called 'real' in a mental, not sensual, sense.

Redefining Empiricism

Modern Western empiricism emphasizes the perception of the five senses—hearing, touching, seeing, tasting, and smelling—and it works with the assumption that the world is definite objects. The sensual version of empiricism succeeds in conjunction with the classical physical model of reality comprising particles and waves, which possess properties such as position, momentum, energy, angular momentum, mass, charge, etc. *a priori*. This is the dominant dogma of science since the time of Newton, but it has become increasingly tenuous since the dawn of atomic theory in the early 20th century.

The new reality discovered by atomic physics has struggled to retain the classical physical dogma because in the new picture the world is not *a priori* definite objects and properties. The world is instead possibilities and how this possibility is converted into a reality remains a huge mystery.

The classical physical dogma also emphasized reason over emotion, adopting reason as the method of science, and relegating emotion to religion, the study of happiness, and ethics or morality. By splitting reason from emotion, the physicalist dogma hasn't just created a problem for the field of human psychology where reason and emotion co-exist and integrate but now even in the realm of physics itself. Finally, the separation between mind and matter created by Descartes made it impossible to create a role for imagination within science, even if science could not work without imagination. The problems of mind-body separation and reason-emotion divide in conjunction with the notion that the world exists as *a priori* definite objects were designed to achieve a model of nature in which objects followed a trajectory deterministically, there was no choice, and nothing was left to chance. The current misery stems from the flawed assumptions incompatible with facts.

The fact is that the world exists as a possibility *before* it exists as sense observation. That we can perceive these possibilities through the mind *before* we perceive the reality by the senses. That choices mediated through emotion and purpose are employed *before* the possibility is converted into reality. That emotion and reason combine *before* the sensations are created. And that the mind produces concepts and purpose through its activities *before* we perceive through the senses.

The deepest problems of modern science originate in flawed assumptions about mind and matter, reason and emotion, purpose and determinism in classical physics. It is now time to bury a flawed ideology and move forward with a new set of assumptions about nature, drawn without the scars that Western Enlightenment carried from the Dark Ages, redefining the nature of empiricism compatible with everyday experiences, and then using it to redefine science in a way compatible with human experience. The bonus from such redefinition would be the solution to all the sticky problems of science spanning from atomic theory to the psychology of emotion.

Misconceptions on Emotion and Chemicals

The chemical basis of emotional changes is prevalent at present because we can observe chemicals but can't observe emotions in a third-person manner. Of course, we can observe emotions in a first-person manner, but introspection or self-examination are not methods of modern science. Therefore, the reduction of emotions to chemicals always suffers from the yawning gap between first-person and third-person accounts of reality: from the first-person view, we can perceive emotions, but from the third-person viewpoint we can only perceive chemicals. How can we bridge the conflicting ideologies in first-person and third-person accounts when their vocabularies involve different words? This has been the focus of nearly all the physical theories of emotion. They are radically different from purely "psychological" theories where emotion is studied based on first-person reports of what one feels.

The hallmark of physical theories of emotion is that they begin in a chemical trigger. The trigger could be an external event, a physiological change that appears prior to the psychological report of emotional alteration, or an event that is supervised by reasoning before an emotional response is produced. I find this surprising because many of my intimate experiences with desire, anxiety, and fear were triggered without an external event and against all rationality. Anyone who has tried to control anxiety, fear, and desire will testify that cutting yourself from the situations that create emotions generally reduces the emotional occurrences but doesn't eliminate them. By leading a solitary life, I can decrease the incidence of unwanted emotions, and the resulting mental disturbances, because I have removed the surroundings that could trigger emotions in me. But I would also be the first person to acknowledge that freeing myself of the emotions by cutting off the connection to the external world doesn't imply freedom from desire, anxiety, or fear.

There is a commonsense belief in most of us that desire, anxiety, or fear are innate in all living beings, including humans. The richest, most powerful people also suffer from insecurity, and incessantly feeding our desires causes temporary cessation of the desire but, afterwards, the desire returns more vehemently, and no matter how much your material surroundings seem to present a happy situation we continue to feel empty inside, looking and searching for that meaning and purpose to make ourselves happy.

External situations may sometimes make us happy, but one can be happy without them. Meditative traditions teach us how to be happy without the external trappings. Similarly, the inner desires for happiness are not always due to external triggers. Even if we cut off all our external connections, we will still experience that desire for happiness. External situations may modify the innate desires—e.g. inciting me to seek happiness *through* the acquisition of goods, relationships, and encounters. But these are changes in the medium, not the message. The external situations can create a desire for objects, which are vehicles for attaining happiness, but even if these vehicles were removed from our vision and experience, the desire for happiness would remain.

We can therefore note two kinds of exceptions to the chemical theory of emotions. First, the emotions are not necessarily triggered by an external event; they may be caused without external contact. But the skeptic might still equate such internally-caused emotions to a mechanism like hunger, sleep, or pain that are caused internally. Therefore, it is important to note the second key difference which is that the chemical state is a possibility and not a reality. Emotions can always accompany cognition, and similarly, there can always be pain and pleasure associated with the physical state. That association doesn't mean that the emotion, pleasure, or pain is the cognitive or physical state. They are both *phenomena* produced by a logically prior reality that cannot be sensually experienced but can be mentally intuited.

The Origin of Emotions

The fundamental mental intuition in all of us is that we desire happiness. All emotion originates in the desire for happiness, which is the original emotion and the cause of all other emotions. The desire leads to the search for avenues for happiness, and such avenues can modify the sought–after vehicles for happiness but never the need for happiness itself. Furthermore, the quest for happiness sometimes leads to unhappiness when the sought vehicles of happiness aren't found or found but lacking in happiness. If we weren't seeking something for happiness, where is the question of unhappiness upon not finding it? Fear, anxiety, and insecurity arise from the perceived possibility that one might lose the means for happiness. They too are triggered from the innate desire for happiness, because if we were not seeking happiness then we would not be anxious, stressed, fearful, or insecure about not finding it.

The flaw in modern theories of emotion is that they neglect the *origin* of all emotion in the innate desire for happiness, and only study the modifications of this desire for happiness through worldly interactions—describing how we sometimes meet happy and unhappy situations—and attribute the emotion to the external situation when, in fact, it originated in the innate desire for happiness. If the innate quest for happiness disappears, then no external situation can make you happy or unhappy because happiness and unhappiness are *interpretations* of the world relative to our *goals* and *purposes*.

If we don't have a purpose, then nothing is, relatively speaking, closer or farther from that goal. How can the worldly situations then create happiness or distress within us? Emotion arises because we designate a specific goal as the means to achieve happiness, and progress towards that goal makes us happy while the regress from that goal makes us unhappy. The entire gamut of emotions rests on the existence of goals, and the choice of the goal in turn depends on desires for happiness. In that sense, the study of emotion cannot be complete without the study of goals and purposes[12], and their root in the innate desire for happiness. The quest for happiness is the main goal. From that goal emerge other subsidiary goals and purposes. If these goals are satisfied, we are happy. If they are frustrated, we become unhappy. The mechanism for emotions rests on the process of goal formation for happiness.

When we disconnect our theories of emotion from the psychological mechanisms of goal formation and their origins in our innate need for happiness—which itself has no mechanism because it precedes all others—we produce a caricature. We delve into the biological mechanisms of stress and unhappiness, the fact that happiness and distress imply physiological changes, or that thought mediates the understanding of the world and therefore the interpretation of whether we increased or decreased the proximity to our goals. These ideas are not the problem. The problem is that we fail to recognize that they cannot alone constitute a theory of emotion without acknowledging desires and goals as the centerpiece for any theory on emotion.

The true theory of emotion must begin in the innate desire for happiness, the modification of that desire to form specific goals by which happiness can be achieved, followed by a cognitive component that measures our progress or regress relative to those goals, which then produces emotions.

There is, hence, an involvement with the external world, an engagement with perception and cognition, and a relation to biology and physiology, but these make sense only when we understand goal formation as the route to happiness. If the goals were internal rather than external, then the interaction with the external world, reliance on outward triggers, and some physiological consequences such as the rate of breathing or sweating or heartbeat, would become less important, relatively speaking, although our theory would still be robust because it describes happiness as the fulfilment of goals. These facts are empirically confirmed today because as the mind is freed of desire, the body is automatically calmed, even under adverse conditions.

A Soul-Based Theory of Matter

We saw in this first chapter how space and time are produced from the observer; we can now recall that discussion on possibility and purpose which creates space and time and connect it to the theory of the soul outlined above. The possibility we discussed previously is produced from the *chit* of the soul and constitutes all that "I have". The primary example of this possession is our body itself, and it exists as the possibility of knowing and doing in the senses, mind, intellect, ego, and the moral sense. We normally call them *abilities* that exist in the body, but they cannot act by themselves unless combined with a desire or purpose. The purpose is produced from the *ananda* of the soul, and it constitutes "I want". The body of the soul is expanded into the space of abilities and the desire of the soul expands into the time that employs the ability for a purpose. The possibility and the purpose—which create space and time—are produced from the *chit* and *ananda* of the soul.

The above space and time are, however, *subjective*. It is what we have and what we want. To fulfill these wants, we must interact with something that we don't already have, which now requires relationships to other bodies with their own wants, and these relationships require an *inter-subjective* space and time. In modern science, we call this *objective* because the subjective space and time of desires and abilities is never studied. By neglecting the subjective space and time we come to believe that the world exists objectively. In the objective space and time, there are only objects and no roles, because every object is simultaneously interacting with every other object. In the inter-subjective space and time, one subject interacts with a few subjects at any time, although it can *potentially* interact with any subject at any time. When the interaction between subjects is limited, we can speak about the *role*, which did not previously exist in the objective space and time.

What we consider objective space in modern science is the inter-subjective space in which the 'object' is a collection of abilities, the relation between different such objects creates their respective 'roles', and the abilities are exploited under a given role by our desires. The inter-subjective space and time creates our sense of *proximity* and *distance* from other subjects. This interaction can be carried out at several different *levels* because the subjects are also hierarchical; we can thus interact with their bodies, senses, mind, intellect, ego, or morality, which are successively more subtle and abstract. As we interact with the other subject only at a deeper level, there is proximity at a deep level, but distance at gross level. Or, as we interact only at the gross level, there is proximity at the gross level, although there would be distance at the deep level. There are, hence, different kinds of proximities and distances created by the level of interaction we have with a subject. The idea of "distance" is tiered because you can be close to an object at one level and distant at another level, and two objects can thus have many different "distances" between them based on the level of interaction.

The inter-subjective space is unlike the objective space of modern science because in the objective space two objects always have a fixed distance between them but in the inter-subjective space the distance between objects can vary depending on their interaction. The notion of "size" manifests because of this interaction. For example, when we look at bacteria through a microscope, they seem large because our eyes are interacting with lower regions of the material hierarchy. When seeing these details, we cannot simultaneously see the big picture, although it exists independently of the details. The microscope reduces the inter-subjective distance to the molecules, but it increases the distance to the whole bacteria. As a result, when we see the molecules, we cannot see the bacteria, and vice versa. What seems bigger or smaller is not because it is factually big or small. It indeed has its own *absolute* size given by its position in the hierarchy, but it also produces a *relative* size based on the level at which the senses are related to the object.

We can sensually perceive the relative sizes, but those are not the reality. To know the absolute sizes, we must know the entire hierarchy and then see an object in relation to that hierarchy. Sense perception only gives us a relative understanding of the world, and many perceptions must be connected by a theory (of hierarchy) to know the reality. When the theory is known, then the sense perception can be explained due to (1) the absolute size, and (2) the observer's relation to it. In that sense, the observation can be explained by the reality, but the observation is itself not the reality. Hence, no amount of sense perception tells us anything about the nature of reality. Only when we know the reality can we explain the sense perception.

The cause, in this case, is the interaction, and the size or distance is the effect. Nothing is therefore big or small, far or near, just because we see it that way. The inter-subjective space—which science considers *objective*— is wholly an *effect* that must be explained because it is not reality. Similarly, the time we measure through a *relative* motion of objects is also an effect that must be explained. The real time is due to the subjective forward movement created by our intentions; we can call this the *causal-time*. As we change our body due to this time, we create motion, from which an inter-subjective *effect-time* is produced. The effect-time is relative, but the causal-time is absolute. If we remove the causal-time (by discarding the study of the subjective intentionality in science), then we are only left with the relative measure of time.

Einstein's relativity rests on the effect-time. It leads to a now-famous unsolved paradox called the *Twin Paradox*[13] in which one of the twins sits in a rocket and goes into space at a speed close to the speed of light, while the other twin stays on Earth. According to relativity, the speeding twin must age less, and when he returns to Earth, he would still be young while the twin who stayed on Earth has become old. The problem here is that from the perspective of relativity we could also say that the speeding twin was at rest while the twin who stayed on Earth was moving, so, the twin on Earth should have stayed young while the twin in the rocket should have aged. The paradox emerges because we attribute the age of the twin to the *effect-time* rather than the *causal-time*. Factually, the age of each twin is determined by their intentional change (the causal-time), although the twin who enjoys more would also age faster relative to the twin who enjoys less. Nevertheless, if both twins lead similar lives of pleasures then they would be roughly the same age due to the causal-time although in the effect-time there is a considerable gap. For the twin in the rocket, the clock appears to move slowly but that is an illusion because the age of the twin is decided not by the movement of the clock (which is the effect-time) but the changes in the intentionality which is the causal-time. The causal-time, therefore, has empirical effects— e.g. the duration of life lived by a person—but those effects are contrary to sense perception based relative-time emerging as an effect from the motion. In that sense, the effect-time is an illusion and the causal-time is reality. Of course, the illusion is also experienced, so it is phenomenally real. However, we cannot use the phenomenal time to explain the duration of a person's life.

An obvious implication of this fact is that a person who maintains a steady mind of limited and innate happiness will also live longer compared to a person who has an unsteady mind with continuously changing desires and consequent suffering. The process to elongate one's lifespan is the control of material desires. By controlling the mind and focusing it on one object— which we can call 'meditation'—one can increase the duration of one's life. The causal-time flows slowly for this person, which leads to a longer lifespan, although the effect-time of physical clocks continues to move unhindered. This fact is affirmed by narrations of sages in Vedic texts who could do meditation for thousands of years even within the present human body because they are able to elongate their lives by making their minds steady.

We can conclude that the notion of distance, size, time, and duration in modern science are illusory phenomenal effects and should not be the real space and time as they are produced through the interaction between objects. The interactions between objects should be used to *explain* the effects—the phenomenal (relative) space and time—after we know the unobserved material reality. Clearly, that knowledge can only be obtained through first-person experiences. In the third-person experience, a relation brings an object in contact with other objects, creating an illusory distance and duration.

The cause of relation is *karma* and it brings us in contact with different objects, putting us in different *roles* relative to them. As noted above, this relation manifests over time, and pulls in other objects and persons. The object that enters the relation is not the real cause; the cause is the *karma* that creates the relation. For example, when the *karma* manifests, a person would be naturally rewarded or punished, although the reward or punishment could come through different persons. At the opportune time, one will become employed somewhere, although the employer may vary. At the appropriate time, one would meet with an accident although the other party in the accident could vary. In that sense, you can fully predict the *events* in the life of a person, but you cannot say who would be the *material cause* of that event. Causality based on material causes will remain uncertain, but the causality based on the cause that produces relationships would be certain. Accordingly, a science that tries to make predictions based on material objects will be incomplete but a science that predicts based on *karma* will be complete.

The above conception of causality is material, but it is *based* on the theory of the soul because it is derived from the categories—*sat*, *chit*, and *ananda*—which become relation, possibility, and purpose, and what modern science calls "material objects in space and time" are byproducts of combining the three categories. Atomic theory is based on the fact that material objects are *possibilities*, and it remains incomplete because we don't allow for *purpose* in nature. Relativity theory is based on the fact that a phenomenal experience of space and time is created from relations and it is incomplete because science focuses on the phenomena and not the cause that creates them. Using the above soul–based theory of matter, we can not only diagnose the problems in modern science but also see how they can be solved. The idea of a soul is therefore scientifically pertinent, not just spiritually relevant.

Book Overview

I have painted a succinct picture of the landscape into which we will now begin to fill the details over the subsequent chapters. As you can see, I'm opposed to materialism, but only in the narrow sense it is conceived of at present. I have provided motivations for why materialism must be expanded to include other types of matter—which exist as possibility, relation, and purpose—from which observations are produced. This is consistent with tenets of modern physics (e.g. atomic theory and relativity theory) but incompatible with classical physics. I showed how this materialism involves expanding the notion of empiricism from third-person to first-person observation, and why it necessitates alternative forms of rationality that judge the right and the good beyond the truth. Typical arguments for materialism—e.g. that emotions accompany chemicals, so emotions must be chemicals—are incorrect because chemicals are produced from a combination of relation, possibility, and purpose. The fact that we see chemical accompaniments of emotions only means that there is a cognitive component of reality accompanying an emotive component. Just as cognition and emotion are not identical—although cognition can cause emotion or vice versa—the chemicals we measure in science exist as cognitive possibilities collapsed into a reality by the emotion. With this background, we are ready to delve into the subsequent chapters.

Chapter two discusses modern-day theories of emotion, and their shortcomings. A key problem in all modern science is incompleteness: a theory describes some observations quite well, but it contradicts the theories that describe other observations well. You can have either inconsistency (if you use many theories to explain different facts) or incompleteness (if you use one of the contradictory theories). Modern theories on emotion reflect this pattern, like the rest of science; they explain some facts on emotion well (e.g. that an external situation can create emotions, therefore external situations are causes of emotion) but the theory contradicts other obvious facts (e.g. when emotions are created without an external trigger). Typical problems of modern theories discussed in the chapter include (1) not seeing how cognition, emotion, and relation are all essential to create emotions, (2) not seeing that either of these three can dominate and hence be considered the 'cause' of the others, (3) not recognizing the hierarchy in each of the three, and (4) not seeing how the connection between the three changes situationally.

Chapter three develops a theory of personality based on the understanding of the soul. It discusses how this theory is related to other approaches to personality—e.g. the "Big Five" and "Multiple Intelligence" theories—illustrating their similarities and differences. The chapter discusses how the three facets of the soul constitute the ability to perform three kinds of judgments—of truth, right, and good—and the world (as the reflection of the soul) is known incompletely if we only employ one type of judgment (e.g. the nature of truth, as in science). The chapter shows that personality types are different emphases on whether truth, good, or right are relatively more important, but also that no type is in itself well-suited for all situations. Thus, some situations require more emphasis on truth, others more on rightness, while yet others more on goodness, and therefore different personality types are well-suited to different types of situations. There is an 'ideal' personality type for each situation, but no 'ideal' type for all situations universally. In that sense, personality development entails integrating the missing personality types as the situation demands, after reading the situation correctly.

Chapter four focuses on the physical, chemical, and biological aspects of emotion, and describes how the human body can be described in three ways—parts, functions, and purposes. The world we observe by our senses appears to be *parts*. However, each part has a function in relation to the other parts, but the function depends on which parts are related; the function is not guaranteed even if all the parts remain unchanged, while the relation between the parts is altered—e.g. some new relations are created while old ones are destroyed. The parts can be observed but the relations cannot; however, the functioning of the body depends on these relations, which don't reduce to the parts. Similarly, the same function can be employed to achieve a different purpose, and the purpose doesn't reduce to the function. These forms of irreducibility constitute the failure of scientific reductionism and now every observation must be described as the combination of parts, functions, and purposes. This changes many fundamental assumptions in modern biology, such as evolutionary theory, which reduces functions to parts, the negation of free will, which reduces purpose to function, and species classification, which only looks at the body types rather than the mental states. The chapter discusses how the separation of parts, functions, and purposes creates a new way of thinking about health—namely, that we have to *balance* their relative importance and disease is the outcome of *imbalances*.

Chapter five discusses the Vedic theory in which emotions are classified along two dimensions— (1) six basic types, and (2) three distinct modes. The six basic types are desire, anger, greed, pride, envy, and confusion. The three basic modes are fear, hope, and detachment. Their combination produces 18 distinct emotional flavors where deep-seated fear, hope, or detachment become the causes of the other six emotions, although the ideologies of hope and fear lead to suffering, while the mode of detachment leads to happiness. The chapter then goes on to discuss three distinct social models based on the ideologies of fear, hope, and detachment; while hope and fear lead to competitive social models, detachment results in cooperation. The chapter notes why society can be happy only if based on detachment, compassion, and cooperation, and how the competitive models lead to cyclic rise and fall. This creates a connection between psychology and sociology: that to create a peaceful society, we have to change the individual's emotional state.

Chapter six discusses the different social relations associated with emotions and illustrates how these relations fall into a hierarchy—from a greater mental 'distance' to greater mental 'proximity'. It relies on a notion of space in which proximity and distance are defined based on likes and dislikes, not physical closeness. The hierarchy entails that when the world of individuals is connected through relations, a hierarchy is always necessary in order to *count* the individuals, which contradicts modern-day notions of 'equality'. If everything in the world were equal, there would also be *relativism*—i.e. infinite methods of counting and organizing, and since nobody can agree on the real order (e.g. what is higher or lower), there can never be cooperation among the diverging viewpoints. The chapter discusses that relationships are not accidental features of nature; they are, in fact, fundamental and begin in the relation to the self—created through self-awareness. The chapter delves into the Vedic descriptions of how the self divides into knower and known through self-awareness, and then into many through other-awareness. The 'other' in this case is all that the self is not; knowing the self means knowing what the self is not, but that knowledge creates other things distinct from the self. Vedic texts describe how self-awareness and other-awareness create the male-female distinction as the known object and the power by which it knows itself and others. This forms the basis of 'male' and 'female' archetypes which are separate and yet only two aspects of the same experience as knower and known. The chapter discusses different 'male' and 'female' archetypes and how they are reflected at different stages of man-woman relations, and how these relations can be understood as reflections of divine nature.

31

Chapter seven explores the expression of emotion across symbolic domains from literature, music, art, economy, and politics, to science and mathematics. That matter is a symbol of the mind is evident when it comes to expression in literature, music, and art, because they not only express the ideas in the mind but also the accompanying emotions. This implies two things. First, that symbolism reveals not just the conceptual meaning and the intentional reference, but also the emotive content. Second, we must subordinate the cognitive and emotive content to the questions of what is true, good, and right, and symbolic expression is not just about our mental states, but also which states are true, right, and good. In short, symbolic expression is not *meant* to imitate life; it is rather meant to depict the *ideal* life. The preference of ideals over ideas changes everything from mathematics to science, art, and social life as we not only realize that symbolism is *incomplete* unless both cognitive and emotive content is deciphered, but also that it is *inconsistent* if some expression doesn't meet the full criterion of truth, right, and good.

Chapter eight discusses the role of emotion in religion, highlighting a traditional conflict between personalist and impersonalist viewpoints. The impersonalist view has dominated Western philosophy where the ultimate reality is portrayed as Platonic ideas—which leads to logical thinking and modern science. The personalist view has dominated most modern religions where the ultimate reality is a *person*—which leads to the emotive basis of religiosity, often in contradiction to logical and scientific thinking. Both these ideologies are incomplete on their own because "science without religion is lame and religion without science is blind"[14]. Just as science deals in the question of truths, religion has traditionally dealt with the questions of right and good. Their conflict emerges only because all the truths are not pleasing, and all that is pleasing is not right. When we consider the notion of a soul, we don't omit all that is false, wrong, and bad. Rather, we seek that *subset* that is compatible with the nature of the soul—i.e. true, right, and good—while explaining how things that are not true, right, and good, are also temporary, ignorant, and painful. Religion, therefore, is not a separate endeavor from science; it is science defined in a broader sense of truth, right, and good.

As you can see, the scope of this book is vast because it covers wide-randing topics, from philosophical materialism, to personality theories, to the description of body and mind, to the notion of symbolic expression and social organization, to human relationships, and religion. Each of these is a disparate area of inquiry at present. But all of these are aspects of human experience. In that sense, what transcends individual experiences—the soul—can be used to unify the understanding of these different types of experiences. The book is ambitious in undertaking such a wide-ranging unification. And yet, once the soul is understood, everything else is naturally demystified.

2

Theories of Emotion

A theory is something nobody believes, except the person who made it. An experiment is something everybody believes, except the person who made it.

—*Albert Einstein*

The Outside-In Worldview

A hallmark of all modern theories on emotion is their outside-in worldview: the presumption that external stimulus creates an "arousal" in the body—a physical state change—which then leads to emotion. What about dreams that lead to fear? Or that fear which comes from the contemplation of what might happen even though it hasn't happened? Or the anxiety arising from one's inadequacy? Or the love that one feels by remembering children and family? Do you desire tasty food after you see it in a restaurant, or do you go to a restaurant because you desire tasty food? What about innovation—do you desire the innovative thing after it exists, or do you desire to create it? What is the stimulus, in these cases, that is supposed to cause emotion?

Modern science grew out of the need to control nature, and behaviorist psychologists have treated the mind as something that responds to stimulus. In behaviorism, 'mind' is the correlation between stimulus and response. The correlation may be explained using emotion, cognition, perception, etc. but everything must begin from a stimulus. Nothing could be a worse caricature of the mind, which in the simplest understanding of the self, involves *free will* in the sense that the person can act without a stimulus. This is an inside-out view of the self, and it is the commonsensical ground on which society is built. For example, we are all urged to conquer our inner—often irrational—fear, just as we extol the virtues of spontaneous and unselfish love.

When love and fear—the most powerful emotions—drive us forward even without a stimulus, while all the behaviorist theories pretend that emotion follows a stimulus, there is something fundamentally wrong with these theories regardless of what else they seem to explain about emotions.

The fundamental flaw in theories of emotion is that we are stuck in the outside-in view of perception, mental development, cognition, and emotion. The man at birth is a "blank slate"—to quote John Locke—and he acquires everything through sensual stimulus thereafter. As a result, man has no innate *nature* because everything is caused by *nurture*. You can therefore pass the buck of responsibility to what you have experienced due to a stimulus in which you had no choice and have no accountability for not attempting anything completely out of your own accord by changing the stimulus.

What could be more important to man if not free will, responsibility, and accountability? And what kind of society—economics and politics—is possible without a central role for choice? If man is only a system to be stimulated for an appropriate response, then who are those stimulators that are not themselves stimulated? The philosophical, psychological, and sociological ramifications of a theory on emotion are as important as the theory's empirical usefulness given that emotions have a bearing on these broader questions. The question of emotion is therefore not just about how we elicit the desired response via a stimulus, but also the fact that we desire a response before it is elicited. Are we to suppose that society has reached a point where we only respond to others' desires and have no innate desire of our own?

I will spend no more time on suggesting that I disagree with the premise of modern theories of emotion because it contradicts experience, has disastrous outcomes for philosophy, sociology, and economics, and is morally and spiritually hollow. In fact, I believe that there can be no understanding of humanity without an understanding of the soul that was born into a body and will survive its death. The "blank slate" view emerges because we suppose that there is no past prior to birth, and there will be no future beyond death. What happens between these two points is no more significant than a chemical reaction, which begs not just explanatory questions (how chemicals become thoughts and emotions) but also moral questions (why is happiness better than sadness if both are only said to be chemical reactions)?

In the remainder of this chapter, I will focus on the explanatory gaps in the theories on emotion, leaving their philosophical ramifications aside. This is deliberate because how a theory is used to build a society, and how people in that society come to view themselves are *normative* questions—they try to answer the question: What should society and humanity *be*? The more important question is whether the assumptions on which we build that society are empirically and theoretically sound explanations of the human mind. A theory's primary purpose is to explain how the world is, rather than what the world should be. Only if we can find a good explanation of experience, can we talk about how to improve or alter that experience and remove its shortcomings. If we don't have a good explanation of experience, we also cannot diagnose the causes of that experience, and hence the ways that might fix it.

With this background, I will now proceed to survey the current theories. What they claim is as important as why they claim it—there are motivations underlying the theories on emotion, and we can tap into the purpose that breeds a type of theory, analyzing the desire it fulfills. For example, the author of the theory cannot say that he started liking the theory after he formulated it. He must say that he wanted to formulate a theory and had a purpose to begin with, which presumes the motivation to pursue a certain ideology. What emotional states might underpin the choice of a theory on emotions? I think the best way to critique a theory is to show it the mirror. What better way than to reveal the motivations underlying a theory of motivation?

The James-Lange Theory

Proposed independently by psychologist William James[1] and physiologist Carl Lange[2], the James-Lange theory[3] claims that emotions follow the physiological reactions to external stimuli. The external stimuli are the cause, the physiological changes are produced from the stimuli, and emotions are caused by physiological change. The cardinal examples of emotions that this theory explains are lust and fear. For instance, a man may be attracted to a woman by the smell of her perfume, the dazzling colors of her dress, the gloss of the makeup on her skin, or the revealing curves of her body. A mortal threat to one's life or limb, similarly, results in a fight-or-flight response before a person even realizes that there is something dangerous and experiences fear. In such cases, there is an external stimulus which causes an emotional response, so it seems that the stimulus is the obvious cause of emotions.

This theory of emotion stems from the examination of animal behavior and rests the understanding of human emotions on the primitiveness of animal feeling. Biology is given greater importance than the mind, and primal instincts like lust and fear—which dominate the animal kingdom—are treated as the cardinal examples of facts to be explained. No doubt, lust and fear are the most dominant forms of emotion even in modern human society, although they are not necessarily the only possible types of feelings. Some people still experience subtle and nuanced emotions like affection, admiration, or envy, which are dominantly found in humans instead of animals.

One cannot feel affection, admiration, or envy without cognition, and the complexity of cognition increases as the emotion gets more subtle. This suggests a far greater role for the mind than this theory permits. For instance, to feel affection, sensations are not enough. One must also infer the relationship to the person—e.g. that this is *my* child—which involves a mental recognition of facial features followed by their correlation to determine that this is a child, that the child has a resemblance to my memory of my child, and therefore it must be my child. Affection follows the mental recognition of an object followed by the assessment of one's relationship to that object—established previously. To experience admiration, one must have sensations, but also a cognitive understanding of reality, followed by *comparison* to previously cognized realities before one realizes that this experience is far superior to previous ones and hence worthy of appreciation. There is no admiration without a comparison and the comparison involves both cognition and recall of previous facts from memory. To feel envy, again, one must have a cognition of a person, recall from memory their understanding of themselves, perform a comparison between the self and the other, and judge that the self is inferior to the other before one can feel envy. You cannot feel envy unless you compare the self to the other, *after* you have a cognitive image of both, and a *yardstick* has been established which indicates you are relatively inferior.

We have noted that emotions are also hierarchical—that there are gross sensual pleasures and subtle or deep feelings. The emotions produced by physiological responses correspond to sensual pleasures (or pains)—these include carnal lust and mortal fear. But emotions don't end there. As we delve into the deeper recesses of the mind, we can find subtle emotions such as affection, admiration, and envy, which may not even be expressed through a bodily response—e.g. fight-or-flight, or inexorable attraction that leads to a person staring. The subtle emotions are not only produced after far more mental processing, but the effects of this processing may not even be visible to others. There is far more complexity in their causation and far fewer observable effects as a result of that causality. Therefore, not only is it harder to explain their origin, but also harder to detect their presence empirically.

The idea that emotions follow a physiological change is therefore problematic when we consider subtle emotions, which arise more in the human world—with more sophisticated and developed minds—than in the animal kingdom, with a primitive mental life. To reconcile the production of gross and subtle emotions, we first must recognize a hierarchy and then accompany the emotions to the level of complexity commensurate with how deep the hierarchy goes. The deeper the emotion, the more subtle is its experience, and that subtle feeling rides on a more complex psychological explanation. The gross emotion, therefore, has a simple explanation, but the subtle emotion has a very complex explanation—which is when the James-Lang theory fails.

Schachter and Singer's Two-Factor Theory

Stanley Schachter[4] and Jerome Singer[5]formulated the two-factor theory of emotions[6], and like the James-Lange theory, it claims that physical arousal plays a primary role in emotions although the arousal is similar for a wide variety of emotions and could not be the sole arbiter for emotional experiences. The two-factor theory attributes emotions to a combination of physiological arousal, and its *cognitive interpretation* derived from the person's environment. For example, if you are waiting for an interview, and your body is perspiring because the surroundings are hot, you are likely to feel anxiety—thinking that since you are perspiring while waiting for an interview, you must be anxious. Conversely, if the surroundings are cold, you are less likely to feel the heat, and that should somewhat calm your nerves—i.e. feel less anxious. Unlike the James-Lange theory where the surroundings create the arousal which leads to emotions, in the two-factor theory, the arousal and the emotion are created separately—the emotions based on the interpretation.

The idea is that there is some correlation between anxiety and heat, and therefore heat can cause anxiety. The problem is that when we posit that emotions are caused by physiology, we forego the inverse relation in which anxiety makes the body hotter and peacefulness makes it cooler. Clearly, in such cases, the emotions are the cause of physiological changes.

The two-factor theory applies to the self the same kind of interpretation that we typically apply to others. That is, the emotions are caused because we *interpret* our physiology to create the emotions quite like we interpret others' body language to derive their emotional state (although we don't feel those emotions). For instance, if you saw that a person waiting for an interview was perspiring, you would naturally infer that he must be anxious, because you have no recourse to their actual mental state and you are *unlikely* to attribute perspiration to the heat in the surroundings and more *likely* to attribute it to anxiety based on typical mental modeling of the people around you (who tend to perspire while waiting for an interview). However, that interpretation depends a lot on your previous background. For instance, if you don't know much about the anxiety that precedes an exam or an interview (because you never saw others getting anxious in such situations) and you come from a colder climate such that your body recognizes that the environment is hot, then you would attribute the perspiration to heat rather than anxiety.

Sometimes perspiration leads to anxiety (when the interpretation cor-relates interviews with fear) and at other times it doesn't (when interviews are nothing to be worried about). Given that contextual interpretation cre-ates the emotion—although based on a physical state—the two-factor theory attributes emotions to both physical states and their cognitive interpretation (which are the "two factors"). Thus, the person who associates the interview and perspiration to the mental anxiety will feel the anxiety, but one who does not make that connection would simply find the environment hotter. In this picture, emotions are outcomes of establishing cause-effect relationships based on the observation of facts. The cause-effect relation is speculative and based on whatever mental model one carries from the past. But once the mental model has been established, the emotions naturally follow.

Thus, if you have been watching horror movies in which a person gets mugged in a dark alley, you will feel fear while walking through a dark alley because you carry a mental model that says— "people get mugged in dark alleys". You *situationally anticipate* a mugging although you haven't been attacked. In such situations, there is some sensual stimulus—e.g. walking in a dark alley—but the most critical stimulus that would decisively explain the emotional outcome may not exist (e.g. fear comes from an attack, but nobody has attacked you). You still feel the fear because you mentally extrapolate the situational outcomes based on a previously formed model of reality.

The two-factor theory nicely explains why one feels fear in a dark alley and it overcomes the shortcomings of the James-Lange theory in being able to attribute subtle emotions like envy, admiration, and affection based on previously formed mental models mediating the production of emotion. That is, because a cognitive interpretation is involved in the creation of emotions, therefore, it is possible to see how subtle emotions such as envy, affection, and admiration can be produced *after* a cognition of the situation.

However, this theory would also entail that lust is excited not merely by the scent of a woman or the curves of her body, but also by the mental model that good smelling women with curvy figures are desirable because others have socially constructed this model of attraction, and I should model my desires based on these previously assimilated social constructs. The idea that a woman is attractive because others will find her attractive is a false caricature of most man-woman attractions. No doubt social sensibilities play a role in a long-term decision whether a man and woman get married, but to say that all attraction is mediated by such social constructs is also false. Horror movies can lead to the fear of dark alleys, but romantic movies—in which a nice-smelling curvy woman is found desirable—are not the sole cause of attraction to nice-smelling curvy women. The right approach would be to say that sensations create arousal, but precisely how certain scents and sights create that excited state cannot be explained just based on chemistry. Rather, we have to say that even physiological arousal can be explained only when we attribute the biology of the organism a *purpose*—i.e. likes and dislikes. We cannot explain these likes and dislikes just based on chemistry, although the excited state can be *detected* by the change in bodily chemistry. How the chemistry is caused by an intentional purpose now becomes a unique problem in chemistry itself, in order to explain physiological changes in the body, even *before* they are interpreted cognitively to create emotions.

The two-factor theory suffers from the opposite problem relative to the James-Lange theory. In the latter, all emotion is caused by physiological states and in the former, by mental models and social constructs (apart from physiological arousal). The problem is that deeper emotions involve deeper levels of mental and intellectual reality while the superficial sensual pleasures involve shallower levels of material reality. For example, deep bonds of attraction between a man and woman are based on mental models—e.g.

the social acceptability criteria—but the superficial attractions are based only on physical beauty. If we have to explain emotions, we have to account for both—superficial and deep attractions—and the emotions that accompany them. This is not achievable without distinguishing the superficial from the deep attraction through a hierarchy, attributing deeper levels of emotions to mental models while attributing superficial attraction to physiology.

In other words, we cannot just say that purpose and interpretation are cognitive functions. We have to say that these are physiological functions too. The cognitive interpretation has no special status in causing emotions because even with the cognition we don't have to get excited unless we like or dislike the cognition—i.e. we have a purpose. This purpose must exist both physiologically (e.g. as the carnal desires for sensual pleasure in the body) and cognitively (e.g. the social and individual interpretation of when something is desirable) which lead to deep or superficial levels of feelings.

Cannon-Bard Theory

Walter Cannon[7]—a physiologist at Harvard University—formulated this theory with his student Philip Bard. The theory claims that both physiological changes and emotional experiences are created in parallel and independent of each other by the hypothalamus in the brain. The theory challenges the key tenet of the James-Lange theory that emotional responses are caused by physiological changes. It is based on experiments in which afferent nerves[8]—neurons from the skin to the sympathetic nervous system (which control autonomic responses)—were cut, removing the stimuli that cause physiological arousal. With the connection intact, we expect an organism to react spontaneously to touch—e.g. in a fight-or-flight response[9]. But if the connection is severed, the physiological arousal is absent and according to the James-Lange theory, the emotional response should be missing too. Cannon and Bard showed that the emotional response is intact even when the physiological arousal is absent, thus disproving a key tenet of the James-Lange theory.

The Cannon-Bard experiments have similarities to the *phantom limb*[10] phenomenon where a person's limbs have been severed (due to an accident or surgery) but the person continues to experience the sensations and pain in the limbs as they would prior to the dismemberment. The 'cut' in this case is even more drastic than performed by the Cannon-Bard experiments (the entire limb and not just the afferent nerves are cut in the case of phantom limbs phenomenon), and the outcome is therefore even more surprising in the phantom limb cases because psychosomatic pain continues to be experienced in the imaginary limb even when the limb itself does not exist anymore.

The existence of pain in a body part when the part doesn't exist indicates a need to separate the part from the feeling associated with that part. If emotions can exist without physiological arousal, physiological arousal can also exist without emotions. An example of the latter is that the body is active, but the person is not anxious. Meditative traditions and martial arts teach the practices by which the body remains active, but the mind becomes free of stress. Phantom limbs and the Cannon-Bard experiments are the converse of meditation in which the bodily activity is not sensed although the emotional state is felt. These phenomena point to the need to view cognition and emotion as being logically distinct, and yet, in most cases, they are associated.

In all cases, the body parts exist as possibilities, and the emotion selects among possible relations to other objects, creating a perception and a feeling. The feeling is, however, not the cause; it is rather caused by a *purpose* and one gets upset if the purpose is unfulfilled, or joyous if it is fulfilled. If a person's purpose is not material success, then successes would not make them happy, and failures would not make them unhappy. Both success and failure would be the completion of a task, which must be followed by more tasks. Thus, it is possible to become emotionally 'detached' from the acts of the body. This detachment doesn't mean the end of the bodily activity. It only means that one is using the body for a purpose that is not enlivened by a material success and not frustrated by a material failure. Both success and failure are just outcomes of actions, which then lead to more such actions. The purpose continues to exist, but the emotional outcomes cease to exist.

When a limb is severed its possibility of being used is removed, but one's purposes which aim to employ the limb may not be gone if the purpose exists materially. Just because the body part is cut, the desire to use that part is not. The pain in the case of phantom limbs is the consequence of a purpose trying to use the limb, although the limb is not available. The pain is the outcome of the frustration of the purpose. Similarly, even if the afferent nerves are cut, these nerves only pertain to the hierarchical connection between the parts. Cutting a connection doesn't cut the tree of purposes, and because the purpose exists in all parts of the body, the feeling can still be created by the purpose tree, producing an emotional arousal even though one doesn't have a sensation.

The key point is that experience has three different pathways— (1) a relation to an external object, (2) a cognition of that object, and (3) a purpose in relating to that object, which creates a feeling. In the case of phantom limbs, the relation to the object and the purpose of that relation exists even though the limb itself doesn't. Therefore, the subject feels that they are touching something and experiencing a pain, but there is no cognition of the object itself being touched. Thus, two of the three parts are present, and hence experience is created by the existing parts. Similarly, in the Canon-Bard experiments, there is a relation and a pain, but no cognition of the object, because the cognitive component has been cut, as it is the visible component, but the relation and the purpose are invisible and cannot be physically cut.

Once we explain the experiments differently, we can note that the premise of emotion and cognition being 'independent' and 'parallel' doesn't work because sometimes bodily heat can lead to anxiety, and at other times anxiety leads to bodily heat. Therefore, sometimes the emotion is the cause, and at other times it is the effect. In most cases, every cognition involves some emotion and every emotion involves some cognition. However, because both emotion and cognition are hierarchical, sometimes the physiological effects of emotion and cognition may not be very apparent, especially if the emotion and cognition are *subtle*. As we saw above, affection is a deep emotion and lust is shallow. Therefore, lust will produce more physiological change and affection, less. Just because we see less or more physiological change relative to an emotion only means that the emotion and cognition are deeper. Lust will have far greater physiological implications, while affections may not.

The relation between cognition and emotion is also varied. Some cognitions lead to strong emotions, others don't. This is because emotions are mediated by *desires*. If the cognition is as desired, there is happiness. If the cognition is not as desired, there is unhappiness. If the cognition has no relation to one's desire, then there is no emotional change and the person remains neutral. Thus, small cognitions can lead to big emotions, while big changes that result in big cognitions may have no emotional response. The fact that these two *seem* to vary independently doesn't mean they are independent. It just means that physiology doesn't create emotions. The main cause of emotion is our purpose, and varied responses to the same cognition follow because that purpose exists materially. We cannot observe the purpose in a third-person manner, but we can experience it in a first-person manner.

Emotion and physiology are indeed "parallel" in the sense that they are separate. But in every scenario, there will always be both emotion and cognition because there is no experience unless we combine them. However, we can cut off the physiological response and the emotion and cognition could still exist at a subtle level but not at the gross level. Thus, a person may feel an emotional connect upon a touch even if the afferent nerves to the skin have been cut because the skin is only one of the pathways of experience—purpose and relation are others. Even if the cognitive signals have been cut, the relation and purpose will give the experience that a person is being touched and the purpose of that touch is affectionate, although the person may not cognize if the touch is soft or hard. This fact is often shown in movies where a person in a coma is touched by a family member; while the doctors insist that the person cannot feel their touch or hear their voice, the movie shows the person having an experience though not through the body.

The Cannon-Bard experiments are variations on coma scenarios and the phantom limb phenomena, but their explanation in the theory is not accurate because (1) in most cases emotion is the key decider of alternatives selected by the purpose to produce a cognition, and (2) there are situations in which physiological changes such as heat lead to stress or vice versa. In the former case, emotion is the cause and cognition is the effect. In the latter case, cognition is the cause and emotion is the effect. In neither case are emotion and cognition parallel phenomena, as the Cannon-Bard theory claims.

The Cognitive Appraisal Theory

The cognitive appraisal theory[11] suggests that an appraisal—mediated by a cognition—is involved in emotional experience, and the cognition must precede the emotion. This theory overcomes the shortcomings of the James-Lang theory where physiological arousal precedes emotions because in many cases—e.g. admiration and envy—appraisal is indeed involved. However, cognitive appraisal does not always precede emotions. As noted in the two-factor theory, one can feel anxious simply because the surrounding is hot or have anticipatory anxiety that is not driven either by rational thought or by real-world cognition of facts. In other words, there is a subtle difference between perceiving a danger because it exists or imagining and projecting a danger when it doesn't exist. The appraisal theory attributes the feeling to the perception of danger, although it could easily cover the imagined danger as well. For example, it is not necessary that a cognitive appraisal be involved before the emotional feeling is produced. It is quite possible that our fears are irrational, and they are produced *despite* reasoning to the contrary.

The appraisal theory comes close in identifying the mechanism of emotion by dividing experience into three distinct aspects: relation, motivation, and cognition. There is always a relationship between a person and the environment, where the environment causes the emotions. The motivational aspect assesses one's goals relative to the current situation, to determine whether the situation is relevant or irrelevant relative to those goals. The cognitive component involves the appraisal of the situation, or an evaluation of the implications of the current situation for one's life's goals. There is hence a great amount of synergy between the appraisal theory and the Vedic model we have been discussing. There are, however, several nuanced distinctions that don't exist in the appraisal theory relative to the Vedic model.

First, the appraisal theory talks about cognition in the sense of deciding whether the situation is good or bad for me, but it doesn't invoke the *conceptual* aspect of the cognition in which you recognize that something is a table or a chair. It's noteworthy that we all carry a theory of the world and data from the world is succinctly summarized into a concept—e.g. when perceiving the world, we aren't aware of every minuscule sensation; we rather perceive a 'chair' which summarizes the sensation into a cognition. Cognition also involves the understanding of whether things are related to me—in the sense of me and mine. Is this *my* chair? Or is it someone else's chair? The relation is thus different from the cognition of relation: we establish a relation to everything we experience, but we don't necessarily conclude that we are masters of all that we see. Emotions arise when we cognize the relation to ourselves because if things are not related to us, we won't be bothered emotionally. But that relation to what we perceive is cognitive; it is not just a relation, it is not yet motivational, and it is not an appraisal of implications.

Second, once we have a cognition that the situation involves something related to me—e.g. it concerns my family, house, job, country, race, society, etc., all involving the cognition of 'mine'—then we bring our personal *goals* into play. The motivational aspect in this case follows the cognition and the so-called 'appraisal' is not cognitive but motivational—i.e. given that this is my family, and the family is in danger, and I am motivated to protect my family, the motivation will make me angry, anxious, or fearful. Once the mind is overwhelmed by an emotion, then the cognitive functions are hampered by it. For example, if we are angry, cognition will assign the responsibility for the situation to someone else and blame them for what is happening rather than start finding a solution. Similarly, if one is fearful, then the emotion will cause a person to start imagining what would happen if things don't change, rather than causing them to act to change those things. Conversely, anxiety will cause a person to alternate between action and inaction, making their actions less effective than if they weren't overcome by emotion.

The appraisal theory confuses these different aspects: it calls the assessment of one's relation to the world motivational when it is cognitive, it separates a person's desires from their emotional response when the response is due to the desire, it doesn't distinguish between the cognition that precedes the motivational response and the cognition that is controlled and conditioned by that response, although the cognition that follows fear and anxiety is different from the one that precedes fear or anxiety—in the first case cognition dominates emotion, and in the latter emotion dominates cognition. If a person is overwhelmed by emotion—e.g. fear—then subsequent cognition is tailored to fit that emotion; we start imagining things that magnify and justify that fear and make it bigger than it must be. Conversely, if we are not fearful, then cognition makes the same situation seem trivial.

Cognition is not always the cause of emotion, nor is emotion always the cause of cognition. Either cognition or emotion can be the cause, and when they are the cause, they also *dominate* the experience. Thus, rapid emotional response results in a cognition being tailored to fit the emotional response, while a delayed emotional response results in the emotion being tailored according to the cognition. Clearly, no alternative is universally appropriate—sometimes (e.g. when the danger is severe) it is better to respond quickly and imagine the worst, while at other times (e.g. the situation is not dangerous) it is better to respond after deliberation and careful planning. The issue is not whether emotion or cognition always follow each other because they do follow. The issue is that emotion and cognition become the dominant determinants of the overall response in different situations, and the order between them is not predetermined. Therefore, sometimes emotion dominates cognition and at other times cognition dominates emotion. For instance, many fearful responses may be tempered by detailed rational cognition, and many cognitive judgments may be hijacked by emotional overwhelming.

The appraisal theory is great because it identifies the relational, cognitive, and motivational parts of experience. It is flawed in that it mixes up the roles performed by motivation and cognition, because of the use of the term 'motivation', which is ambiguous: motivations can be rational or emotional. For instance, if your boss tells you that you will get promoted if you complete a task, the emotional motivation is the promotion (because it will make you happy) while the rational motivation is to complete the task. Completion of the task does not make you happy if you don't get promoted, in fact, it would make you angry and frustrated. The emotional motivation creates subsidiary rational motivations and we might sometimes remember the emotional motivation to fulfill the rational motivation (if the rational reasons don't motivate you enough) and at other times just focus on the rational motivation ignoring the emotional motivation (because being overwhelmed by desire doesn't help you complete the rational goals faster). The appraisal theory does not recognize how emotion and cognition can alternatively dominate each other, controlling the overall experience and emotional outcome.

Motivation must itself be viewed as an emotional state in that it prompts us toward goals, which are created due to the basic need in each person to be *happy*. The purpose is therefore not to simply do some things but to do them because it makes us happy. The motivation cannot be separated from emotion, although in some cases we use that goal to find the rational path to achieve it. Similarly, if the goal is not achieved, emotions follow because the goal was to become happy, and not fulfilling the goal leads to unhappiness. Likewise, certain relations to the world alter our cognition and make us think different ideas, which then alters emotions. The relation, emotion, and cognition are thus dominant at different times, but their combination is always essential to produce an experience. It is futile to imagine that just because some cognition precedes emotion in many cases, emotions will not precede the cognition (and alter it) in other cases. Similarly, emotions (as desires) are the cause of seeking certain relations and thinking in a particular way.

Materialist theories of nature are, for example, motivated by the need to eliminate the soul from the description of reality and there is as much pleasure in finding an explanation of our observations as in the fact that such an explanation doesn't invoke a soul. One, therefore, doesn't always begin in a cognition—e.g. a theory of nature—and conclude that it makes us happy. We also begin in motivations (e.g. to eliminate the soul from the theory of nature), find the necessary relationships—experiments and data collection that don't seem to involve the observer—followed by a theory (cognition) that explains the data without invoking that soul, thereby fulfilling the motivation. The fact that science can be motivated toward specific kinds of explanations, therefore, tailors the choice of relationships and the conceptual cognitions.

The Facial-Feedback Theory

Everybody knows that happy people tend to smile. The facial-feedback theory says is that if you smile you will feel happy. This idea can be easily proven in many scenarios. For example, if you are feeling stressed and weak, you can stand with your legs apart with hands on your waist and you will feel confident and strong again. If your head is bowed due to unhappiness, just looking straight or slightly upward will inject a sense of positivity into your life. If you are feeling scared with your legs and arms crossed, just sitting with open legs and arms will make you feel more confident and less afraid. Doing the things that people do when they are happy—e.g. jumping, talking, eating, or having sex—will make you happy even if you were unhappy. You don't have to be happy to express that mental state into the *symbols* of happiness. Just pretending to be strong, confident, and happy also makes you happy. Conversely, if you don't express your sentiments into bodily symptoms, they tend to die. For instance, if you don't smile on seeing someone who makes you happy, after a while you will stop feeling the happiness on seeing them.

The facial feedback hypothesis[12] claims that our emotional experience is influenced by our bodily expressions, and by changing that expression we can change the emotional state. Just by repeating the motions of smiling and laughing you can gradually begin feeling happy and positive. If we thought of the body as the symbol of the mind, then the mental state of happiness can be expressed into the bodily demonstration of happiness, but even if the mind is not happy, but the body enacts the symbolism of happiness, the mind will eventually derive the mental meaning of happiness from the body.

The practice of bodily discipline to control the mental state is now well-known through *aṣṭānga-yoga* since people who practice yoga can alter their negative emotions into positive feelings. Indeed, *yoga* is described as an eight-step progressive practice in which physical exercises are the preliminary step toward controlling the mind. There is hence empirical evidence to prove facial-feedback. However, to assume that because physical states cause the mental state, they are indeed the mental state—as facial-feedback theories claim—is false because some people who don't express feelings may continue to feel, and while good posture generally makes you happy, some happy people also have bad posture. Bodily expression is neither a necessary nor a sufficient condition for experiencing a particular type of emotion although in many cases one can see a strong correlation between the two. The theory must be able to explain both the observations and their contradictions.

The central problem here is the nature of the mind-body interaction. Clearly, the feeling of happiness is felt in a first-person manner, but the bodily changes can be known in a third-person manner. Mind-body inter-action is an intractable problem when the body is treated as physical parti-cles because in the cases described above, they are expected to be *symbols* or *symptoms* of happiness. Even if you don't experience happiness, by just seeing others happy you can know that *they* are happy by just observing their bodily posture, facial expressions, confident walk, or carefree hand movement. In short, the mental state of happiness is inferred from the physical state, and this is possible only if we treat the physical state as a symbol of the men-tal state. There are cultural nuances of cognition involved in interpreting physical states into emotional ones because different behaviors are treated as expressions of emotional state in different cultures and societies. So, there is a language that helps us translate the physical state into mental state, but if that language has been learned through experience or practice, we can do that translation.

The mind-body interaction problem tells us mind and body are in one sense identical because the body is a symbol of the mind. In another sense, they are different because the body is the symbol and the mind is the mean-ing. Therefore, if we acquire the bodily symbols—e.g. we start laughing—then we can change the mental state (e.g. we start feeling happier). In this case, the symbol appears before the meaning is cognized. In other cases, the meaning appears before it is converted into a symbol. Therefore, either the meaning or the symbol can be the cause of the other's appearance and we cannot definitively claim that the mind or the body are universally the causes. It is more appropriate to say that the mind *or* the body could be the cause in different cases. The facial-feedback theory tells us that the body can be the cause of the mental states, and we can purposefully attain and body-to-mind change (if we were previously unable to change the mental state purposefully).

Modern science began from the study of inanimate objects like the collision of billiard balls, or metallic weights falling toward the ground. You don't have to treat such objects as *symbols*—even though they are symbols of ideas (e.g. the idea of a billiard ball or a metallic weight) because any such object is only one *instance* of the idea of a billiard ball or metallic weight. Therefore, even though ordinary objects are also symbols of ideas, you could disregard this symbolism as an artifact of our mental state and just study the physical properties. For instance, if you did not know about billiards, and you saw a billiard ball, you would just think of it as a colored round object, and that change in thought would not make a difference to the object. This belief gave rise to the notion that the ideas we attach to objects are purely mental constructs and our thinking makes no difference to the external world—creating the now-famous mind-body duality. The problem with this duality is that the mental states are indeed expressed through the body, and changing the mental state alters the physical state too. In other words, the physical state is not just an object; it is rather a *symbol* of the mental state or the concept.

The idea of matter has to be revised from physical objects to symbols of meaning. We don't just sensually perceive the symbols; we also mentally understand them, although the meanings we attach to these symbols can't be reduced to the physical states of the symbols. In other words, we separate the mind and the body and yet connect them as the meaning and its symbol.

The question now is: how is meaning expressed into symbols? This problem can be demystified if the meanings were also symbols—of even deeper meanings—which constructs an inverted-tree *hierarchy* where each node is a symbol if you look upward and a meaning if you look downward. Now, you don't have to suppose that there is a special 'substance' called mind or matter. There is just matter, but it is *subtle* when situated higher in the tree and *gross* when situated lower. Mind and matter are not separate kinds of things that interact in a unique way that physical particles don't. Mind and matter are simply two locations on the inverted tree. Obviously, relative to the number of leaves, there are fewer twigs, relative to the twigs there are fewer branches, relative to the branches there are fewer trunks, and there is only one root. Therefore, it is far easier to observe the leaves, but the trunks and root exist too. Furthermore, if you indeed saw the twigs or trunks you could not tell the difference from the leaves because they are both *particles*—physically speaking. To know that some particles are subtle while others are gross you would have to know the hierarchical *relation* between them. In effect, knowing the isolated particles is not all the knowledge, because the meanings are in the *hierarchical relation* between the particles.

This brings me back to the issue of whether the mind is the bodily state. Materially speaking, yes, both mind and body are comprised of particles, but the physical state of the particle is irrelevant to determining whether it is part of the mind or the body; to know which particle is the mind or the body, we have to know the hierarchical relationship between them.

When the bodily state is changed, a new branch of the tree is created which has both subtle and gross components. However, in the third person way, you cannot be sure the subtle component is indeed happiness if the person is smiling because the person may indeed smile, with the aim of pretending to be happy while feeling empty inside. The third-person observation can be deceived but the first-person observation would clearly know if the smile is indicative of happiness or a pretense of happiness. Therefore, if you know the mental state, you can understand what the physical state is a symbol *of*. But if you only know the physical state you might be mistaken about the mental state. However, if you want to feel happy, and you create the symbols of happiness (such as smiling), then you can obtain the needed *interpretation*—i.e. happiness. The happiness will arise if you want to interpret the bodily state as happiness rather than as the pretense or deception of happiness. The interpretation of bodily state is no different than the interpretation of the external world by which we judge if someone else is happy. The difference is that in this case we identify with the body and knowing that *this* body is happy is equivalent to *my* body is happy, which means that *I* am happy.

The process of creating happiness from the physical state is the *interpretation* of the physical state to derive the meaning. That meaning is also a symbol and we call it a mental *representation* but in the tree of meaning, the mental state is higher than the physical state. The act of interpreting our bodily state to derive happiness is the converse of expressing our happiness into the bodily state. Hence, it is incorrect to suppose that all happiness comes from the bodily state, just as it is wrong to suppose that one could not display a happy face without happiness. When physical theories of matter are revised to understand the role of meaning, and how it *organizes* material particles into *structures*, then we can see that meaning is a scientific property, which converts particles into symbols. If science studies matter as particles, then it misses the meaning. Thus, the body is *organized* in a way to express the mental state, but the particles in the body are not that mental state. Rather, the mental state is given by the *relationship* between the material particles.

Theories in Perspective

The above analysis of present theories is by no means an exhaustive survey of all theories on emotion, although I hope it served as a sample exposure to the various theories and their shortcomings. A complete theory has to take into account the fact that there is relation, cognition, and purpose, that each of these is organized hierarchically, that the hierarchy produces three kinds of trees, which are combined in experience, that the three propensities can become dominant or subordinate, and that they are *rooted* in the *sat, chit,* and *ananda* of the soul. We could only look at part of the whole reality and presume that it is the whole, but that produces a caricature of all that exists.

The above theories look at different parts of the three trees and proceed as if they were the whole. The James-Lange theory looks at the lower part of the tree and presumes that the gross perception is the cause of the subtle reality, when, in fact, the subtle reality often creates the gross experience. The two-factor theory gives importance to the surrounding environment from which the gross perception is obtained and claims that the emotional interpretation depends on that environment, but, again, the ability in the emotion to cause physiological changes is ignored. The Cannon-Bard theory realizes that physiological arousal and emotional states are distinct, but it connects the two *physiologically* in the hypothalamus when phenomena like phantom limbs indicate that pain in the limbs can be experienced even when the limbs don't exist. The separation between cognition and emotion is not taken deep enough—i.e. they are not treated as separate hierarchies. The appraisal theory incorporates an active role for both cognition and emotion but doesn't recognize that both can dominate the other, and become their cause. The facial-feedback recognizes that physical states create the mental states, but the role of interpretation—in which the mental state is *interpreted* from the body—is not recognized. Thus, we treat the body and the mind as physical particles rather than as symbols of meaning, which begs the question of how we know the emotional state in others even when we don't experience it.

The above theories are true in the data they collect, but false in the interpretation of that data, in most cases. To find a better theory we must reconcile the contravening data from different situations. For example, we need the data of physiological arousal, the observation of cognitive intervention, the interpretation of the bodily expression into mental states, the observations that separate emotion from cognition, how we are able to correctly judge one's emotional state from their bodily expression in most cases, and that we might sometimes be deceived by that expression, besides others. Only the theory that explains all the data is ultimately correct, but as we noted earlier, data collection typically follows the formulation of a hypothesis, and only the data that ratifies the hypothesis is typically collected. Our ability to repeat that experiment and confirm the data doesn't necessarily ratify the theory because the theory would be disproven by contravening data.

There are philosophical and methodological issues present even in the theories of emotion, and the primary issue is that a theory can never be verified—it can only be falsified[13]—if we only look at the data from a third-person perspective. However, we don't necessarily have to only look at the world from the third-person perspective, especially when it comes to emotional experience because emotions can only be observed in a first-person manner. The theory derived from the first-person experience should not be counteracted by the third-person experiments. But such experiments only mean that the theory isn't *falsified*. To know that the theory has been *verified*, we must rely on the first-person experience. If a verification has been performed from the first-person perspective, the fact that third-person experiments don't falsify the theory is only additional evidence for its truth. The lack of falsification is only necessary but not sufficient to prove its truth.

The philosophical and methodological issues in psychology not only reinstate the primacy of first-person observation but also require us to revise the outside-in view to the inside-out thinking. The inside-out worldview tells us that a subtle mental state is generally the cause of the gross bodily expression, although once the mental state has been expressed into the body, other bodies can also grasp that state through interpretation although they may not necessarily experience the mental state. The third-person experience followed by its interpretation can therefore create the mental state, although in many cases the mental state is the cause of the bodily expression.

That revision in turn necessitates the idea that the world is hierarchical—i.e. involves subtle and gross levels of material reality—rather than flat and linear. It also implies that matter by itself exists as a possibility to be selected by the relations and purposes and that the combination of these three produces the conscious experience. In these things, we can completely observe the physical states, intellectually infer the relationships, but we cannot explain the reason why someone makes a choice without delving into their desires and emotional states. In that sense, empirical observation, and rational inferences are inadequate to complete the picture of nature.

3

Emotion and Personality

The Theory of the Soul

As stated, in Vedic philosophy, the soul has three properties—*sat* or aware-ness, *chit* or meanings, and *ananda* or pleasure. Quite simply, these three aspects of the soul mean that (a) the soul exists as awareness, (b) that it has cognition which includes the body and the mind, and (c) that there are things it wants because it doesn't have them. The three aspects of the soul are layered on top of each other: awareness, cognition, and desire. One can give up desire without losing one's cognition. Similarly, one can give up cognition without letting go of awareness. But one cannot forego one's awareness. In that sense, awareness is the most fundamental, followed by cognition, fol-lowed by the desires that seek to possess what one does not already possess.

These three aspects of the soul are also reflected in matter and pervade the body—the parts of the body are due to *chit*, the functional role of each body part (in relation to other body parts and other bodies) is due to *sat*, and the purpose associated with the functions of each part is due to *ananda*.

The *sat* of the soul expands into a variety of functional roles. Examples of such roles include ordinary relationships such as father, mother, child, citizen, employee, friend, lover, etc. They define our identity through a mutual relation, and they draw our awareness toward the individual we are related to. So, awareness is both a relation and an awareness. Originally, the soul has a relation to itself, which constitutes its self-awareness. It is focused internally on the self. It can be directed outwardly to other indi-viduals. All experiences entail my awareness of myself. I could not exist unaware of my existence, and existence can be equated with awareness. In principle, awareness and existence are separate ideas, but when applied to the self, they entail each other, because if I exist, then I must be aware of my existence. This is the source of much-unwanted confusion when *sat* is sometimes translated into "existence" and other times into "awareness", when they are the same thing.

Even in this life, the material appellations such as "father" and "mother" are modified; however, the awareness of the self, or the relation to the self, is never lost. Therefore, my existence is continuous and eternal while my being a father is temporary. Owing to this fact, the *sat* is also called the *eternity* of the soul. This adds to the confusion because *sat* was previously called existence, and then called awareness, and it is now also called eternity. These ideas may sometimes even be combined by calling the soul "eternal existence" or "eternal awareness". These are not contradictory. Once we understand the nature of awareness there is no conflict among the varied descriptions.

Awareness is the need in the soul to relate to something. We all have the need to relate with families, societies, nations, and cultures. Every living entity exists in a tribe—it could be family, race, society, culture, or humanity. The origin of our instinct to exist in tribes is the soul's awareness, which compels us to identify ourselves in relation to other things that are not us. Once the soul relates to something other than itself, it obtains a role in their relation. Thus, for instance, we can take on the role of a father, mother, or employee. When the soul adopts an identity, which is entangled with another identity, then it becomes aware of the person who is entangled in their identity. Thus, awareness of the self leads to awareness of the other, just because the awareness of the self is externalized. Through such externalization, awareness becomes a relation to something else. Therefore, the material counterpart of *sat* is a relation to something else. Notably, it started as the relationship to the self, but when the self identifies with other individuals, then, that relationship to self becomes the relationship to the other individual.

Now we are led to an unintuitive position in which existence equals awareness (because we cannot exist without knowing our existence), and awareness equals a relation (because to be aware of something is itself to be situated in a relationship to it). The introverted nature of the soul is converted into extroversion. This extroversion—which we call "consciousness"—is identical to material relationships, and the counterpart of the soul's awareness in matter is relationality. As a result, these relationships are equated to awareness and the *mahattattva* where these relationships originate is now equated to "consciousness". However, this "consciousness" is temporary world-awareness, not the eternal self-awareness. We can say that world-awareness is a material element and can be described scientifically, however, self-awareness is non-material, and hence outside material science. The scope of material science can therefore be extended all the way to the origin of world-awareness, which begins in the externalization of awareness.

The technical term used to describe the relationship to other things is *sambandha* but it is no different than world-awareness, which originates in eternal existence. In a sense, we *exist* in a relationship, our experiences are produced through that relationship, and even our material identity is defined by that relation. Therefore, we can equate existence to eternity, eternity to awareness, awareness to relationship, and relationship to (material) identity once we understand the gradual process through which this comes about.

Why does a soul's introversion (i.e. self-awareness) become extroversion (i.e. world-awareness)? Why are we tempted to identify the self with things other than the self and enter relationships? The short answer is that the self-awareness is not satisfying enough. Sure, it is better than the suffering caused by material entanglements, and if someone is suffering, he or she desires to exit these relationships. Once the suffering has ceased, the soul is satisfied in the relation to the self, although this satisfaction is temporary. The soul is incomplete, and it seeks the other in order to complete itself. Thus, no one can stay isolated and just being self-aware. As a result, even if the soul transcends material relationships to be situated in self-awareness, it again falls into the same cesspool of material entanglements in order to find the completeness which it lacks in the self-awareness experience.

The awareness of the soul has a material counterpart in relationships between objects, through which these objects interact with each other. The material interaction is called *causality* which puts one entity in contact with another entity, and science ordinarily calls this cause a "force". The scientific notion of a force is flawed because forces spread everywhere in space, which means that all objects must always interact with all other objects. You cannot speak about a specific relationship between a specific pair of objects precisely because the force spreads to all existing objects and is expected to cause all objects to interact at once. In contrast, our consciousness is only aware of one thing at a time. When causal relationships are simultaneously enacted between all objects, the idea of a directed awareness—originating in the soul—becomes scientifically irrelevant because the material counterpart of the awareness (the relationships between objects) is evicted from science by postulating that all objects interact with all other objects. The notion of awareness, due to which we know specific things at any given time, would be scientifically relevant if all objects did not always interact with all objects because then we could posit a specific interaction as directed awareness.

In a revised notion of force, we could say that the force puts specific objects into "contact" with each other, and the role of force would be the selection of a specific pair of objects for interaction. The *choice* involved in the selection of a pair of interacting objects would now correspond to the choice of being aware of something specific, which manifests as a relation between specific objects, not all objects at once. We might note here that this new notion of force has now become real in atomic theory because force is mediated through *particles*, which create a source and destination pair of interacting objects. An object no longer interacts with all other objects. Rather, it *chooses* an object to interact with, although atomic theory is unable to describe this choice, making the theory incomplete. This incompleteness is the counterpart of the fact that the idea of force has now changed from a universal interaction between all particles to a selected pairwise interaction between two objects. In this modified notion, we can think of force as a material counterpart of the soul's awareness, which is always directed towards a specific object, not all objects. The choice in awareness is reflected in the creation of a specific pair of particles between which the energy is transferred due to 'force'.

From Awareness to Cognition

So far, awareness is not *cognition*. That is, we have only established a relation between things, but we haven't yet defined the properties of those things. Before we can attribute properties, we must identify the observational relation to that thing through which its properties are cognized. This observational relation originates in the relation to the self or self-awareness by which we construct an identity of the self. The idea here is that everything has a relation to itself before it has a relation to other things. In physical theories, for example, we speak about the *self-field* of an object. In the case of gravitation, for example, each massive particle exerts a force on other things. But the field of the particle also exerts a force on itself. This force is often disregarded because the distance between the object and itself becomes zero which means that the force for itself must be infinite or a singularity. And yet, this singularity constitutes the individuality of the object. It is the means by which we can construct a *relational* definition of the object's identity. That is, what we mean by an object is that it bears a relationship to itself. This relation can be conscious in the case of observers, which we call their self-awareness. But this relation can be material as in the case of self-field.

Once we construct this relational identity, it becomes the *object* to which the properties can be attached. This object constitutes the unchanging entity underlying the changes. In the case of material identities, the identity does not persist because material particles can split and combine, thereby producing a greater or lesser number of particles. In the case of the soul, however, the identity always persists, which is why we also designate it as eternity. Nevertheless, even in the case of material particles, we must postulate the existence of an identity aside from the properties. The identity, however, is constructed from a *field* of relationships. It is a different kind of identity than when we suppose the existence of *a priori* real individual particles, which subsequently form a relation (of force in case of material particles) to other particles. The situation here is the opposite—the relationship constructs the identity. We can say that it is an interpersonal or contextual identity that is different from a personal or absolute identity (which we will discuss subsequently).

The objects are identified by *names* while the properties are identified by *concepts*. For example, you can say that "the apple is red" where the "apple" is a name, while redness is a concept. The irony here is that "apple" can also sometimes be a concept, which leads to confusion. This dichotomy can be resolved through the notion of a *semantic space* in which locations indicate concepts[1]. The location by itself is a physical property but locations are defined only in relation to other (higher) locations, so the "concept" is the distance between locations. This semantic space—we will see later—exists as a *tree* in which the more abstract ideas are closer to the root and the more detailed ideas are closer to the leaves. Each branch on the tree acts—relatively speaking—as a root and can therefore be called the "object" whose "properties" are the twigs emanating from the branch. Likewise, each branch can be viewed as an emanation from a trunk, and thus a property of the trunk.

The conceptual objects are different from the identities we spoke of above. For instance, a 'table' is a conceptual object, but it is different from the identity produced through a field of relationships. The field-identity is a relational object. The 'table' is a conceptual object. And we will subsequently speak about a third kind of object—which is a personal or absolute object.

The entire tree of concepts originates from *chit* or the ability of understanding meanings. When the awareness is directed toward the self, the soul has knowledge of itself. When it is directed outwardly, then it acquires cognition of the world. This cognition includes what we normally call our body and mind and includes external material objects. The *chit* has two aspects—knowledge and action—due to which we have the senses of knowledge (seeing, tasting, touching, smelling, and hearing) and the senses of action (hands, legs, sexual organs, etc.). The key takeaway is that *sat* is prior to *chit* and relationship is created logically prior, and then a body "enters" that relationship. This is the foundation of the theory of *karma* in which relationships manifest in time, and they attract somebody for rewards and punishments. The cause of that reward or punishment is the relationship, and not the body, although we attribute causality to the body. When *karma* manifests, the specific person who rewards or punishes you is not fixed, although once the relation is manifest, someone will come and do so. If it is not body X, then it would be body Y. Thus, causality is not attributed to the body. It is rather attributed to the relation which 'attracts' some individual body to act appropriately in that relation. The relation manifests as an *opportunity* that sucks in a body. Thus, we often hear people say, "If it wasn't me, it would have been someone else".

The *chit* is also sometimes called "awareness" because we do not distinguish between the awareness and the content of that awareness. The *chit* is the content of awareness, while the *sat* is awareness itself. The content of awareness follows the existence of awareness; in that sense, *chit* is secondary to *sat*. The *chit* constructs the branches of the tree of cognition, while the *sat* constructs a tree of relations. In the real world the conceptual objects interact with other objects through a relation, which means they are combined.

From Cognition to Pleasure

Once we have the cognition of the world, we have the experience of emotion, which may be pleasure or pain. Alternately, to seek pleasure, we may have desires. This potency to enjoy is called *ananda* because it manifests the desire for happiness. The desires for different things ultimately emanate from the desire for happiness, but the need for happiness is innate. The objects of the desire—just like the objects of awareness and cognition—can keep shifting and therefore they are different from the desire itself. The desire for something is the root cause of all other emotions—both happiness and suffering. From that desire stem greed and pride if the desire is fulfilled, or anger and frustration if the desire is unfulfilled. If one is unclear on how to fulfill their desires for happiness, then confusion is created. Unfulfilled desires lead to jealousy if we see others having what we want, and fulfilled desires lead to revulsion if others don't have what we possess. Desires also project our consciousness outwardly, just like the awareness of things and the cognition of things. However, this outwardly projection is toward the future. Sometimes, due to lamentation, we might also project our awareness in the past. The best emotion is that which is caused by the existence in the present and remains free of hankering and lamentation—i.e. focusing toward the future or the past. Due to the focus on the future, we can say that *ananda* manifests as *purpose*.

The purpose for something is its absolute identity. Let's illustrate this with some examples. Consider for instance a carpenter who has the purpose to build a chair. He is however not adept at carpentry and builds an imperfect chair. This imperfect object can also be contextually utilized as a table. We can now discern between three types of identities. The relational identity is that someone can use this thing as a table in some context. The cognitive identity is that it is an imperfect chair. But the absolute identity is the purpose that existed in the carpenter's mind while building the chair. This problem also appears in linguistic meaning comprehension. There is a purpose in the mind of the speaker which he or she articulates through some words. What the speaker intended to say is the absolute meaning of what was said. However, this purpose must be articulated through some words, which through the rules of phonetics and grammar constitute an objective meaning. This objective meaning may also be interpreted differently by readers. So, the linguist asks: What is the real meaning of the sentence? Is it the contextual interpretations of different readers? Or is it an objective meaning to be derived from the syntactical construction of phonetics and grammar? Or should we delve into the mental state of the speaker to understand what he or she meant? Ultimately, the meaning in the mind of the speaker is the real meaning. This meaning may be imperfectly expressed by the sentences. And those sentences may be variously interpreted by different listeners. What a listener gets out of the sentence is their contextual interpretation, subject to their own purposes, knowledge of linguistics, and understanding of the speaker. But there is also an objective reality—the sentence—which encodes meaning. However, there can be variation between what is *said* and what was *meant*. This is the main reason that if someone misunderstands you based on what you have said, you will clarify through subsequent utterances what you meant. You might say—this is not what I meant; what I meant is this.

The objective understanding based on phonetics and grammar is better than the contextual understanding of a person because at least it is not biased by the personal goals, limitations in understanding, or the context. For instance, something said in one context can be interpreted differently in another context, and context therefore can lead to misinterpretations. However, even better than the objective understanding is the intentions behind the utterances because what you intend is only partially expressed by utterances. Therefore, expressing a single idea can sometimes take many sentences and paragraphs, because, in addition to describing what you mean, you must also explicitly eliminate what you don't mean. The cognitive component of the meaning involves opposites; there is something you mean and there are its opposites which you reject. However, if you merely state what you mean, and you haven't explicitly rejected what you don't mean, there can be misunderstandings about what you mean because the rejections are absent. But when you intend something in your mind, these rejections are missing. You know what you mean but you may not communicate it well as the medium of this communication—i.e. language—cannot embody what you *don't* mean.

Thus, the intention is absolute because it doesn't involve the rejection of what you don't mean. The objective expression of this intention involves such rejections. Despite such assertions and rejections, if someone interprets your utterances contextually, they can arrive at different interpretations.

Therefore, we must distinguish between intended meaning, objective meaning, and contextual meaning. The intended meaning is subjective, but it is the absolute reference for what is being said. The objective meaning is empirical evidence for what was said and if the intentions were properly expressed with both assertions and negations, it is possible to logically derive the intention provided you are situated in the same context as the speaker. If, however, you change the context, the meanings become prone to biases.

When we speak about the three aspects of the soul, therefore, we can distinguish between relational (contextual), objective (cognitive), and subjective (intended) meanings. When you listen to a speaker, these three aspects are combined because there is an intention in the speaker, an interpretation in the listener, and an objective expression of the meaning. Nevertheless, if there is confusion about what is meant, or the listener wants to double-check what is being said, he or she would cross-question the speaker: Do you mean this, or do you mean that? This cross-questioning presupposes that the objective expression is imperfect, or the listener's intentions may have biased the interpretation. The most authoritative meaning can be sourced only from the speaker. This is what I mean by *absolute* identity. It is the intention underlying the expression subject to varied interpretations.

The origin of these intentions is the *ananda* of the soul. It constitutes desires, purposes, intentions, ultimately driven by the need for pleasure. So, objective expressions originate in subjective intentions, and these intentions are in turn caused by the desire for happiness, or the pleasure tendency.

Desires are hierarchical just like concepts and relationships. Some desires are deep-seated and long-lived while others are shallow and temporary. Coming into a relationship with something can incite desire, and when that thing disappears from our awareness the desire may also disappear. Similarly, desire sometimes brings us into awareness of things, and at other times revulsion pushes us away from them. Thus, desire and awareness are different, but one causes the other. Nevertheless, because desire is also a choice, just like awareness (of our body and mind, and of other bodies and minds), therefore *ananda* is also sometimes called "consciousness", or "feeling", such as pain and pleasure, happiness and distress. Factually, *sat*, *chit*, and *ananda* are all choices and awareness, although of three different kinds: *sat* is awareness and choice of the other, *chit* is the awareness and choice of concepts and properties of the self and other objects, while *ananda* is the awareness and choice of the pleasure and pain associated with knowledge. The terms "choice" and "awareness" are therefore to be associated with the soul, although these are divided into three parts as *sat*, *chit*, and *ananda*.

We cannot establish a strict causality between awareness and desire because sometimes awareness leads to desire (or revulsion) while at other times desire (or revulsion) leads to awareness. Similarly, cognition is both a cause and an effect of awareness and desire. All three exist in all experiences, but different things can be the causes and effects at different times.

Thus, it is said that the soul is always *sat*, *chit*, and *ananda*, but there is a *hierarchy* between them. Sometimes, *sat* is the decider, which means awareness leads to cognition, which then leads to desire; for example, you might encounter a person, become aware of their beauty, and then develop a desire for them. At other times, *ananda* is the decider, which means that one gets a desire, finds a way to fulfill the desire, and finally becomes aware of the object of that desire. Finally, there are times when *chit* is the decider in which your own body and possessions incite you into desires and awareness; for example, you might possess wealth and observing that wealth leads to the desire for spending, and then you go about shopping for different things.

Different features of the soul—*sat*, *chit*, or *ananda*—"dominate" at different times. The dominant feature is the cause, and the subordinate feature is the effect. There is always a hierarchy between *sat*, *chit*, and *ananda*, but this hierarchy is not fixed. Different features of the soul go to the top or come to the bottom, allowing others to dominate. However, all three must be combined to create an experience. Thus, all experience involves a relation, a cognition, and an emotion. There is no cognition without emotion, and there is no emotion without a relation. All three must exist simultaneously, although one may be the cause of another because one arises before the others but remains incomplete without them. Philosophically, *sat*, *chit*, and *ananda* are at the same "level" because they can alternately become dominant or subordinate, but all three must be present simultaneously to create experience.

Therefore, just having concepts or sensations is not complete because we don't know what those concepts and sensations correspond to—i.e. the individual identity that we are experiencing through a relation. Similarly, we might desire happiness, but that desire is incomplete without cognition and the object to which that cognition pertains. Since one of the three aspects of the soul can appear before the others, there is an associated experience of emotions, cognitions, and relations individually, although it is incomplete because it has to be complemented by the other two aspects. Thus, we can have knowledge without emotion, and relationship without knowledge, but in all cases the three must be combined to complete the experience.

The Six Types of Personalities

We can conceive of a personality of the soul based on the relative dominance of the three different aspects of the soul. Some soul is mostly dominant in desire, while knowledge and relationship are subordinate, while in another soul the relationship is mostly dominant while desire and relationship are subordinate. There can be one of the three features at the top, two in the middle, and one at the bottom. This leads to six kinds of personalities in which the three different aspects of the soul are dominant and subordinate.

Type	Top	Middle	Bottom
Conscientious	Relationship	Meaning	Desire
Agreeable	Relationship	Desire	Meaning
Open	Meaning	Relationship	Desire
Extroverted	Desire	Meaning	Relationship
Neurotic	Meaning	Desire	Relationship
Pragmatic	Desire	Relationship	Meaning

Table 1: Six Personality Types of the Soul

Table 1 lists the six personality types. Of this, the first five are drawn from the "Big Five" theory of personality, which started with the *Lexical Hypothesis*[1] that assumes that the most dominant personality types must be found in the most recurrent *words* used to describe personalities and that each type of personality will have a unique word identifying it. In other words, one could begin by listing all the words by which personalities are described, then conduct tests to see if people identified with these words, then unify the personalities based on the synonymous words, grouping them through that semantic similarity to identify the smallest set of types.

The approach is classificatory and relies on empirical measurements, but it begs the explanation of why a certain number of unique types exist. We can certainly classify people by putting the words used to describe them into separate classes, but that classification doesn't explain why a certain number of classes exist, or why only those specific classes exist. Personality theorists don't have good answers to such questions. They attribute the personality types to things like gene evolution, brain development, social organization, linguistic enrichment, and so forth. The approach that I present here differs radically in this respect because we don't use the data to identify the types and then speculatively evolve a theory that explains the types. We rather begin in the theory of the soul which then explains the production of personality types which can then be measured empirically, verifying the theory.

The first type—conscientious—includes those people whose lives are defined by hard work to earn and provide, who are preoccupied with duty and commitment, and who take pride in their relationships as the source of meaning and purpose. The middle-class people in most societies largely belong to this type. This class believes that doing your job, earning an honest living, providing for your family, raising kids with education and moral values, doing your due diligence to society—e.g. by charity to the poor—and following some religion with an emphasis on moral duty is the essence of life. Routine makes them happy and satisfied and they thrive on doing the same activities over and over, without getting bored or frustrated. They generally make good parents and caretakers, security officers, accountants, nurses, or factory workers. The stability of job and home makes them peaceful and happy. They are not well-suited to innovation and disruption, new ideas, or risky propositions. They cannot be wanderers, explorers, thinkers, or pioneers.

The second type—agreeable—includes those who believe that happiness comes from making others happy. They thrive on friendliness, having a helpful nature, kindness, and gentleness. They make friends easily, they bring stability in relationships, and they tend to be liked by everyone. Such people are well-suited for service industries such as airlines, medical care, hospitality, education, and customer support. They may be good negotiators and mediators because they generate trust with others. Due to this trust a lot of people rely on them. However, agreeableness can be problematic if one foregoes promises to agree with someone else. As time passes and situations change, their agreeable nature can cause them to forget their commitments, and forego the trust previously built due to their friendliness. Ultimately many of them become confidants of others' secrets, but not very practically useful to others. You might turn to them when you need a shoulder to cry on, but you may not turn to them to become business partners or co-workers. You don't go to a battle with a soldier whose primary need is to be agreeable.

The third type—open—is an explorer of new ideas, and he or she seeks these ideas through new relationships and encounters. There is a proclivity to be creative, which means that the person enjoys music, art, literature, and innovation. People in this type get easily bored with routine, and seek thrill from exhilarating novel experiences, with the emphasis on novelty. They might enjoy going on hikes and touring other countries, reading about new theories and discoveries, or creating innovations themselves. They might enjoy debates and conversations, discussing politics and society, science and nature. Such discussions unburden them from the boredom of routine.

The fourth type—extroverted—is the classical go-getter. He or she is motivated by inner desire, identifies plans and schemes to achieve them, and goes after encounters and relationships to fulfill them. The person is generally self-centered, and everything else remains subordinate. As the desires change, the plans are quickly modified, and previously formed relationships are discarded while new ones are formed. Such a person doesn't dwell on what others think or feel because he or she is focused on what they want to achieve. Such people tend to become ruthless and cruel, and they are seldom known for their pleasantness, although they are generally high achievers. This personality type is often found in the higher echelons of society; they know what they want, and they are not shy to ask for it. Due to the clarity of their desire, followed by adroit planning, they tend to become leaders.

The fifth type—neurotic—has a very vivid imagination. He or she traverses the universe of possibilities in their mind, to find something they desire, and finally try to achieve it through worldly relationship. Most of the time is spent just imagining the possibilities, evaluating their pros and cons, before deciding on what should be done. The greatest scientists and philosophers fall into this category as they spend most of their lives just thinking about the possibilities and their pros and cons before arriving at a prescriptive model or theory of the world. There is so much rough and tumble in the mind that the person is sensitive to small changes outside. They prefer to live in solitude and emerge from their caves only after they have evaluated alternatives and found the answer. That a person will indeed successfully complete the evaluation and find an answer is not guaranteed, so there is also a proclivity toward madness in which the mind becomes very unstable because it sees all the possibilities at once but is unable to make a clear decision. Neurotic persons can therefore remain indecisive and in the exploratory phase. Pushing them towards a commitment generally angers them. They are prone to unstable relationships—e.g. multiple marriages.

The sixth type—pragmatic—has many desires but no preferred plan to achieve them. He or she relies on whatever is available to move toward their goal and has little commitment to a theory of the universe. For them, whatever works is the correct path. Pragmatic people are attached to their goals, but not attached to the method of achieving them. If lying, cheating, manipulating, or deceiving gets them to their goal, they will take the path because there is nothing right or wrong in the path itself, and the ends justify the means. They adapt to new situations and are generally not disturbed by changes because they did not begin with a mental model of reality. They are street-smart and troubleshooters. Most politicians, bureaucrats, salesmen, businessmen, and middle managers fall into this category as they believe that they need to achieve their goals and targets by hook or by crook. They may not be crooked per se, but they are so focused on the results that the means don't matter.

We can think of these six personality types stereotypically in terms of the jobs they are ideally suited for. The table below summarizes them.

Conscientious	Accountant, Factory Worker, Security Officer
Open	Artist, Author, Innovator, Musician, Actor, Comedian
Agreeable	Counsellor, Customer Support, Housekeeper, Nurse
Extroverted	Business Leader, Military Commander, Administrator
Neurotic	Philosopher, Scientist, Mathematician, Inventor
Pragmatic	Salesman, Politician, Businessman, Bureaucrat

Table 2: Preferred Job Roles of the Six Personality Types

Generally, it is hard to find a person who only matches one personality type because these personalities are based on the relative domination of one of the three characteristics of the soul. Every soul is capable of every personality type although their type is created by a bias by which some soul's proclivities dominate others. This domination may be enduring but not persistent. That is, we can find patterns of dominant personality types, which occasionally change into other types. In some cases, all six personality types can be found in the same person at different times. Ultimately, the idea of a personality—as something fixed for all times—is flawed because the domination changes. The personality type also changes with the evolving situations. For example, if the desire is present but the opportunity is not available, the personality can change from Extroverted to Pragmatic—from seeking what they desire to what is practically achievable. Similarly, one might have artistic abilities but the personality manifests only when the opportunity is created through relationships. Likewise, the latent desires may only manifest after the abilities have been acquired and the opportunities are present. There is no denying the existence of clear types, but we should be cautious about the academic tendency to stereotype individuals into specific types forever.

This flaw manifests in empirical studies which test a person at a specific time. Depending on their current behavior or based upon what the person feels about their personality at that moment, the answers could be true only in that context and time. The results of such measurements and psychometric tests will vary with time, although the types are themselves invariant. This leads to the false impression that the individuals fit into one type when the fact is that a person might shift from one type to another over time. Most people who undergo life-changing events face a shift in personality type.

The study of personality must not just explain the dominance of certain types, but also how a person changes their personality from one type to another. A personality theory that only identifies the types is incomplete, and a theory that relies on measurements to conclude a type is generally stereotypical, although there are a fixed number of personality types. A complete theory is one that describes the types along with the evolution of the person through the different types. The shift emerges because a person realizes that the type that worked in previous situations doesn't work anymore. Sometimes you need to be extroverted and other times you must create or think to find answers. Typically, a personality type continues to use the tools of the past even in the new situations except when their application leads to spectacular failures. The shift from one type to another is therefore not easy; generally, it would be caused by a change in the situation, which impacts one's survival or success unless a radical shift in personality type is made.

No personality is suited for all roles and situations. The ideal persona is one that adapts to situations, shifting from conscientious, to open, to agreeable, to extroverted, to neurotic, to pragmatic, as the situation demands. The study of personality types can be illuminating in what areas a person is weak and therefore must build upon. For example, the neurotic would benefit from being more pragmatic, and the extroverted from being more conscientious. The idea that one has a fixed type of material persona is ultimately flawed not just because the personality changes over time, but also because one is required to exhibit a different personality in a different situation.

Three Kinds of Intelligences

The need to develop alternative kinds of capabilities in our persona is articulated in modern times through the theory of multiple intelligences[1], first described by Howard Gardener[2]. His work has been extended by others like Daniel Goleman[3], who emphasize social and emotional intelligences beyond the traditional cognitive models of intelligence widely used in tests of IQ (Intelligence Quotient). Following the recognition of additional types of intellects, terms such as EQ (Emotional Quotient) and SQ (Social Quotient) are now prevalent, each bringing a new set of tests and numbers. The point of such testing is that having a high IQ but a low EQ, for example, is a lower indicator of overall success because EQ and SQ are as important as IQ.

This fact attests to a contradiction in the study of personality because on one hand the theories that identify personality types suggest that no personality type is better than the other and one should not judge the different types as superior or inferior as each person has the advantages of their type. In fact, before beginning the test, the questionnaires often placate the subject that low scores on any dimension do not indicate a personality flaw. On the other hand, the tests that measure the different types of intelligences imply that low scores on some test (e.g. EQ vs. IQ) entail an overall lower chance of success in life. Neither of these approaches clearly bring out the fact that personalities and abilities change over time, new forms of intellect can be acquired through education and experience, and many practice techniques used to score high on the quantitative tests—e.g. GMAT and SAT in the United States—which are designed to test intellect, only test exam preparation.

I am of the view that a well-rounded person is one that can exhibit all personality types, choosing the correct type for the given situation. Similarly, I am of the view that a person must acquire all forms of intelligences, choosing and adapting them to the situation. There is limited merit in personality type testing if the results of these tests are employed to judge a person's capabilities because they change over time. There is however usefulness in this testing for the individual being tested as he or she can identify their personality-related shortcomings and see how adopting other types can improve their life. There is also limited value in quantitative tests because they can be beaten with education, experience, and practice. The real merit is to identify the education and practice needed to improve on the type of intelligence. The net value in such testing is that a person can identify their improvements and seek opportunities to develop a well-rounded personality of multiple dimensions as all personality types are valuable and often required in a person's life, while also teaching them which type of personality is suited when.

This fact becomes even more evident when the six personality types (described previously) are deconstructed into three fundamental properties of relationship, cognition, and emotion. There is a very close resemblance between these three properties of the soul and the three kinds of intelligences noted above. The cognitive ability of the soul called *chit* can be identified with cognitive intelligence measured as IQ. The emotive ability of the soul called *ananda* can be equated with emotional intelligence measured as EQ. Finally, the relational ability of the soul to connect to other individuals is the basis of social intelligence measured as SQ. Given that the different personality types are in turn byproducts of the relative dominance of three distinct properties, we can now appreciate the intimate connections between the theories of personality and the theories of different kinds of intelligences, and how these theories can be improved by grasping the nature of the soul.

We can see that different types emerge through a relative dominance of a type of intelligence, and the three types of intelligence are more fundamental than the six personality types. A person is likely to encounter situations in which different kinds of intellects must dominate, for them to exhibit the right kind of personality. In that sense, all the intellects are important, provided we can decipher the relative priorities of the different intellects in the given situation. Furthermore, the three types of intellects are nothing other than the three fundamental properties of the soul. The approach both simplifies and unifies diverse forms of personality studies, laying greater emphasis on personality development than upon personality measurement.

Our experiences are created from the combination of objects, relationships, and purposes and no individual can be totally devoid of these three types of intelligences because that would entail a lack of experience itself. We can, however, find specific areas of deficiency in individuals. For instance, cognitive intelligence is defined as the ability in people to understand the world and act in it, but autistic individuals can, for example, have far superior observing and memorizing abilities, while suffering from speech and other motor impairments. Autism, therefore, is the impairment of *chit* specifically regarding some of the senses of action—speech, hand, and leg movement. The notable point here is that the *chit* is not fully impaired because that would make it impossible to understand and do anything. In fact, when the activity aspect of *chit* is impaired, the knowledge aspect may be enhanced. Thus, there are rare instances of autistic individuals being savants.

Similarly, many people are very comfortable working with tools and things but have great difficulty in interacting with other people. They like working with controllable things which don't react spontaneously, because they cannot handle things that behave impulsively and unpredictably. We are prone to thinking that such people are impaired in their social intelligence although they make some of the most stable relationships, albeit in smaller circles like a team or family. We contrast them to other gregarious people who network easily but who cannot make stable relationships, attributing the socially outgoing people a greater amount of social intelligence.

These are flaws of viewing personality monolithically rather than hierarchically. Just because a person is socially outgoing doesn't mean they also understand other people at deeper levels such as mind and intentions. Similarly, just because a person works well in smaller groups doesn't mean he lacks the ability for relationships. In both cases, there is a cognitive impairment to perceive deeper levels of a person, although the socially conservative people spend time to obtain a deeper understanding of other people and form strong relationships while the socially outgoing don't spend time in this understanding and hop from one relationship to another. Both classes of people can be distinguished from those who are adept at social interactions—both in close-knit and broad-based settings—because they can read the minds and feelings of other people. Such people, on the other hand, may be poor at working with tools and things. They too are cognitively impaired, but in the opposite sense, because they can understand others' minds but not the things that don't seem to have minds. The contrasts between these different personality types require a hierarchically nuanced theory of personality.

The key point is that no one is ever so impaired as to completely lose cognition, relations, or emotion because that would entail the cessation of experience. However, they can be selectively impaired in one or more of the functions, while remaining average or excellent in others. The personality differences arise not just due to the relative dominance of one property of the soul over another, but even due to the relative strength of these properties within the same dominant-subordinate structure. This idea can be understood very well when each of the three—relation, cognition, and emotion—are viewed as *trees* rooted in the soul. The *form* of the tree— i.e. the relative development of different branches—dictates the relative strength of each of the properties. Both abilities and disabilities are different kinds of trees. As a particular branch on the tree grows, the abilities are pronounced. As a branch shrinks, the abilities are deficient. The level of intellect—cognitive, social, or emotional—can therefore be attributed to the extent and type of the tree.

Intelligence as Choice and Judgment

The three functions of the soul manifest into three kinds of judgments and the cognitive, emotional, and social intelligences can be viewed as the ability for these judgments. Cognitive intelligence manifests into the judgment of true and false, social intelligence into the judgment of right and wrong, while emotional intelligence results in the judgment of good and bad. Life is carried through the combination of these three kinds of judgments.

The judgment of true and false is the easiest to understand. It involves sense perception and mental cognition along with the judgment of true or false. It can also involve the assessment of the person's intentions, and what the person considers ideal. For example, when someone says "the President is waiting for you" the senses hear and judge whether the words are correctly spoken based on the speaker's accent. The mind then derives the meaning of the above sentence. The intellect judges whether the statement is true by including other relevant facts—e.g. the president could be traveling, or be under surgery, or might have other appointments due to which they could not be available, etc. Once the truth has been determined, the ego interprets if the statement is uttered seriously, jokingly, or sarcastically, based on which you could determine the intended meaning of the statement as a fact, or meant to fool someone, or intended for laughter. For example, the intellect might judge that the claims are false, but the ego might decide that the purpose of the false claim is not deception but lighthearted joking. Finally, we judge a person's nature based on their statements; for example, whether the person is a habitual liar, honest and serious, or goofy and fun-loving. We also judge their deepest values—or what they consider virtuous and ideal. The problem of perception is complex because of the multiple levels at which perception operates. As we saw above, from the same sentence we can judge everything from the words being spoken to the character of the person who speaks it, with the concepts, the context of speaking, and the intentions in between.

```
┌─────────────────────────┐
│        MORALITY         │
└─────────────────────────┘

┌─────────────────────────┐
│       INTENTIONS        │
└─────────────────────────┘

┌─────────────────────────┐
│        CONTEXT          │
└─────────────────────────┘

┌─────────────────────────┐
│       CONCEPTS          │
└─────────────────────────┘

┌─────────────────────────┐
│      SENSATIONS         │
└─────────────────────────┘

┌─────────────────────────┐
│     SENSE OBJECTS       │
└─────────────────────────┘
```

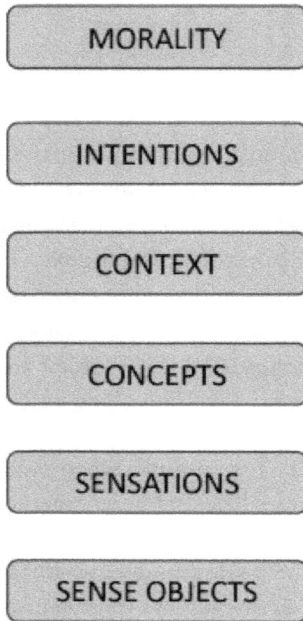

Figure-3 The Hierarchy in Perception

Ideally, one begins to process meanings top-down, rather than bottom-up. We first try to understand the character of the person, because if the person is a habitual liar, his claims would be suspect before you even know what he is saying. We then try to determine the person's intent—e.g. serious, goofy, sarcastic, etc.—because once you know the intent everything else based on that intent could be taken seriously or rejected regardless of what they say. Then we bring to attention all our beliefs about what we consider true or false, which if violated would automatically render everything else false. Then we bring to the situation the understanding of language, culture, customs, and practices which are used to interpret the meanings of sense perceptions. Finally, we pay attention to the utterances, and automatically, the meaning, judgment, intention, and character are brought to bear.

On initial encounters, however, the reverse process is typical. In this act, the words are heard first, then over time we understand the unique ways in which words are used in specific contexts to find the linguistic conventions, then we gather facts about the environment to formulate our belief system, we then judge a person's intent based on previous encounters with them, and finally over longer periods of time we understand their character.

Cognition can stop at any of these successive stages. For example, it can stop if the senses don't hear the words. It can end if the mind does not know what the word means in a given context. It can terminate if the listener finds that a speaker is not telling the truth due to a mismatch with the listener's beliefs. The listener can stop paying attention to what is being said if the intent is judged to not be what the listener was expecting. Finally, the cognition can stop if we dislike a person's character. The cognition of true and false is a complex and multi-tiered problem because it depends on deeper and deeper levels of a person's reality, which can be understood over longer and longer periods of time. It is thus easier to understand the words, but somewhat more difficult to understand the contextual meanings. It is much harder to get a full understanding of all the facts, even harder to judge a person's intent, and nearly impossible to fully understand a person's true character. And yet, all these judgments exist in us to greater or lesser extents; they manifest from a soul's ability called *chit* to perform the judgment of truth.

The Origin of Moral Judgments

The judgment of right and wrong is the next type of judgment we make in relation to our worldly interactions. It involves questions not about the true nature of an object and its properties, but how one should interact with that thing. For example, the cognitive judgment will decide whether something is a gun, but the moral decision will determine when, where, and whether it must be used. We perform moral judgments based upon a moral compass that determines when, where, and whether we interact with things and people. It determines how we speak to friends, colleagues, family members, strangers, elders, juniors, and superiors because there is a "right" way of interacting with each type of person. Similarly, there is social etiquette while driving, eating, working, dressing, and walking. There are rules for playing games and sports, laws of government for citizens and immigrants, and there are edicts on conduct in the workplace. Each context and situation involves different guidelines which decide what is right and wrong.

Moral judgments are also hierarchical like meaning judgments. At the lowest level, we judge if an action performed by the senses is right or wrong. For example, we might say that hitting somebody is wrong. Then we judge the same action in the given context—e.g. hitting someone in self-defense could be right. Then we judge if we have left out relevant facts or added irrelevant facts. For example, the fact that a person is a dutiful father or husband may be irrelevant to the moral question when the person neglects his professional duties. However, including the fact that the person was asked to do something else at that time by a relevant authority, taking away time or opportunity to perform his duties is relevant to the moral question. Including the right facts and removing the irrelevant facts is the job of the intellect. Then we judge if a person's intentions are pure or malicious. For example, we might say that a person went to a friend with the intention to murder. Finally, we judge whether the person is moral or evil. For example, we might say that a person is righteous, but he might have behaved inappropriately as opposed to saying that the person is evil although he sometimes acts courteously.

The moral judgments of right and wrong have the same type of hierarchy as the judgments of truth and false. The same observations are thus judged right or wrong, and true or false. However, moral judgments are not based only on the sensually perceivable material reality; they are also based on *rules* of activity that can't be seen by the senses. For example, when we see a speed limit road sign, we could interpret it as a metal surface with some numbers or letters painted on it, rather than as a rule that should not be violated. Rules of ethical conduct may be written in books and manuals.

The study of matter in modern science disallows the ability to interpret objects as symbols of meaning; we can measure the symbol's properties such as shape, size, color, etc. but we cannot perceive meanings. Meanings—such as descriptions and rules—are relegated to the "mind", which ultimately has no existence apart from matter, and therefore meanings and rules don't really exist in the material world. Ultimately, when the mind is material, the rules and concepts must be pushed into another Platonic world, which begs the question of how those ideas and rules could descend into this world.

The fact is that meanings and rules exist materially, but this is a type of matter that spans multiple objects. If materialism is defined as individual objects, then we cannot conceive of concepts and rules materially because they span many objects. To see this kind of matter we must treat even the individual objects as concepts, spawned from higher concepts, in a tree structure. The concepts and rules spanning many objects are the higher nodes of the tree—they span those objects because they *spawned* them originally. In this way, rules and concepts become materially real because materialism is altered to include them. Matter must be described as symbols rather than as objects, which means that meanings and rules are embedded in each object, although perceptual advancement is needed to see them in the objects. This is because the perception of meanings and rules requires mental intuition beyond sense perception. Modern science is based on sense perception alone and it therefore facilely eliminates meanings and rules from its ontology.

Once we begin to perceive the meaning, we realize that there are two kinds of meanings—*descriptive* and *normative*. When matter is described as a possibility, descriptive and normative alternatives denote *could be* and *should be*. Thus, descriptively, a gun *could be* used to shoot anybody anytime, but prescriptively it *should be* used only for self-defense. The normative alternatives are materially possible, as well as morally permitted. Ideally, we must perceive the normative rules and use them to *eliminate* some of the descriptively allowed possibilities (which do not comply with the moral rules). In effect, materially speaking, there are far more possibilities than those morally allowed. But every moral imperative must be materially possible, or it cannot be an imperative. For example, a soldier cannot be responsible for not defending the country if he has not been trained or doesn't have a gun.

The key point is that moral judgments are also material because matter exists as the possibility of what it *could be* and *should be*. Since we don't describe this matter as meaning, we are unable to distinguish between descriptive and norms, and we not only eliminate the meanings from the study of matter, but also the moral rules. This doesn't eliminate the normative rules per se, but they become invisible to our perception. This is important for the *reduction* of possibilities because out of the many allowed options, only a few are morally allowed. If the morally allowed alternatives are treated as material rules, then these rules can themselves reduce the uncertainty of many alternatives. Therefore, the objective study of such rules can aid in the resolution of the problem of reducing the possibilities—in some cases, there is only one moral option, and the moral rule can therefore reduce the possibility to reality. Even with multiple morally allowed options, morality still reduces the possibility by eliminating many immoral alternatives from reality.

Similarly, an observer's desires—which exist materially—will further reduce the morally permitted alternatives to the choice of what one wants. In this way, the material possibility can be reduced both by morals as well as desires, and this is a practical scientific solution to the problem of how a definite world emerges from the possibilities: the solution is that possibility is just one kind of matter; two other kinds of matter—morality and desire—reduce possibilities into reality. The judgment of right and wrong originates in the *sat* or awareness of the soul, which creates a role. As this awareness is modified by appellations such as "soldier" to form a soldier's role, normative rules of behavior automatically appear. In this case, there are rules of how a soldier must behave. Similarly, as we add more appellations such as citizenship, employment, family membership, growing relationships lead to increasing rules. We can never be free of rules unless we are out of all relationships but being out of all relationships means lacking in worldly experience. In that sense, awareness brings relationships, and relationships bring rules.

We cannot separate the relationship from the rules. Each object exists as a set of possibilities of what it can be, but those possibilities are not meant for all relations. For example, a gun has different rules in the hands of an ordinary citizen vs. a law enforcement officer. I am entitled to drive some car, but not all cars. I can live in some house, but not any house. Some job duties are supposed to be performed by me and not by others. A superior can chastise his subordinates, and a mother can chide her children. Morality simply means that the rules of engagement vary from person to person. The possibilities of what an object can be are not meant to be realized universally. Instead, there are specific guidelines on who can realize which subset of possibilities.

In modern science, the distinction between objects and roles doesn't exist. Therefore, we can study the gun, and how it could be fired, but we cannot describe who is morally obligated to fire the gun and who is morally forbidden from using the gun. In modern science, objects interact according to universal laws of force based on some properties of objects and the distance between them. In a moral science, each object has a *role*, on which the moral imperatives are based. The *role* determines which interactions are appropriate or inappropriate, and the relation between objects is defined not as the distance between the objects but between the roles occupied by those objects.

These roles are expansions of the *sat* property of the soul. The "distance" used in causal interactions is not to be measured between the objects expanded from the *chit* but between the roles expanded from the *sat*.

The distance between the *chit* expansions gives an object its conceptual properties—or what it *could be*. The distance between the *sat* expansions gives the object its moral properties—or what it *should be*. The object and the role are distinct, and two notions of "distance" are involved—one that defines the object's properties and the other that defines its roles. Morality is not outside science *per se*. It becomes scientific when we separate objects and roles and define a "distance" which indicates normative rules. The fact is that the objects and the roles are combined in all situations but as we defer to the study of objects and neglect the roles, we arrive at an incorrect picture in which causal interactions are mediated by object-distances. The problem emerges because we confuse object-distance with role-distance.

Judging the Nature of Good

Object and role distances are not the only types of distances. There is also distance created due to our likes and dislikes. You might be close to a person physically but far mentally due to a dislike. You might be far physically but close mentally due to your liking. The distance due to likes and dislikes corresponds to our desires and emotions, and it creates the personal judgments of good and bad. There is a difference between the truth of a statement, the appropriateness of uttering the statement in a situation, and the likeability of the statement to a person. The speaker might be truthful, and their speech might be righteous activity, but I might not find it appealing.

The judgment of good and bad represents what I find relevant, appealing, interesting, and attractive, based on my desires and goals. To make that judgment for others—i.e. if they are attracted to something—we have to judge what they consider good and bad, likable or dislikable. The emotive capacity in a person is not just about their ability to feel the emotions but also being able to judge the emotions and their causes—preferences of likes and dislikes—in others. Generally, those who have a heightened sense of their own emotional perception also have a better understanding of other's likes and dislikes—often called 'empathy'. Conversely, those who don't feel strong emotions themselves are also unable to perceive those emotions and their causes in others. This is similar to the fact that those who have a rich conceptual repertoire perceive nuanced meanings in others but those minds which are not as richly informed tend to slot others into predefined categories.

Some individuals have the capacity to be empathetic to others, but their own emotional experience overwhelms them to a point that they fail to recognize the emotional needs of others because they remain preoccupied with their own feelings. This is like the cognitive state where a person is preoccupied with their ideas and fails to understand the ideas of others. Or they might be so convinced about their beliefs that they fail to recognize that others have a different viewpoint. This difference arises due to the relative dominance of *sat* and *chit*. As we noted earlier, *chit* is the perception of one's own body and mind, while *sat* is the relationship to others. When *chit* dominates over *sat*, we fail to see the emotions and ideas in others, but we can see them in ourselves. Thus, we might humanize ourselves and dehumanize others.

Intellectual and emotional people tend to feel their mind and body, but they fail to recognize similar things in others. It is not because they lack the capacity to perceive, but that they are overwhelmed by their own ideas and emotions because the *chit* and *ananda* dominate the *sat*. If this dominance were inverted, a person would prioritize ideas and emotions in others and deprioritize them in himself or herself. This is the origin of the dominant and subordinate personality types where the dominant person dehumanizes others while the subordinate person dehumanizes himself or herself.

Our desires play an important role in determining our attention to the world. The world presents us with numerous possibilities only some of which become our experiences. For example, while reading this book, you might not be aware of the pressure of the chair you are sitting in, the voices in the distance, or the air circulation around you. This is because we choose to not focus on them. What do you attend to? And what do you ignore? The decision is not just based on the meaning or what is available because we might desire objects that are not available and not desire what is available. Likewise, certain beautiful things might be ignored while others that are unattractive things might be desired. Ultimately, everyone has the free will to choose what they want to pay attention to, and the cause of that free will is desire.

The question of good and bad is also hierarchical like the question of right vs. wrong, or true vs. false. The senses enjoy certain kinds of sensations—e.g. taste, smell, sound, touch, and sight, and we have natural preferences for colors and forms, sweet vs. bitter vs. sour, etc. The mind similarly has preferences for certain types of objects and activities—e.g. some people like quietly reading books, while others prefer to talk to friends. The intellect has preferences for including and excluding facts from a context, thus distorting the context in one's perception. For instance, someone who dislikes formality may exclude the facts that indicate a formal setting and continue to talk informally as if the context was informal. The ego has likes and dislikes for goals. Finally, the moral sense has an innate judgment of what type of pleasure is desirable and based on that if others are good or bad persons.

When you interact with someone, you judge everything from whether they speak sweetly, to whether they say something interesting and likable, to whether they are comfortable in the given context, to whether they have good intentions, to whether they are good persons. This hierarchy means that we might not like what someone says, but we might consider them good persons. Similarly, we might like their intentions, but we might dislike their actions. Generally, the deeper perceptions have greater importance than shallower ones. Therefore, if you dislike a person, even their good intentions, ideas, and actions would be disliked. Conversely, if you inherently like a person, then you may be more tolerant even of their bad ideas and actions.

Emotion is generated from the judgment of good and bad. It involves distaste and dislike on the one hand, and desires, likes, and love on the other. Both likes and dislikes can be instant or gradual. Sometimes we encounter people who might have a pleasing appearance or manners, and we start liking them until we find that they have bad motivations and desires. The likes eventually turn into dislikes, but it takes a while. Similarly, a person may develop an instant dislike for someone, which may be hard to understand for others who find them to have a pleasing appearance or manners. Over time, however, their apprehension might be gradually converted into liking. This is caused due to the hierarchical nature of perception where a deeper sense develops a dislike even though the superficial facts are likable. Or the superficial sense develops a like, and the deeper sense hasn't yet perceived the true nature of a person. In the longer run, when one has understood the full hierarchy, the like or dislike becomes either more sustained or more nuanced. For example, if you like the person at a deep level, but dislike their appearance or action, your liking would be tempered by the discrepancy between deep and shallow perceptions. If, however, the person is disliked at more levels and liked only at a few levels, the overall result would be a disliking.

The Hierarchy in Perception

In every perception we simultaneously perform three kinds of judgments—the judgment of true and false is tied to the concepts, the judgment of right and wrong is associated with the relation, and the judgment of good and bad is connected to our purposes. Therefore, we are not only deducing—from the observation—its underlying causes (concept, purpose, and relation), but also judging if these are true, right, and good. The mind is involved in gathering the causes—i.e. attributing an observation to a specific combination of concept, purpose, and relation. The intellect judges if the concept is true, the ego judges if something is pleasing, and the moral sense decides if that thing is right. In this way, the sensations are interpreted by the mind into a three-fold division of concept, purpose, and relation, followed by the intellect, ego, and the moral sense performing a judgment on whether this division is true, good, and right. What we commonly call the "mind" in Western philosophy is actually a more complex mechanism of interpreting followed by judging.

If the world were things, then sensations would suffice. But if the sensations are giving us symbols, then we must understand what the symbols *mean* followed by *judging* if that meaning is true, right, and good. The mind becomes important when the sensations are treated as symbols rather than things, and to adopt this view, the material world we perceive sensually must be treated symbolically. If the world is things rather than symbols, then only the senses are necessary, and the mind is an unnecessary addendum not to be given any importance in the study of the world. The existence of the mind changes the nature of reality that exists outside the mind from things to symbols. Considering this fact, everything we perceive through sensations is a symbol of the ideas in the mind; the ideas are in turn produced through judgments about what the author of the symbols considered true, right, and good. The symbol comes about not because there is a material reality which we sense, but because it originates in our view of truth, right, and good.

The mind in Vedic philosophy performs three functions—thinking, feeling, and willing. The mind is also the agency that *interprets* the symbols into their meaning. These two descriptions are identical because there are three kinds of meanings derived from the same symbol. The "thinking" faculty of the mind derives the concepts based on *chit*. The "feeling" ability of the mind understands the emotions based on *ananda*. The "willing" potency of the mind decides where our attention is directed based on *sat*. The mind is the capacity of grasping and creating two types of concepts—those of knowing and acting. For instance, 'apple' and 'house' are knowing concepts, while 'running' and 'swimming' are action concepts. Similarly, an action can be performed in different roles, and with different kinds of emotions and purposes. Owing to this, the triad of thinking, feeling, and willing is further augmented by knowing and acting, producing either five (if you add knowing and acting to thinking, feeling, and willing) or six (if you divide thinking, feeling, or willing by knowing and acting) types of mental faculties of interpretation.

Memory is associated with the mind as well as the three judging faculties. The mind holds the memory of linguistic, cultural, and social conventions by which it interprets the observations into concept, relation, and purpose. The judging faculties similarly hold pre-formed beliefs about what is true, right, and good, due to which we might interpret the situation favorably or unfavorably. For instance, if you hold the belief that a person is evil and manipulative, whatever he or she says would be automatically imbued with a negative emotional state. Conversely, if you think that a person is truthful and righteous, you will attribute their negative emotional state to the circumstances. Since everyone tends to think that the world is just like them, manipulative people read even the honest and truthful as manipulative often, thereby coloring the judgment and interpretation by their own personality. Conversely, the truthful and righteous fail to see manipulation more often and tend to interpret other's actions according to their own nature.

Those who are truthful and righteous tend to often be emotionally weak and are prone to emotional manipulation. Conversely, those who are not truthful and righteous tend to emotionally manipulate others in order to derive a favorable outcome. Both the interpretive and judging faculties can therefore be dominated by emotion, concept, or relation. As we saw previously, a person can have six types of personalities based on a relative dominance of the three faculties of *sat*, *chit*, and *ananda*. When emotion becomes dominant in a person—due to their incessant desires—but they don't see a way to fulfill those desires through truthful and honest means, or their judgment of truth and wrong is dominated by the emotion, they resort to emotionally manipulating others to meet their goals. This is seen in people who play the victim to get what they want and appeal to other's compassion although they are wrong. Similarly, some people when losing an argument using truthful and honest means start attacking a person's character by hurting them emotionally. Once a person is hurt emotionally, he or she might react adversely, and the argument shifts from the content to a person's character.

By the very nature of the dominant-subordinate structure, if a person is high on truth and right, he or she will also be low on perceiving emotions in others and themselves. They are prone to neglect the motivation in others and seek only the right and the truth, and as a result those who are not high on right and truth tend to manipulate, ignore, or fight such a person emotionally—attacking their weakness rather than strength. Thus, it is not enough to be righteous and truthful if you are not also emotionally strong. This emotional strength doesn't have to be used in manipulating others; but it should be used in defending oneself from those who manipulate you emotionally.

One can defend oneself from a manipulator by realizing when the manipulator has lost the argument based on truth and right but wants to fulfill their desires, and the game will shift to appealing to your compassion or attacking your lack of sympathy. Most truthful and righteous people are drawn into this kind of situation and given their need to preserve their clean, truthful, and honest image, start defending themselves from the attack using a counterattack. The situation spirals downwards then on, and the truthful succumb to the machinations of the manipulator, allowing the manipulator to get what he could not obtain truthfully and righteously from the start.

The egoistic person has a strong sense of purpose (what they want) but a weak sense of truth and right (intellect and moral sense) and they rely on manipulating others. The intellectuals have a strong reliance on facts, but they may not know the situations in which to apply the facts (i.e. when it is righteous) and how to attain their goals, but they talk about the truth. The practical person knows how to interact with others but has a lesser sense of truth and their goals; they rely on their ability to work hard and fast relative to the others. None of the different personality types work well in all situations, as we have seen previously, which gives rise to the need to balance the types. Finally, in the ultimate analysis, only the truth that is right and good wins. Interpreting the worldly situations and judging them as truth, right, and good, is thus as important as being truthful, righteous, and happy oneself.

All these facts about the nature of experience are summarized in Sāñkhya philosophy as the four-four division of the *antahkaran* or the "internal instrument"—a euphemism for what Western philosophy calls the "mind". In Sāṅkhya, these are respectively called the mind, intellect, ego, and the moral sense. The mind is the lowest of the four; it does the job of interpretation, deriving the cognitive, emotive, and relational meaning out of the sensations. The mind, however, does not judge their truth, rightness, or goodness. These three are performed by successively higher functions called the intellect, ego, and the moral sense. The intellect is the next higher than the mind; it determines the truth. Since the truth is contextual, and the mind has already derived the meaning from the context, the intellect's job is to judge if the context is correctly framed—i.e. whether all the relevant facts have been included, and all the irrelevant facts have been excluded. After the intellect comes ego; its job is to judge good and bad, or whether we like something or not. While the intellect judges the truth of the context, the ego relates the facts to the self to determine likes and dislikes. Finally, above the ego is the moral sense; its role is to judge the nature of right and wrong. The right and wrong is contextual, so the judgment of context by the intellect is important. Similarly, to judge right and wrong, one must know a person's true motives and goals, not just the superficial facts and the truth of those facts. In legal judgments, for instance, it is very important to establish the motive for a crime. The moral sense takes the truths and motives, along with an understanding of a person's role to decide if the action was appropriate or not.

The hierarchy illustrates several important ideas. First, the judgment must follow an interpretation, and the interpretation depends on sensation. Hence, the senses that create sensations are the lowest. Following the senses is the mind which derives the meaning, and higher than the mind are the three judging instruments—intellect, ego, and moral sense. Furthermore, the hierarchy within the judging instruments means that truth is of the lowest priority because there are many facts, but we don't necessarily like all of them. Our likes and dislikes correspond to our ability to choose from among the available facts, due to which not every truth is the truth for every person; each one has some ability to create their own reality by choosing from the available options. Thus, the judgment of good or bad is higher than the judgment of true and false. The judgment of right and wrong is higher than that of good, which means that our likes and desires have to be subordinated to the consideration of moral conduct. We can choose what we want, so long as it is also moral; that is, our choice of good must also be righteous.

The hierarchy of the cognitive apparatus, therefore, creates a sophisticated picture of the world. At the bottom of this hierarchy are *facts* which the senses perceive. However, the meaning of these facts is deciphered by the mind, and there is freedom to interpret the facts. But all the interpretations are not valid because the context in which they are drawn may not be appropriately demarcated. The intellect represents the freedom to choose the context, but there is also a real context, so the choice only amounts to the ability to pick falsities in the face of truth. The ego represents the choice to form goals in order to become happy, but these goals must be subordinated to the moral conduct given by a role. Thus, certain goals are forbidden in the current roles, and other goals are mandated for the given roles. Moral conduct in a particular role creates a limited freedom of goal selection, compatible with moral action. Just by understanding this hierarchy we can see how facts are reconciled with interpretation, and judgments of truth, good, and right.

The personality of a person is manifest in the relative emphasis given to the tiers of this hierarchy. Some people, for example, are preoccupied with sensations—e.g. eating, drinking, sex, hearing, and seeing—and lead a life of mindless stimulation of the senses. Somewhat higher than this tier of people are the creative people who use their minds to produce new ideas, stories, works of art, music, theatre, etc. Their pleasure rests at the level of the mind. However, they are not concerned whether their creations are true, or whether they depict the nature of reality. Their creativity, for instance, may involve writing fiction, composing songs, or painting art, but all this work is pure imagination disconnected from reality. Higher than those who enjoy via the mind are those who enjoy through the intellect. They seek not just new ideas, but only those ideas that are true. They want to find the universal truths, or at least the truths in a given context. However, their preoccupation with the facts and reasoning makes them insensitive or unaware of the emotions in other people. Higher than them are those people who seek the truths to make the world a happy place, selecting those truths which will improve life and rejecting those that will make everyone unhappy. They believe in the sanctity of life and whatever makes everyone happy is the highest good for them. The problem is that they don't understand that our happiness depends on right action—i.e. that which produces the right *karma*. Therefore, higher than the do-gooders are those who do good deeds with the understanding of *karma*—i.e. the roles and responsibilities of individuals that dictate moral action.

The hierarchy in perception creates yet another way of studying personality although the hierarchy of *sat, chit, ananda* acts through the perceptual hierarchy. Thus, a scientist may conduct experiments to know the truth, the artist creates sensual objects in order to enjoy, and the moral person acts in order to perform their duties. They are all sensing and acting, and yet they have different emphases in their actions. Similarly, the mind may be dominated by the quest for truth, pleasure, or morality, recording history and creating scientific theories (dominated by truth), producing fiction and art (dominated by pleasure), or formulating ideals of socio-economic behavior (dominated by morality). The intellect dominated by the quest for truth debates the truth of claims, when dominated by pleasure seeks only facts that will create happiness, and when controlled by morality that subset of truth which is also righteous. The ego when controlled by truth enjoys the pleasure of seeking truth, when ruled by pleasure enjoys the selfish happiness, and when led by morality seeks the collective happiness. Finally, the moral sense when ruled by truth considers knowledge the highest value in life, when overcome by pleasure regards happiness as the highest principle, and when dominated by morals considers the execution of one's duties the highest virtue.

The dominance of *sat, chit,* and *ananda* nuances the dominance of different levels of perception. Thus, for instance, either of *sat, chit,* and *ananda* might dominate the different perceptual levels, creating variety in personalities. The highest personality is that which finds the intersection of truth, right, and good, at all levels. He or she senses, thinks, and judges only that which is true and right and good. Personality development is ideally about living that rare type of life in which the truth, right, and good are exhibited at all levels from the senses to the mind, intellect, ego, and the moral sense.

The Role of the Unconscious

Only a part of our judgments of truth, right, and good are based on what we are aware of. Most of these judgments are founded on that which remains unconscious. For example, we might have a bias for science, and everything published in a scientific journal or said by scientist would be regarded true. Similarly, we have cultural notions of right and wrong, and we might automatically judge things based on these pre-formed cultural biases. Likewise, we have personal likes and dislikes and we judge things to be good or bad based on these personal preferences. In so many ways, judgments are automatic rather than conscious and deliberate. The collection of these biases constitutes our unconscious and it plays an important role in judgments.

But all these are relatively innocuous examples of the unconscious. One might even argue that they are not truly unconscious because if we carefully analyzed one's culture, intellectual biases, or personal likes and dislikes—something that people do at a psychotherapist's clinic—all these examples of the unconscious can be gradually made conscious. While they are all important, this is not what I mean by the 'unconscious' at this point.

Earlier in this chapter, I talked about how the personality changes over time due to the relative domination of ability, desire, and opportunity. We also discussed the six types of personalities and how they originate in the three kinds of intelligences that create these six personalities. While these are good explanations of the lived and experienced persona, they are not good explanations of why a soul enters the material existence. The origin of the soul's sojourn in the material world—which we study as changing personalities—is not ability and opportunity (the body and its interactions with other bodies). The soul enters the material world due to *desire*. The real unconscious is that realm of desire that causes the soul's entry into the material world, and, subsequently, abilities and opportunities might subordinate that desire to what is possible. When the desire is subordinated, one seeks not what one wants, but that which can be achieved in the given circumstances. That might entail a frustration of the desire, which then leads to anger and fear. If the desire is fulfilled, one might be gripped by pride and greed. The origin of all material experiences lies in desire and its many consequences.

In Vedic philosophy, this desire is called *māyā*—which literally means *I am not that*. Desire originates in a sense of *inadequacy*, which leads to insecurity, which prompts the soul to seek those things which can overcome the experienced incompleteness, and we call that quest for completeness *desire*. Desire is therefore not the origin of experience. In fact, when desire manifests, we are generally conscious or can become conscious, of its existence. What we often remain unconscious of is the sense of inadequacy, insecurity, and fear that prompts the soul to seek fulfillment and completeness.

Every soul is an individual, but it is a *limited* individual in the sense that it has certain innate abilities, certain innate desires, and to fulfill them the soul needs some opportunities. There is no need for fear and insecurity if you realize that you are limited because under that recognition you don't aspire for everything that other souls might naturally aspire for. You might, for instance, feel completely content in who you are, and secure in the fact that you can obtain what you truly desire. *Māyā* means that the sense of contentment and security is lost, and one is reminded of one's limited nature—not in the sense of what one *is* but what one is *not*. Vedic philosophy thus distinguishes between two kinds of *māyā* or limited individuality: (a) *yoga-māyā* is the sense of what one is not, but that distinction creates a relation to the others by which one recognizes that others are different from the self, but there is nothing to fear because they too are different from me, and hence related to me by that distinction, and (b) *mahā-māyā*, which is also the sense of what one is not, but that realization creates fear and insecurity in the soul because he competes with the others to attain their position and feels threatened and insecure by the qualities which they have but are missing in the self.

Yoga-māyā results in cooperation based on the realization that I am not what others are, and yet we can play complementary roles, and cooperate with others. Conversely, *mahā-māyā* creates competition based on the recognition that if I am not what others are then I have reason to fear their power and position, and I must therefore feel threatened by their superiority.

In every definition of what one is, there is an inherent description of what one is not. Our individuality always brings a distinction from others. However, that distinction can be a source of cooperation or competition, depending on how we interpret that difference. The difference is caused by a relative change in emphasis. If one focuses on what one is, rather than what one is not, he would be naturally content, satisfied, and secure in his ability to contribute to others what they don't have. Unhappiness emerges when we focus on what we are not, resulting in a perceived shortfall relative to others. Now we seek what might be outside our reach, which leads to suffering. Thus, unhappy people are often advised—focus on what you have, and what you can achieve, rather than what is impossible and unattainable, because we neglect what we can achieve and obtain in search of what is unachievable.

The secret to happiness lies within each person: focusing on *yoga-māyā* instead of *mahā-māyā* and becoming satisfied with whatever is available and possible with our abilities in the present opportunities. But that is not easy because the soul tends to focus on all that he is not, fights the limitations, remains fearful that he will not meet his goals, suffers in the struggle of trying to fulfill these unattainable dreams, and becomes frustrated on failure.

When I speak of the unconscious, I mean the sense of what one is and is not. Our true spiritual identity—of what one *is*—is hidden from us, and it is therefore unconscious. Our current material identity—of what one is *not*—is also generally hidden from us; it is the *cause* of desire and fear; while desire and fear become manifest in us, the cause (namely the incompleteness) is not. The cause is our sense of inadequacy, incompleteness, and insufficiency.

If one considers what one *is* then everything else constitutes what one is not. In comparison to what one *is*, what one is *not* is far bigger. However, we are not perennially aware of all that we are not. Each person is focused on a limited sense of inadequacy. For example, I might not be a successful sportsperson, but it doesn't bother me. I might not be the president of a nation or a much-decorated military officer, but it doesn't bother me. I am bothered by a different set of needs and desires, which are relatively small in comparison to all that can be desired by others. This doesn't preclude the fact that I might wish to be a successful sportsperson or a decorated military officer in the future. Therefore, my identity created by what I *am* can be eternal, but my identity produced by what I *am not* is temporary. We can distinguish between a 'spiritual' and 'material' identity—the spiritual identity is that which I am eternally, and the material identity is that which I am not temporarily. If one finds the spiritual identity, all other identities are immediately known to be material and one stops trying to fulfill what one is not because there is natural satisfaction and fulfillment in what one is. Until the spiritual identity is found, one keeps trying to quench the needs of what one is not.

Both spiritual and material identities are currently unconscious, but I will here focus only upon the temporary material unconscious (I will return to the question of the spiritual identity in the last chapter). It is constituted of a very complex set of ideas that define everything that we are not—i.e. all the ways in which we are inadequate, incomplete, and insufficient.

The fact is that nobody wants to be told of all the ways in which they are inadequate. That knowledge makes us unhappy and fearful. Therefore, even if there were opportunities to bring the inadequacy to the conscious surface, without knowledge of the spiritual identity, inadequacies would be suppressed. We try to get away from people who criticize us, we leave the relationships that expose our limitations and weaknesses, and we quit talking to those who are constantly advising and correcting us. Even if we sometimes open to others about our problems, it is almost never to point a finger at our inadequacies, but only to blame others for our problems. We seek solace in a friend who will give our story a patient, compassionate, and sympathetic hearing, and we avoid those who might blame us for our own problems. We fundamentally don't want to be reminded of our limitations and inadequacies. In that sense, this world of inadequacies remains unconscious. It is not because it cannot become conscious. It is because we don't want it to be.

The soul is trapped in the material world because it has forgotten its spiritual identity and focuses on the material identity of what it is not. Even this identity is suppressed because it represents what we can never be, and we don't want to be reminded of it. We focus on that limited set of inadequacies that drive us towards the desire to surmount it, and are successful in overcoming, even if only temporarily and partially. That limited set of inadequacies that are partially and temporarily conquered becomes conscious *after* they have been overcome. We then tell stories about how man overcomes his limitations, overpowers his fear, and fulfills his desires. All that remains unfulfilled remains hidden, but it pushes us toward new aspirations.

Desires are conscious but their causes in inadequacies are unconscious. We can speak about what purposes we have, but we are unaware of why we have precisely those goals because explaining them would bring us face to face with what we don't want to know. The desires we attend to are not actually free will because these desires are automatically created by the unconscious and forced upon us due to our hidden sense of inadequacy, which changes with time and prompts us toward new directions. Nevertheless, there is free will precisely because we can discard all these inadequacies and understand who we really are. There is also limited free will in whether we permit the desire, or suppress it. Free will is thus not desire. Free will is rather the selection of one desire vs. another, while desires are naturally produced. Free will is indicative of two facts—(a) we can choose from among the desires by prioritizing them, and (b) we can discard all such desires. Free will, however, is not the only agency involved in prioritizing desires; the desires themselves are relatively dominant or subordinate over time.

One key difference between spiritual and material desires is that material desires bring fears, but spiritual desires involve no fear. Recall that in the spiritual desire there is no latent inadequacy. In the material desire, there is always latent inadequacy and hence fear. If you want to be successful, you have the fear of failure; if you want to be rich, there is fear of poverty. The material desires and fears are created as a pair, but we can choose to attend to either side—desire or fear. Free will is selecting which side we attend to.

Sometimes we face the desire and neglect the fear, and sometimes we face the fear and neglect the desire. The stories of greatness are based on embracing the desire and ignoring the fear, while the stories of degradation are based on embracing the fear and ignoring the desire. Factually, these stories are not great because happiness is possible only when we are free of fear, not just when we conquer fear. Conquering fear gives us a sense of material happiness because we feel empowered and independent, but this sense is temporary.

Depression, on the other hand, appears when fear overpowers desire. The fear of failure makes us incapable of fulfilling any desire and we lose interest in life. We are paralyzed by our inner demons because we choose to pay more attention to the fear rather than its counterpart—desire. All mental illness is caused by the unconscious and it emerges from fear. Many of these illnesses are triggered by bad experiences in which fear becomes more prominent and our desires are frustrated. As we begin to focus on the fear, we lose sight of what we desire. Life then becomes a downward spiral in which we avoid fulfilling the desires to become happy and spend all our time in fear mitigation, which can factually never be mitigated because the material world is created from inadequacies. The path out of depression is realizing that when the soul is covered by fears, it fights back. Of course, in the ultimate analysis, this fight is futile because the space of possible inadequacies is infinite; if you overcome one, there would be many more. Therefore, even those who are not depressed (because they focus on desire over fear) are fighting a futile battle. However, the same battle can become useful if the battle against fear is meant to become free of fears, not just conquer specific fears.

The unconscious is our collective fear. It is what we feel we cannot be. From that fear emerges the rage and passion to conquer the limitations and inadequacies. That rage and passion is called desire. It is not our innate desire. It is rather a response to a provocation. You would be provoked only if you accept the challenge of a material limitation and decide to fight it. The soul suffers from continuous provocation and the rage to fight it. If the limitation doesn't provoke you, there is no rage, there is no fight, and no need to prove oneself again and again. Then, you become happy and peaceful.

Emotion plays a very important role in our lives because the limitations are factual but the response to that limitation is emotional. If the response is depression, life goes into a downward spiral. If the response is rage and passion, life goes up and down in a cycle because sometimes we are successful and at other times we fail. Life can only go upward only if we realize that these limitations are indicating what we are not; these are facts, and nothing to be depressed or angry about. We must accept them as facts because that acceptance opens the door to the realization of what we truly are. Depression and rage are thus not appropriate responses to the discovery of the unconscious. The appropriate response is acceptance that it is not who we are.

4

Emotion and Biology

Introductory Background

In the first chapter I described how it is possible to reconceive material nature—the idea of space, time, and matter—based on the three features of the soul, and how this revision is consistent with modern theories in physics, although inconsistent with the dogmas of classical physics. The classical physical dogma holds that the reality we perceive is caused by something beyond that perception, so it must be grasped by conceptual speculation—postulating ideas such as particles and waves—which cannot be perceived. The philosophical problem emanating from this dogma is that reality is forever unknowable because we can never *directly* experience it, and we can never have *enough* data to irrevocably prove a speculative idea. Every theory is in principle tentative, which is now (following Karl Popper) called *falsifiability*, because a theory can never be proved; it can only be disproved.

I also described an alternative in which the world that we consider to be 'outside' is *projected* from inside, and the causes of this projection are available to us through first-person introspection rather than speculative guesswork. Philosophically, this is better because it makes reality knowable, and the approach is no worse empirically. It does, however, require us to reconceive space, time, and matter—based on the nature of the soul. I also noted how the new conception addresses long-standing problems in science—e.g. the problem of incompleteness in atomic theory, and the incompatibility between atomic theory and relativity. We noted how the alternative resolves paradoxes (e.g. the Twin Paradox), and how the resolution is compatible with new kinds of phenomena—e.g. one's lifespan—currently outside science.

I will now use this chapter to expand on the above ideas, specifically in the context of biology. As we saw earlier, we are not trying to study the soul directly, but using a theory of the soul to describe material phenomena. This theory is compatible with well-known psychological facts—e.g. personality types, how these types emerge out of intelligence types, how everyday life is carried out through three types of judgments, and how the unconscious plays an important role in determining our subsequent experiences. In that sense, the idea of the soul is understood in terms of psychological facts and then used to demystify the problems in physical and chemical sciences.

Biology presents some interesting examples of this usefulness as well. Of particular interest is the fact that the body is comprised not just of material *parts*, which are created from the *chit* or cognition. The body of the soul also includes two other things—corresponding to *sat* and *ananda*—which can be called the *function* and the *purpose* of the part. The need for additional ingredients in the body arises because the parts are not definite objects; rather, they exist as *possibilities* or *abilities*. Something is needed to make them real.

Each part can be many things, in relation to other things. The *function* of the part emerges when a part is related to another part, and this function cannot be *reduced* to the part, because the part is capable of many functions one of which materializes through a relation. To know why a part functions in a specific way, we have to look beyond the part, see other parts, and their interrelation. This means that a part is capable of many functions, but a *relation* selects one of them. The part is like the dice and the function of the part is one of the six faces of the dice that turns up on a throw. The selection of the face depends on the relation between the hand of the player and the dice, not the dice itself. Similarly, molecules are not functional by themselves, because they are not definite objects in themselves. They are only possibilities of being many things, one of which becomes real within a relationship. The relation is therefore the cause of the *function*, which we can observe.

Now, this raises new questions about why a part is interrelated to only specific parts such that a function emerges out of the infinite possibilities through a relation. Given that a part could have relations to any part, what determines the relation between two parts? The answer to this quandary is that just as functions are selected by a relation, similarly, the relations have to be selected by a *purpose*. The purpose, in this case, targets an ability toward a specific object, as opposed to the numerous possible objects.

The body that we observe is produced from the combination of parts (which are possibilities), relations (which select a function), and purposes (which select from among many possible relations). Thus, the possibilities are selected by a relation, and the relation is selected by a purpose. This is, however, only one possible scenario. In other scenarios, the possibilities in a part limit the relations to other parts, which then limits the purpose that can be achieved. The parts, relations, and purposes are not logically prior to one another. However, they must always be *combined* to create a reality.

This idea can be understood through everyday examples. For instance, a plank of wood has the potential to be the leg of a chair or a table. To convert the plank of wood into a chair's leg, we must put it in a specific relation to the other planks of wood, which then through the specific relation become the back and seat of the chair. But these relationships can be instantiated only if we have the goal of building a chair because based on that goal we choose the relationships. Generally, we begin with a purpose of producing a chair. Then we come up with a *design* that defines the specific relations between the parts. Finally, we choose the parts to fit that design. The final outcome—the chair—combines the parts, relations, and purpose, but we sensually perceive the parts, we mentally see the relations between parts, and we use the chair (e.g. sit upon it to eat, study, or work) because it fits our purpose.

Design and Purpose in Science

This fact about designs has now become evident in atomic theory where the atoms are possibilities of being many things, and to realize those possibilities they must be put into a relation to another atom. Unlike classical physics where the effect of an object spread universally, now the effects are *quantized*—we call them *bosons*—which are particles that don't spread universally; they are emitted and absorbed by specific particles, and the destination of that particle is known before the particle is emitted. In other words, the boson represents a unique relation between some chosen particles, and atomic theory is unable to predict which source will emit a boson to which destination when. The boson is just like a hammer in your hand; it is an ability that can be used, but when and where you use the ability cannot be predicted. There is hence a "choice" involved in closing the gap between what the theory can predict and the facts which can be observed empirically: the theory doesn't predict the facts about (1) what event will occur, (2) the specific pair of objects between which it will occur, and (3) when the event will occur. These gaps in theory can be bridged only if science includes *purpose*.

In current atomic theory, we recognize that atoms are possibilities. We also recognize that interactions between atoms are quantized and hence not universal. But because we don't recognize purpose, quantum theory is incomplete. In the standard interpretation of quantum theory this purpose is called a "collapse" of the possibility, but the mechanism of this collapse is unknown. Physicists don't accept a non-material agency—e.g. consciousness—that could make a choice, owing to the legacy of mind-body problems. And physicists are unable to show that this collapse can be avoided while remaining in the current material ontology. What I present here is a new category of matter called *purpose* which is related to consciousness but not consciousness itself in the sense that purposes can be objective, and yet not objects.

Without bringing about such changes in science, there is a never–ending stream of interpretations that try to recreate the classical world from the quantum world, and as such attempts continue, the classical physical dogmas continue to dominate chemistry and biology. The fact is that atomic theory is consistent with our everyday experiences about the world, so the theory is not the problem. The problem is that we *want* the theory to look like classical physics where atoms were not possibilities, a relation between atoms was not required to interact, and a purpose was not needed to select a relation.

Biology, too, operates under the presuppositions of classical physics. Biologists think that molecules are *things* rather than *possibilities* of things. The chemical reaction is believed to be an outcome of physical forces acting between molecules, although the forces are quantized, and the specific pair of reacting molecules can't be predicted. To first select the interacting molecules, and then select the specific behavior of a molecule, a new kind of agency is required which doesn't exist in biology today. Biologists haven't realized that in classical physics particles and forces were both fixed, but in atomic theory particles and forces are both uncertain, and therefore chemical reactions are undetermined. The molecules are inadequate to cause reactions. They must be activated by force particles, and those forces must be triggered by a purpose. We can say that matter is still moved by force, but force doesn't move by itself. This is not merely philosophy. It is rather a direct outcome of quantum physics, and how it differs radically from classical physics.

Every physical effect is an outcome of determining a source and a target, which constitute a specific relation—this is what I previously called inter-subjective space. The effect also depends on choosing a time of interaction—which is caused by the purpose. The objects constitute a space called Hilbert Space in atomic theory[1], which I previously called the objective space of possibilities. The objective space exists as the abilities, the inter-subjective space selects a particular ability toward a specific object and it exists as opportunities, while the purpose exists as the subjective space of intentions and it triggers the conversion of that ability into an action that causes change.

The description of the body in terms of parts, functions, and purposes is a *quantum* description of the body. We cannot observe these individually in a third-person manner because observations are produced by their combination. But, we can speak about these ingredients in a first-person manner because the purpose exists in a person before it is used to select a relation, which then manifests an action. We have thus reached a point in atomic theory where third-person observables (called "hidden variables") cannot be used to complete atomic theory. If, however, we look at that situation from a first-person perspective we can find variables that are not hidden, and which can be used to complete the theory. In fact, everything about atomic theory involves a first-person perspective because the senses cannot see possibility, relation, or purpose. The mind can see the world as possibility which is yet to become reality. The mind can perceive relations between objects because relations are observable entities. Finally, the mind can perceive purpose which exists before an action is performed, a relation is chosen, and a possibility is selected. Therefore, if we look at the situation from the first-person perspective, we have everything needed to complete atomic theory. But seen from the third-person perspective, atomic theory is forever incomplete.

This incompleteness is the imminent virtue of the first-person viewpoint over the third-person view, or what I have called the "inside-out" thinking–what we can perceive through the mind is logically prior to what we can gather through the senses. Only when science discards its "outside-in" view, in which the mind is produced from what can be empirically observed by the senses, will the problems of atomism be solved. Of course, the fact that the mind can perceive possibility, relation, and purpose doesn't mean that all possibilities are eternal, all relations are right, and all purposes are good. But just recognizing that the mind is superior to the senses in terms of its ability to see what the senses cannot, gets us started on a new journey in which higher faculties—intellect, ego, and the moral sense—can be added to the mind incrementally. Ultimately, this ideology entails that the material world reflects the properties of the soul (as objects, functions, and purposes), but they are so deeply enmeshed that most people generally tend to think that the part is itself the function, and the function is itself the purpose.

I will use the remainder of this chapter to elaborate upon the above understanding of material nature produced from the combination of parts, functions, and purposes. Each of the components of experience is hierarchical and organized as an *inverted tree*, which emanates from a root into trunks, branches, twigs, and leaves. The trees are also connected such that a part can perform different functions, and a function can be used for different purposes. In a simple sense, the body of an observer experiences different objects (higher or lower in the hierarchy), which is then associated with different pleasures (higher or lower in the hierarchy). Only the nodes on the tree thus connected are *experienced*; any part of a tree unconnected to two other nodes on other trees remains "unmanifest" and is not experienced. Thus, a very limited set of abilities, a very limited set of relations, and a very limited set of pleasures are experience at any time, although they are always possible.

The material world, as the cognitive, emotional, and relational possibilities is eternal. But, a small subset of these possibilities is visible at any given time because that vision is the outcome of their *combination*. Everything that lies uncombined remains invisible. And because the combinations are performed by specific individuals, they are only visible to them. The experience of the material world therefore must be explained by who combines the eternal possibilities in a certain order. Matter, in this sense, is neither created nor destroyed. However, matter becomes visible and invisible to varying extents to different observers. Once we view matter this way, we can see why free will is important because it creates a material combination. Free will makes no changes to matter, because matter exists as possibilities and all possibilities are eternal. But free will changes our experience by creating the combination of eternal possibilities. Instead of worrying about how the soul can change matter, we should be worrying about how free will combines possibilities.

The Whole-Part Distinction

In classical physics, each particle is *independent* of other particles, and the material world has no *boundaries*. While we isolate the study of macroscopic objects into "closed systems", factually there is nothing in science that corresponds to this closure. Accordingly, we only think of reality as atomic objects and not *macroscopic objects*. The idea that the macroscopic object *reduces* to its components has now become problematic in atomic theory because each particle has an *orthogonal state*—energy, momentum, angular momentum, and spin—which means that particle states are defined *collectively* rather than *individually*. Classical particles could change state independent of the other particles, but if an atomic object changes state, all the other particles must change state as well. You cannot, therefore, manipulate an individual object without 'disturbing' the state of the whole system, which entails that you are manipulating the entire system, not just a particle.

A collection of particles acts like a team of people in which each member of the team performs a different role. Because the same role can be performed by another person, the team can be abstractly described in terms of roles, and tangibly described in terms of the people. If a team is large, there is a greater division of labor among the members, and the roles of each member are altered accordingly. If the team is small, there is a lesser division of labor among the members, and each person's role is again modified. We could envision a team that has unfilled roles which exist as *possibilities* to be filled by another person joining the team. We could also envision a team in which there is a person who doesn't have a role because all the roles have already been taken. If a team role is vacant, the team naturally tends to attract new members so that the current members can continue with their present roles. If all roles are filled, the team has a natural tendency to repel redundant members. Now, you don't need mechanical forces to attract and repel, because you have the occupied or redundant roles to achieve that.

Current atomic theory doesn't distinguish between the scenarios in which all the roles are filled, and some roles are vacant because it doesn't separate the roles from the parts. The parts of the team are the people who work in it, while the roles of the team are which types of people could join or leave the team. The role of a team member is called the quantum *state*, and the member is called the *particle*. A particle could exist in different states, and the states could be occupied by different particles. The particle is therefore not identical to the state, but whenever a measurement is performed, a particle is in a state. The particles have to be distinguished from states because there could be vacant states which a particle from outside the system could occupy. Similarly, a particle could leave a state vacant for other particles.

The ensemble of particles is distinct from the ensemble of states, and present atomic theory only describes the ensembles of states. When a particle enters a state, it takes on a role within the ensemble, and by that occupation of state, it is designated by that state in the context of the ensemble.

This is like a person who takes a role in a team and gets designated by the name of the role. For example, we say that the team *has* an accountant, and a person *is* an accountant. The *has-a* description pertains to the person, and the *is-a* description pertains to the role. If we observe the person in the team, we could call him or her by the role—e.g. an accountant. And yet, the person could leave the team, and be replaced by another. Therefore, the person and the role are distinct, although every person is in some role (although sometimes that role can be doing nothing within the team), and our observation is produced by the combination of a person and a role as we designate the person by the role—e.g. an accountant—although he or she could be in another role. There is a possibility associated with the *person*—i.e. that he could be in another role. There is also a possibility associated with the *role*—i.e. that someone could occupy the role. These are, however, different.

The distinction between person and role—or part and function—leads us to two different notions about space. The person or the part is *inside* the team due to which we say that the team *has-an* accountant. But the role connects the person to other roles which are *outside* the role, due to which we say that the person *is-an* accountant. Thus, from the team perspective, there is a space of people who are "inside" the team. But from the person's perspective, there is a space of other roles "outside" the person's role, but which define it relationally. The *has-a* perspective begins from the whole and considers the parts inside the whole. The *is-a* perspective begins with the individual role and sees other roles outside of it, typically in relation to the next higher role. Owing to these complementary descriptions, we can describe space as something *inside* the whole, and something that is *outside* of a part.

If we collapse the distinction between an individual and a role, then the inside and outside descriptions become identical, and we could use them interchangeably although now we would have to describe the effect of other parts on each particle. That effect is, in classical physics, universal, which means that the universe is a single very large team and every role affects every other role. However, in atomic theory, it is possible to think of the universe as smaller teams—ensembles—in which roles only affect other roles within the team, although the team can play a role in a larger collection. Therefore, by collapsing the role and the person, we don't truly get rid of the role; we just inherit the description of the role as the *effect* of the other persons on all persons. In physical theories, the 'role' is called the 'field' and to know that field one must know all the other particles. There are still two things—particle and field—and you cannot reduce it to just one. A far better approach is to keep that distinction between person and role. If, however, we distinguish the individual from the role, then two notions of space are required—one that distinguishes individuals and the other that distinguishes roles. The relation between the particles identifies a macroscopic object with parts. But the relation between the roles attributes each part in the whole a new role.

The *chit* or cognitive space is the space of individuals and the *sat* or awareness space is the space of roles. To identify a person across different roles we use the *chit*. To distinguish the different roles of a person, we use *sat*. Thus, one type of space is used to identify an individual, and the other space is used to distinguish the person's role. The *sat* creates the soul's awareness—we contact other individuals through role-play. The *chit* creates the individuality—we remain unchanged across these different roles.

The *chit* or individual space corresponds to what we call 'objects' in modern science. Each object has an identity although that object can enter a different state. The *sat* or role space corresponds to 'state space' in science; it describes the states of objects. The term 'position' thus serves different purposes in relation to objects and roles. One position individuates the objects, and the other position individuates the states. At the point of experience, the *chit* and *sat* are always combined, which means that there is an individual and a role, or an object and a state. The combination of individual and role, or object and state, may be temporary but the roles and individuals (or objects and states) are always possible. The possibilities may not be experienced although they exist, because experience needs their combination. In fact, we can distinguish the possibility from its experience: the individual and the state are always possible, but their combination is a temporary experience.

That temporary combination is caused by *time*, which exists as *purpose*, and corresponds to the third aspect of the soul—*ananda*. A person enters a role due to their purposes. In a sophisticated language, we say that a particle enters a state due to time. The terms *sat*, *chit*, and *ananda* are therefore counterparts of scientific terms 'space', 'object', and 'time', and while they exist individually and separately, the experience of the soul is created only through their combination. Thus, we cannot observe a state without an object independent of time. Whenever we observe, we will see an object in a state at a time. Space, time, and object are conceptual constructs that can't be experienced individually; to experience them, we must combine them.

The novelty now is that what we call 'space' is no longer constructed from the distance between objects; it is constructed from the distances between roles or states. In atomic theory, this space is the *Hilbert Space* mentioned earlier and its dimensions identify states. Similarly, what we call an 'object' is not identified by its states; it is rather identified by the succession of states which constructs a *trajectory* for the object—i.e. the series of experiences. Finally, by time we don't just mean a universal arrow; we rather mean that each individual has a purpose which pushes them forward from one state to another, which creates the succession of states, which *appears* to be change and time. The real time is not the appearance of succession; the real time is the purpose that lies behind that succession and produces it.

In this way, the ideas of space, time, and object, are redefined by the theory of the soul. This change is consistent with our understanding of the self, but also consistent with science. The new ideas of space, time, and matter are incompatible with classical physics, and with nearly five centuries of dogmas about nature. To change the dogma, we undertake a philosophical discussion, not because the goal is philosophy but because the dogmas run very deep.

The Necessity for Hierarchy

When we think of reality in terms of individuals, roles, and goals, we arrive at the difference between the old and the new viewpoints—the difference is *hierarchy*. Our goals are hierarchical—we have top-level goals and then subordinate goals to achieve the top-level goals and then smaller goals which achieve the subordinate goals, etc. The roles are also hierarchical—there are individuals in top-level positions, in mid-level positions, and in low-level positions. Finally, the individuals are also higher and lower due to the whole-part relationship in which the whole is the higher individual, the part is the lower individual, and the part of the part is even a lower individual.

In modern thinking this hierarchy has been discarded because objects don't contain other objects, locations in space are not higher and lower because all locations are considered equivalent, and instances in time are not higher or lower because we don't conceive time as caused by a purpose.

The top-level goals take more time to be fulfilled, but the smaller goals are fulfilled in shorter times; therefore, if we thought of time as being caused by purposes, we could think of longer durations and shorter durations as different kinds of time. This time is compatible with our everyday notions of time where months are inside years, weeks are inside months, days are inside weeks, and hours are inside days. Everyday time is hierarchical, and you can refer to the year, month, or day just as easily as we refer to microseconds. Modern science collapses this hierarchy and we arrive at a flat, linear time which is universally progressing for every individual, thereby discarding the fact that each individual can have different purposes, which drive them towards different directions in their personal lives at different rates. Time becomes a much-nuanced concept when treated hierarchically; it is stripped of all its nuances—and causal properties—when hierarchy is discarded.

The top-level objects have more parts and subparts than the lower-level objects. Thus, planet Earth has many countries, which then have many states, which are divided into many cities, which have many homes and offices. When sending a letter to someone, we address it to their home or office, and that address traverses the hierarchy from the country to the state to the city to the street to their home or office, which *contains* their body. The body is identified hierarchically, and we refer to a country or a city just as well as we refer to a house. The fact that a country is reducible to smaller parts doesn't stop us from treating it as a real entity. Objects become nuanced when we treat them hierarchically due to the whole-part relationship which allows them to be treated as *symbols*. The relation to the higher-level object—the whole—acts as the *context* of the object, and the object is given a *meaning* in that context. When space is stripped of its hierarchy, the symbols lose their meaning. The world is reduced to a collection of meaningless things.

The top-level roles have a greater span of control than the lower-level roles. Due to this, their causality spreads over greater or smaller distances. Thus, the effects are sometimes extenuated over great distances, and at other times confined to a local influence. Common examples of such hierarchies are seen in organizations, government, and even within families. A person may be physically the same size as other persons, but their influence sometimes spans over many persons, and sometimes they are unable to even control their own lives. The causal influence of an object, therefore, is not defined by its physical properties; it is rather defined by its current role—higher or lower. When space is defined as the hierarchy of roles, then it is possible to explain why an object in that role can influence many more objects as opposed to other objects which are unable to influence anything other than their own behavior. When this hierarchy is discarded, every object's influence spreads equally in all directions, making them capable of influencing everything in the universe simultaneously, when in reality the scope of causality—i.e. the objects to which it spreads—depends on the type of the role they play.

Hierarchy is a scientific concept because it brings new scientific and causal properties. Time under a hierarchy has causal properties by which it pushes objects forward. An object under a hierarchy acquires semantic properties, and we don't worry only about its physical constitution but also what it denotes and represents, beyond its physicality. Space under a hierarchy changes the scope of causality by which the influence of some objects spreads to many objects, while the influence of other objects is limited in scope.

The concept of the soul—*sat, chit,* and *ananda*—corresponds to the ideas of space, object, and time, but these are *hierarchical* as opposed to *flattened* constructs as in the case of science. The hierarchy moves the causality from physical properties to time. The hierarchy makes physical properties inadequate without the semantics. And the hierarchy alters the scope of an object's influence based on the state in which it is presently situated.

These ideas in the context of atomic theory would mean that atoms in some states can react with many more other atoms than in others. At present, atomic theory only considers the *kinetic* concept of 'energy' as the basis of reactivity, which means that the atom is prone to react, but the scope of this reaction—i.e. the number of atoms changed by a reaction—is unknown. A minor change in the higher state could dramatically affect many lower states, but a large change in a lower state would not affect the higher states. Thus, some large-scale changes remain confined in their influence, while other small-scale changes reverberate through the system. Quantum theory is said to be *linear*—i.e. small changes have small effects, and vice versa. However, hierarchical space means some small changes have large effects—which would make quantum theory *non-linear*—like the so-called "Butterfly Effect". Non-linear effects must produce a logical contradiction in atomic theory. But this logical contradiction is imminent because thermodynamics is non-linear, and we cannot explain biological phenomena without thermodynamics. To allow for a theory to be sometimes linear and at other times non-linear, we need hierarchy states in the theory. Hierarchical states will allow us to reconcile atomic theory linearity with the thermodynamic non-linearity[2].

Without hierarchical time—that manifests as a choice driven by a purpose—we cannot solve the quantum 'collapse' problem by which a particle is emitted or absorbed at a time without us being able to explain what that time would be. Quantum theory remains incomplete because it cannot predict when an event occurs—e.g. when a radioactive atom will decay. In fact, when the world is described as possibilities, there is nothing that converts it into a reality, which creates the problem that we see a reality, but we can't explain how it emerges from a possibility. The answer is that we experience reality because we have a purpose—we *want* to experience the world. That wanting creates purpose, which selects from the possibilities. The 'collapse' of the possibility is due to a purpose—which creates change and time. Randomness is the outcome of a *macroscopic* purpose without a *microscopic* purpose. Therefore, if we see the world macroscopically, it seems to move deterministically because the top-level purpose is well-defined, but the lower-level purpose is not. The system is like a person who knows where to go but doesn't know how to get there; he bumbles through steps, but still moves forward.

The world is not uncertain and not deterministic because purpose is a hierarchy in which top-level goals can exist without the lower-level goals. To the extent that you can make the lower-level goals more certain, the uncertainty is correspondingly reduced. Empirical results show that the Uncertainty Principle can be overcome[3], but it creates an inconsistency because quantum probabilities forbid the ability to predict individual events. Hierarchical time solves this problem because large-scale (statistical) and small-scale (deterministic) predictions are caused by higher and lower purposes.

Without hierarchical objectivity, we cannot explain why quantum particles are *entangled*—i.e. changes to one particle causes the other particles to change. Entanglement or non-locality is a paradox in atomic theory[4] because we think that quantum particles are independent entities rather than *parts* of a whole. The whole is a *higher-level* object and the parts are *lower-level* objects. A coin has two faces, and a dice has six, but these faces don't change independently because they are parts of a whole. The problem here is that we can separate the head and the tail of a coin in atomic theory (as two entangled particles) while the head and the tail were always conjoined in classical physics. This separation can be understood only if the head and the tail are treated as correlated *concepts* and spatial location as denoting the meaning. The fact that head and tail can be separated only means that they are mutually opposite concepts, and their opposition increases as we grow the distance between them. The distance is a signifier of their meaning, and as the distance is increased each side grows in its 'strength'—they are now even more logically opposed. Conversely, as we bring them closer, the semantic difference reduces, but they always remain logically opposed, and therefore entangled.

Hierarchy is essential to understand atomism, and therefore chemistry and biology. By this hierarchy we can explain the system at different levels of abstraction using the same theory. For example, the theory that explains atomic phenomena at microscopic levels can also be used to explain biology at macroscopic levels. The same theory "scales" at different levels of abstraction which is great because we don't need different theories for living beings, subatomic particles, and human psychology. The same theory works because the theory is derived from the principles of object, relation, and purpose, which can be scaled from atoms to humans and beyond. Emotion remains an integral part of this description as the purpose which drives us forward in life. Emotion is, however, not just a human phenomenon. We need it to even explain why the world of possibilities appears to be so definite and stable.

Macroscopic Atoms

The question is: how do we treat the macroscopic system as a real object in a theory that only deals with atomic objects? This is when the classical conceptions of space must be discarded because in the classical view the whole object is a *bigger* object and it could not be treated as another atomic object. A new way of thinking is required in which the whole object and the parts in it are both atomic (i.e. indivisible), but they are not at the same *level*. Space must now be described as a *tree*—which originates in a root, expands into branches, and terminates into leaves. The parts of the whole are like the leaves, the bigger parts are like branches, and the whole is the root. Both the whole and the part are atomic—i.e. indivisible—and yet one is bigger than the other. Therefore, we can talk about whole and part without reduction. The part is at once separate from the whole and yet attached to the whole just as a leaf is attached to the trunk which is attached to the root. By attaching the part to the whole, we seem to "divide" what is otherwise indivisible.

This idea is physically incomprehensible if the space is *flat*. It becomes intuitive if space is a *tree*. For example, in this tree space, a chair is a trunk, and the legs, seat, and back of the chair are branches from the trunk. Each of the parts—legs, seat, and back—have subparts which are like twigs from the branches, and the chair is itself a part of a room, the room is part of a house, the house is part of a city, a city is part of a country, and so forth.

The entire universe is an atom, and the smallest particles are also atoms. They are, however, atomic from different *viewpoints*—for someone perceiving the root, the universe is atomic (i.e. a single indivisible object, whose details are not seen), and for someone at the leaf, the "small" particles are atomic (i.e. indivisible). Big and small are a matter of an observer's *perspective* and therefore they are *relative* to the observer. What we consider big is small for another observer (closer to the root), and what we consider small is, from another observer's perspective, big (closer to the leaf). The whole system and its parts are both atoms. In current atomism we cannot recognize which atom is a whole, and which atom is a part because we believe that the world is a *box* rather than a *tree*. To distinguish between part and whole atoms, we must attribute *types* to atoms—some atom will *denote* a more abstract *type* while another atom will represent a more *detailed* type. For example, the 'chair' is more abstract relative to the 'legs'. The type is nothing other than the *location* of the object on the tree. The novelty is that location is no longer just a physical property; it also denotes meaning. The tree of atoms constructs a type of conceptual hierarchy, which originates from the *chit* propensity of the soul. It constructs a hierarchy in which the whole is divided into parts, such that the chair can be divided into legs, back, and seat, the seat can be divided into four corners, and so on. This is the objective definition of the chair, as it exists by itself. But this is not the only type of definition. Sometimes, a table can also be used as a chair, in a context. This contextual application of the idea of 'chair' is different from the objective application.

In the contextual application, the term 'chair' is the contextual *role* played by something in relation to other things. Ironically, the same words can be used both universally and contextually; for instance, I can use the word 'chair' to describe an object without describing how it is being used. I can also use the same word to represent the contextual role played by the object. These are different things—part vs. function—but we can use the same words to describe them. It can lead to confusion, which is only mitigated when we distinguish between the *modes* in which the words are used.

The key point is that macroscopic objects are also atomic objects in the simple sense that they are concepts, which can be cognized as wholes. And yet they acquire parts, which are also concepts that can be grasped as a whole. Even though the whole is divisible, it is also a whole. However, the whole is not reduced to the parts but has an *attachment* to the part. The whole and the part remain separately atomic, real, and individual. The uniqueness is not in the whole being "bigger" than the part, but in the whole-part *relationship*: a relationship that makes one atom a part of another atom, because the first atom is situated higher up in the tree while the second is lower in the tree.

The Part-Function Separation

Modern biology sees the parts of a body but doesn't recognize the separate reality of the functions of these parts. The functions arise through a contextual relation to *some* parts, not all the parts. Depending on the context, the relationship may exist between different parts, which leads to different functions of the same parts. For example, the hands can hold, the legs are used to move, the stomach helps digest food, the head is used in thinking, etc. But the hands could also be used to move, and the legs can be used to hold. While a part cannot perform every other part's functions (the hand cannot think) some parts can indeed perform the functions of other parts. In a typical body, there is a specific pre-established relation between the parts due to which they also have well-defined functions. However, quite often, if the relation is changed, their functions are also altered. The functional division of the body arises because all the parts don't interact or relate to all the other parts; universal interaction was the principle in classical physics, but in atomic theory only some parts will interact with other parts, creating well-defined functions. The same part can however perform a different function with another part. Therefore, the body when described as a collection of parts is described incompletely because we don't know how the body will behave *a priori*.

The functionality of a body part is an additional appellation of the body part due to which the part acquires a *role* in relation to the other parts. The parts encompass different abilities but only some of these abilities are instantiated in relation to another part. The other abilities—depending on the relation—become hidden. As the relation is changed, new abilities manifest, not because they did not previously exist, but because the relation makes them apparent. This entails a separation between the *ability* in the part and its selection for a specific *function*—which emerges from a relationship.

This idea is easily seen in the case of an organization that has functional departments such as engineering, marketing, sales, human resources, finance, legal, manufacturing, etc. separate from the people employed in these departments. You can describe the organization as comprised of people—which are the observable parts that you can see and touch. You can also describe the same organization as divided into functional roles—which are not observable as parts but become apparent in *activities*. Some people could potentially work in multiple departments, while others can only do one function. But the key point is that due to job mobility the person is not identical to the role.

Many biologists contend that the part is itself the function, reducing the functioning of the body to its chemical composition. This is a wrong idea even though the body is indeed comprised of chemicals but by such reduction we still don't indicate which chemical interacts with which other chemicals. Not every chemical reacts with every other chemical in the body. You can mix the same chemicals into a test tube, but you would not be able to create the body, because it is not enough to just have the chemicals—one must also define the specific chemical reactions by stipulating which chemicals will react with each other and which chemicals would never react with each other.

The biological properties in a living body are due to chemical reactions, but the reactions are not entirely due to chemicals—i.e. parts. Just because two chemicals exist doesn't mean they will react, and just because two parts are present doesn't mean that they will interact. The functioning of the body doesn't reduce to chemicals because the reactions between the chemicals don't reduce to the chemicals themselves. They also need relations.

An auto-immune disease[5] is an example where the chemicals supposed to attack the 'bad' chemicals from outside the body begin attacking the 'good' chemicals inside the body. It is noteworthy that both the immunity chemicals and the tissue chemicals previously existed in the body without an interaction; the immunity chemicals interacted only with the 'bad' chemicals. Auto-immunity destroys the relation between the immunity chemicals to the 'bad' chemicals and creates a new relationship to the 'good' chemicals. The onset of disease—in this case—is caused by the establishment of new relationships between existing chemicals. In other cases, it might be caused by the addition of new chemicals. Thus, many cancers remain 'dormant' for very long periods of time[6] because the chemicals exist in the body—and can be detected by a test—but they don't react in undesirable ways with other chemicals. A cancer can also go into 'remission' when the disease-causing relationships are broken[7]. The cancer relapses when those relationships are established again. To fully cure the cancer, one must remove the parts that enter adverse relations, but the cancer can also be controlled by changing relations to parts.

If we looked at the body chemically, we would still see the same ingredients in the body, and yet they will not react with each other because the relationship between them has been altered. The idea of relation, therefore, has empirical consequences—(a) it can be used to explain how cancers go into remission and how they relapse, and (b) it can be used to find new ways to cure diseases by changing the relations between the chemicals without consuming drugs. The process of changing the relations between the chemicals is in everyone's hands, and if we knew that process we could lead healthy lives. Indeed, the *yogis* of the past could elongate their lives by such methods. Modern medicine doesn't understand this cause because it doesn't recognize the fundamental role of relations. Therefore, doctors prescribe new medicines to cure the diseases, but the outcome of consuming a medicine is uncertain because it depends on the relation the medicine establishes in the body. In some cases, the medicine will work, and in other cases it can cause adverse effects. Thus, medicines generally have many side effects and what works in one body doesn't necessarily work in another. The root cause is scientific: we have to understand that chemicals are not the only cause of reactions.

The problem for the biologist is that they cannot *observe* the functions as *objects* because of the interaction between parts. Each new type of interaction potentially brings a new function. And yet, since all parts don't always interact with all other parts, there can be potentially new functionality in the system. The flaw in biology lies in the thinking which originated in classical physics: that all parts in the universe always interact with all other parts. Therefore, the function of a part is always given exclusively by the part itself. This premise is falsified when all parts don't always interact with each other, and the evidence of that falsification is atomic theory where the *agency* of interaction—called the 'field'—is *quantized* which means that the field does not spread uniformly everywhere, and the interactions do not occur between all the parts at once[8]. Only some parts enter a causal relation and quantum theory is unable to predict or explain why only those parts interact given its classical physical legacy in which all parts interact with each other.

The problem is akin to the fact that a workman's tool can be used in many ways, in relation to different objects. The tool could interact with several objects, but it doesn't always interact because bringing the tool into interaction with another object involves a choice, which can be empirically observed but it cannot be empirically explained because we cannot observe the choice as a material object. The materialist claims that since we cannot see the choice as an object, it must not exist. The problem with this view is that the function of a part changes in relation to different parts and by changing this relation we can produce new behaviors not previously seen in the part. While parts can be observed as an object, the part doesn't exist as an object prior to observation. Rather, the object is created by the combination of possibility, relation, and choice: the choice selects a relation, which then instantiates one of the many possibilities, and hence we observe an object.

A common example of organizational dysfunction is competitive politics between the divisions, where the individuals might be competent, but they have bad relationships. If we apply object-like thinking, then we would blame the people in each division (because we can see them) and not focus on defining their relationships and roles in such a way that they can cooperate rather than compete. Just being parts of a larger system doesn't mean that the parts are truly cooperating. The dysfunctional parts need not be faulted if the head was tasked to digest food, the stomach was required to move the body, and the hands were mandated to think. There is a proper role for each part, and this role can be enacted only through proper relationships to other parts. While we can know which role is suitable for which part, it is not always necessary that the part is indeed involved only in that role. Nor is it obvious that the part is dysfunctional because of the interrelations in the parts. Thus, the root causes of these problems are not sensually perceivable. But they can be perceived by the mind—if one has acquired the ability.

The Hierarchy of Roles

Relationships between parts are also hierarchical because the parts themselves are hierarchical. Every part has a role in relation to some parts, but this relationship can be subordinated to other relationships. For example, the personnel in a department are given their roles hierarchically—some individual is a leader and the others are subordinates under other subordinates. These roles have names such as salesperson, manager, director, vice-president, president, etc. A person in a department has relationships to their reporting hierarchy, and they might have relationships to personnel in other departments. For instance, finance and sales organizations in a company interact with each other even though they belong to different hierarchies.

All living entities perform some basic functions—eating, sleeping, mating, and defending—but the body parts used in these functions differ, and the functions might be executed differently. For example, some animals use claws for defense, others use teeth, while others use poisons. The differences in the functions are produced by the functional hierarchy, while the parts used for functions involve mapping the material parts to the material functions. They are two separate hierarchies, but they are also combined in the body.

When consciousness leaves the body, the body stops functioning, even though all the parts—e.g. head, legs, hands, stomach, etc.—exist. The reason is that consciousness is the *sat* of the soul, and it creates relations between the parts, from which the functionality of the parts is created. When the soul leaves, the functions are destroyed, although the parts themselves remain. Those who think that the functions are due to the parts should be able to explain how a living body becomes a dead body because at the point of death no chemicals might leave the body, although the chemical *reactions* change. Why is it that the chemicals remain but the reactions are altered? The reason is that the function is separate from the parts and the relation between the parts—which creates various functions—varies even in a lifetime. However, since we don't *perceive* the functions as *objects*, we cannot see how the function is added to the part but is not reducible to the parts.

Modern science studies these relations as *forces*, which are defined based on the physical properties—e.g. mass creates gravity, charge creates electromagnetism, etc., and, effectively, the forces are reduced to the object's properties. Under this reduction, we cannot explain how a part performs a different function. These functions in the Vedic system of medicine are called ingestion, digestion, circulation, assimilation, and elimination. We cannot sensually perceive these functions because they are not objects. However, we can perceive these as processes occurring over time. These functions are hierarchical which means that under the top-level functions there are similar lower-level functions. Thus, ingestion involves digestion (e.g. through food mastication while chewing), and digestion involves circulation (as the food moves from the stomach to the intestine), the circulation involves digestion (the digested food is modified during transport to other parts of the body), etc.

Forces in classical physics act *instantaneously* over large *distances*, which makes the action inconsistent with the finite speed of light, and Einstein formulated relativity to argue for a *local action* that 'travels' at a finite speed. When quantum theory was born, light was also quantized as a particle—photon—which was then said to travel at a finite speed. The problem with this formulation is that quantum theory describes the source and the detector to be in a state of possibility and the possibilities in the two objects must match for an energy transfer. For example, if the photon has energy X, then the source must have two states—A and B—such that the difference between A and B equals X. Similarly, the detector must also have two states—C and D—such that the difference between C and D equals X. Thus, the source and the detector must in a sense be 'entangled'—in order to determine that when A goes to B in the source C will go to D in the detector. The photon can be transferred only when the source and the detector are entangled in this way, which means that there is a non-local interaction between source and detector even before the causal transfer can occur. This non-local interaction violates the finite speed of light, and presents a contradiction between quantum theory and relativity, and remains an unsolved problem in physics today.

This problem can be addressed if the photon is not a moving particle. It is rather a change carried out remotely *after* the objects have entangled. To achieve this, we must separate the entanglement from the photon. The entanglement is the *relation* between source and detector, and the photon is a change *after* the relation is established. In other words, the photon is not moving, although the speed of light is a consequence of the fact that it takes a finite time to make a change. The time is, therefore, spent not in a particle traveling from source to detection followed by zero time in causing a change. Rather, zero time is spent in traveling and a finite time is spent in causing the change. The finite speed of light can be accounted for either as the time of travel or the time of change. In classical physics, the time was attributed to travel rather than change, and the same time can be attributed to change rather than travel. The latter approach solves the problem of non-locality.

Now we don't need the idea of a photon—i.e. a traveling particle. We only need the idea of a non-local relation which causes the source and the detector to become entangled, creating the *potential* for a transaction to occur. The transaction still cannot occur because quantum theory attributes it a *transition probability*—i.e. that it is likely to occur, but the time of occurrence cannot be predicted. To fix that time, we also require a *purpose*, which collapses the probability and causes the change. In other words, what modern science calls a 'photon' is actually the combination of two things—a relation and a purpose. It is called a 'photon' because the change is discrete, and attributed a travel due to classical physics. The changes can still be discrete, but there is no travel. Rather the change takes some time, which appears as travel time.

In the same way, we come in contact with objects in the world, but we have the choice to pay attention to these objects or ignore them. For example, if there is an attractive person in your vicinity then a relation is established by which you and the other person are entangled. This entanglement 'attracts' you to the other person, causing you to turn your head, but you have a choice to ignore that attraction. The attraction, therefore, exists as a possibility whose probability increases with the extent of entanglement. Beyond a point, that attraction might seem irresistible but there is always a choice.

The *sat* of the soul exists materially as relations to the world. The *chit* of the soul exists materially as particles—parts and wholes. These two correspond to the bosons[9] and fermions[10] of modern science. But the change doesn't happen without a choice. The *ananda* of the soul—the desire for pleasure—causes the soul to perform an observation or action in which the relation is used to make a change. The *sat*, *chit*, and *ananda* combine to create an experience. The *sat* is also sometimes called *sambandha*—or relationship. The *chit* is also sometimes called *abhidheya*—or exchange. And the *ananda* is also called *prayojana*—or purpose. These don't constitute a multitude of different ideas once we grasp the nature of causality and how it operates.

The key point is that a natural push and pull is created in nature due to relations, but that force is not mechanical. It is caused by bringing two objects (possibilities) into a relation by which the probability of producing a transaction increases. That increased probability appears as "force" by which we seem to be pulled or pushed towards an outcome, but that force is just a possibility not reality. It appears as natural attraction and repulsion in nature but is controlled by purpose. If the two objects are deeply entangled, then the probability of a transition becomes so high that the outcome seems inevitable. But the outcome depends on the prior entanglement—and it can be changed by altering the relation. In that sense, nothing can move without the will, but there are natural forces. This constitutes the resolution of the free will vs. determinism problem which arises in science if the forces are mechanical and effected through traveling particles. The problem doesn't arise if forces are relations that only increase transition probabilities to be collapsed by a purpose. Natural forces and free will are both causes of the change, and they have to be combined with object possibilities to create an effect.

The Hierarchy of Purposes

When the body parts are functioning, we must also question the purpose of this working. Why do we want to live rather than die? And why do some people begin to prefer death over life? The key purpose of life is enjoyment. We prefer life over death when there is abundant pleasure, and we prefer death over life when there is too much suffering. The pleasure of the soul is called *ananda* and it is embedded in matter as material purpose.

Every part of the body affords some type of pleasure, and the purpose of seeking pleasure pervades all parts of the body. The pleasures of the senses (eyes, skin, tongue, ears, and nose) are well-known. However, there is also pleasure in the senses of action. For example, some people enjoy running, others enjoy working with their hands, while yet others derive pleasure from talking, sex, or even defecation. The mind enjoys thought, the intellect enjoys analysis and judgment, the ego enjoys creating goals, and the moral sense enjoys the judgment, production, and consumption of moral values. Body parts like the stomach create pain and suffering when hungry, and satisfaction and pleasure when full. There is rejuvenation in the body through stable breathing and blood circulation, just as there is suffering via disease.

If the desire for pleasure was killed, then the body parts could function, but there would no incentive to live. To keep the body incentivized, there is purpose embedded in the body as pleasure and pain. Just as there is a mapping between body parts and their functions, similarly, there is a mapping between the bodily functions and their associated pleasures. The simple act of touching a person can mean paternal, fraternal, or conjugal pleasure. Similarly, you can look upon a beautiful person with admiration, wonderment, or lust. The cognition of beauty is therefore quite different from our *need* for that beauty and the reason why we seek it. Every part of the body is designed to seek pleasure and avoid pain. The desire for pleasure exists as lust in every part of the body and it makes automatic decisions. This is called the *autonomic functioning*[11] of the body whereby our eyes automatically close when something is very close to it, our hands are naturally folded or extended in a defensive posture to prevent an attack, the body as a whole bends and ducks to avoid pain. The nature of the lust in the body, however, can be quite varied due to which the eyes enjoy seeing particular kinds of forms and colors, the tongue relishes particular kinds of tastes, the ears prefer to hear certain kinds of sounds, the mind appreciates certain ideas, the intellect likes to divide the world into preferred types of situations, the ego relishes the pursuit of certain goals, and the moral sense enjoys certain types of moral values.

The world itself exists as a possibility, some of these possibilities are eliminated by the relation to other objects because the situation would not permit them, but one among the remaining possibilities is selected by the desire for pleasure. When the circumstances are already predetermined, the possibilities to choose from may be reduced to just one, which means that we are forced to suffer or enjoy according to the circumstances, and our desires for pleasure may remain unfulfilled or may be fulfilled without effort. Typically, however, there is always room to choose from the available options, and this choice is mediated by the type of pleasure we like to enjoy.

The quest for pleasure is also hierarchical such that the fulfillment of deeper desires reduces the need for sensual enjoyment, but if deeper desires are frustrated then a person is driven into the search for carnal pleasures. Thus, we find people who are satisfied by their moral values—such as harmony and family—are much less inclined toward the pursuit of gross sensual pursuits, but those who are frustrated in their long-term ambitions, those who are unable to control their situation, and those who are disturbed by unwanted ideas, are pushed toward greater sensual enjoyment. Similarly, a greater focus on sensual enjoyment hinders the fulfillment of the deeper moral values, longer-term ambitions such as career success, and mental peace by clear cognition and intellectual pursuits for development.

As we have seen in the third chapter, our desires stem from an innate sense of incompleteness and fear, and what remains unfulfilled magnifies this fear.

On one hand, we crave that fulfillment, and on the other hand we avoid its pursuit for fear of recurring disappointments. For example, those who have failed in love, idealistically crave for that love, and pessimistically avoid the opportunities to find that love. This is because desire and fear are simply two sides of the same coin. There is desire because there is fear, and there is fear because there is desire. Optimism is experienced when the desire dominates over fear, and pessimism is felt when the fear rules over desire. Most psychologists don't understand this problem and preach optimism over pessimism when the fact is that when a desire is fulfilled there is a natural reduction in both fear and desire, and so one cannot perpetually remain optimistic. As one desire is fulfilled, other desires and fears become prominent, and the next state one experiences may depend entirely on the prior experience with that desire; for example, in the new desire there may be greater fear.

It is important to understand the twin structure of desire to see how our choices are not always made because we want something; they are also made because we wish to avoid adverse circumstances, and that avoidance may not be a genuine dislike, but a fear that the desire may remain unfulfilled. This has been demonstrated by behavioral psychologists[12] in mouse experiments where the mouse is given cheese and then subjected to electrical shocks. Even though the mouse likes the cheese, he learns to avoid the electrical shock, such that he would not touch the cheese even when the shocks have receded. The desire for the cheese still exists, but the fear of the shock prevents the mouse from fulfilling the desire, even though it can be fulfilled.

The Failure of Reduction

Every part of the material body is simultaneously comprised of the three aspects—relation, cognition, and emotion. Take your brain, for example. It is comprised of different regions, which are parts of the brain. Due to this composition, we can say that my brain has a frontal lobe, a parietal lobe, an occipital lobe, etc. This constitutes the cognitive aspect of the brain. But the parts of the brain also perform a functional role due to which some parts become vision, others speech, olfactory perception, and motor control. Each such function of the various parts of the brain also creates a pleasure associated with a body part and function. I can say that I enjoy music—where the pleasure is tied to the ears and the surrounding which provides the music.

Each part of the body has some function, and each function has some purpose. In the body, the cognition, relation, and emotion are mixed in such a way that we could be forgiven for thinking that the parts are themselves the function, and the function is itself the pleasure. This is because the part is invisible (it exists as a possibility) unless combined with the relation and the purpose. Therefore, when you see the part, you see a combination of possibility, relation, and purpose, and you can therefore claim that the part I see is itself functioning and creating pleasure, so the part must be the function and purpose. And yet, they are separate because they are the causes rather than the effects. The cause can only be perceived in a first-person manner, but the effect can be perceived in a third-person manner (via the senses). The scientific theory of nature, therefore, needs to rely on what exists prior to sensation and produces it, rather than what we see after the sensation.

The *evidence* of their difference comes from *conflicts* between them. For example, if the brain part that performs motor control worked the same in all situations, then we would never spill water while pouring it into a glass. If my auditory cortex worked the same always, then I would never hear incorrectly. If my tongue always had the desire for tasting the same thing, then I would never require eating more than one delicacy. And if my ears always desired the same sound, then I would not need more than one song.

The difference between *sat*, *chit*, and *ananda* is evidenced by the fact that they often conflict, which means that the same part may be employed for a function for which the part is inadequate. And the feeling emerging from such an action may not be pleasurable. The molecular changes in the brain can be seen empirically. However, the *role* played by parts of the brain is also evolving over time, because of which there isn't a fixed brain part for seeing, hearing, tasting, or touching, although in most people the function is performed roughly in the same place. It is now well-known through neuroscience that it is impossible to isolate a function to a specific part, although we can still speak about some typical areas of perception in the brain[13]. This is a revelation because the classical view of the brain—called *localization*—held that each brain part was specialized for only one type of function[14].

We can say that a part is ideally suited to perform a specific function (in relation to other parts), and that function would then be ideally suited to achieve some designated purposes. But the body is not ideal, not because the parts have a problem (how can a molecule be problematic?) but because their relationship to other parts changes over time, which creates dysfunction, and we call it dysfunction because it doesn't meet our purpose. The terms 'health' and 'sickness' are only relative to our purpose because a chemical reaction is not healthy or sick. We expect the body to function in a certain way because that's how we fulfill our desires, enjoy life, and remain happy. The dysfunction is therefore relative to our purpose, but not reduced to the purpose because the purpose could be fulfilled through another function. Similarly, the usefulness of a part is relative to the function, but not reduced to the function because the function could be achieved through a different set of parts.

Modern biology is reductionist, in two ways: (1) it reduces the purposes to the functions, and the functions to the parts, and (2) it reduces hierarchy (in parts, functions, and purposes) to the smallest possible parts. The reduction is the legacy of classical physics and encompasses many flawed assumptions: (1) objects are real rather than possibilities, (2) all objects interact with every other object simultaneously, and (3) each object is working according to deterministic laws rather than a purpose. Biology lives under falsified dogmas because quantum problems are not well-known, and those who understand the problems dream of the day when classical definiteness would replace the quantum uncertainty. In other words, nobody is prepared to reject the classical physical thinking about matter, even with all the evidence.

A time will come when reductionism will look as ridiculous as flat earth theories. The main difference is that the flat worldview stemmed from not having observed other parts of the world, but the modern muddle stems from the inability to discard an ideology even after empirical falsification of that ideology. Ideological canons standing in the face of counterevidence are not treated kindly by history. Materialism is not the problem here, because even in the new view there is matter, although of three types. The problem is reduction—of the whole to the parts and of functions and purposes to the parts. The problem is also the rejection of the soul as a reality, which arises because we think that our experience is created outside-in rather than inside-out, and what lies outside the mind must be more fundamental than the mind.

Evolutionary Theory and Purpose

A direct outcome of classical thinking in biology is the Neo-Darwinian theory of evolution in which the body only has parts, which become functional through chemical interactions, and purpose—i.e. evolutionary direction—automatically emerges because organisms that don't adapt perish. Evolutionary biologists don't understand that chemical reactions don't start automatically, since the molecules themselves are possibilities: you cannot even say that a definite set of molecules exist, because the same atoms can be organized into different molecules, the same subatomic particles can exist in different states, and even after a definite set of molecules have been formed, the chemical reaction—involving energy and matter transfer—can occur among infinitely different molecules, at one among infinitely different points in time. Why a specific molecule exists, and why only some out of infinitely possible reactions occur, and why they occur at a specific time, are all indeterminate.

The occurrence of chemical reactions is itself an unsolved problem because the collapse of the quantum probabilities for a subatomic particle is problematic. To solve this, a specific state is created out of the possibility by putting a specific set of parts into a *relation*—which some anti-evolutionary biologists call "Intelligent Design"[15]. The flaw in the intelligent design argument is that it supposes that design emerges *after* the parts are already well-defined when the fact is that design is needed even to select a particular state out of the many possible states for a part. The Intelligent Design argument still operates under the ambit of classical physics and therefore appears very weak[16] because by the time the object is observed, the relation and purpose are already present in it. We cannot, therefore, use the observable objects to definitively argue for design. The argument should be that the relationships created by design select a possibility and the function emerges *after* the design because each part can have relations to other parts, which can potentially create different functions out of the same part. All these relations constitute competing alternatives and one out of all the possible relations must be chosen, which then chooses the functionality. In other words, Intelligent Design is a strong argument only in the context of quantum problems.

Once the function has been selected out of the possible functions, it must be *enacted*. The function is like the relation between a screw and a screwdriver, but the screwdriver doesn't act on the screw automatically. The time of action must be selected, even if the function is well-defined, and this time is unpredictable due to quantum probabilities. Thus, a part is uncertain because it is capable of many states. One of these states is selected due to a relation to a part. And once the state is selected, a transition must be chosen at a time. The system remains unpredictable due to these three uncertainties.

Competition is a fact of reality—as evolution recognizes—but competition involves choice: when two animals strive for the same food, there is competition, but when each animal has the option of more than one food there is choice. Which animal must eat what food, given that each animal could consume alternative foods? When should an animal eat that food, given that there are alternatives? The variety of foods humans eat should be an indicator of gastronomic choices and is one example of choosing among alternatives. There are similarly choices of mating, habitat, social interactions, etc. As an alternative is selected, a relation is chosen, and from that choice a part is created. From that part, a time of interaction with another part has to be selected. Therefore, we cannot reduce the purpose to function and the function to part, because the part doesn't exist without the functional relation, and the functional relation doesn't activate without a chosen purpose.

Evolutionary biology is a false idea that emerges if we think the world is comprised of fixed particles. When we look deeper, we find that each particle is not comprised of smaller parts, but of many possibilities of being in a definite state. In classical physics, big objects are ensembles of smaller *objects*. In atomic theory, the big objects are ensembles of many alternative *states*. The object is therefore uncertain because its state is uncertain, and to fix this state, we must establish a relation to another object whose state is also uncertain. Thus, we combine the uncertainty in two objects, and the surprise is that instead of increasing the uncertainty, the combination reduces the total uncertainty. This is a surprise in atomic theory because classically speaking when you add two uncertainties, the total uncertainty increases. How does the combination of systems *reduce* rather than *increase* uncertainty?

Consider a couple comprising a man and a woman. The man—let's suppose—likes to watch sports, drink beer at a bar, or dine out. The woman—let's assume—likes to shop for clothes, talk to a friend, and dine out. When a couple comes together, the man realizes that he cannot watch sports and drink beer at a bar, because the woman doesn't want it. The woman also realizes that she cannot go shopping with the man, or talk at length with him because he does not want it. To be together, they must settle for what is shared between them—i.e. dining out. Individually, both the man and the woman had three options. Together, they have just one option, because only one option is *coherent* with both. Thus, when a man and a woman come together, both reduce their options, but that loss converts an indefinite potentiality into a definite reality. Both the man and the woman, therefore, make sacrifices to be together. If they didn't, they could not be together due to incompatibility. This example illustrates the basic nature of quantum uncertainty, which reduces when two or more uncertain systems are combined.

In classical statistics[17] when two uncertainties are combined, the total uncertainty is increased because the two systems are *independent*. For example, if we toss two coins separately, the combination has four alternatives (head-head, tail-tail, head-tail, tail-head). The uncertainty of independent systems is *multiplied* and grows exponentially. Quantum statistics[18] employs a multiplication in which the probability of incompatible alternatives turning up simultaneously is zero. This causes an exponential reduction in uncertainty. A classical relation—between *independent* objects—increases uncertainty, but a quantum relation—between *related* objects—reduces uncertainty. Owing to this fact, the relationship *selects* an object state from possible states. A classical relation is like two independently tossed coins, while a quantum relation is like a man and a woman coming together to reduce alternatives.

In atomic theory, the reduction of alternatives is called *decoherence*[19] in which the uncertain states become certain by eliminating the *incoherent* states. However, the selected alternative depends on which objects are related, as each object is uncertain—with different alternative states—and the choice of object pairing decides which states will be eliminated.

When a man wants to drink beer or watch sports, he will choose a relation—e.g. with his male friends—rather than spending time with his woman. It is thus true that the relationship selects a state—e.g. dining out vs. watching sports—but the state (e.g. of watching sports) can select a relationship (of being with a male friend). Sometimes, the relation selects the state, and at other times the state selects the relation. The selecting agency is the *dominant* factor, and the alternatives are the *subordinate* entity. Either the state or the relation can dominate, but both must combine to create an experience.

It is therefore true that the environment selects something in the species. But it is also true that the species selects something in the environment. The selection is *mutual*—which means that two systems will find something *coherent* between them—if they are made to interact. However, the interaction is not fixed and, especially when an organism finds an incoherent situation, it will seek another environment and relation. The environmental selection is automatic, but the environment is not automatic. There is choice in the organism to opt for an environment and a part of the environment it connects to. The organism does not mutate randomly although it has many alternative states which can be *manifest* in a relationship to the environment.

Random mutation and natural selection are identical from the standpoint of quantum statistics because the contact between the organism and the environment decoheres the alternatives in each of them to find a compatible match which appears to be random only because it previously was an unobservable possibility. The mutation is not random but selected through a relation to the environment. However, the selection of the relation to the environment is a choice. Similarly, the environment might support many compatible alternatives and one of them must be chosen at a given time (e.g. the man and the woman could dine together at home or at a restaurant just to be together). The direction in evolution doesn't emerge because of state selection; it rather emerges from a *choice* of environment (from among the available alternatives) and the environment makes a choice of an organism (from among possible alternatives). Once a relation is chosen, the state is determined, and we observe a combination of possibility, relation, and purpose.

Evolutionary theory is false because it posits two incompatible types of statistics. Each organism mutates independently—like a coin toss—thus obeying *classical* statistics. Then, the environment selects an organism (i.e. reduce the mutated organisms) in a relationship—obeying *quantum* statistics. The problem in evolutionary theory is that the mutating entity obeys classical statistics and the selecting environment follows quantum statistics when they could only follow one of them. The practical problem is that even the organism must follow quantum statistics, which means no random mutation. When the burden of selection is on a relationship, a choice in the environment selection also emerges. This choice is the organism's purpose.

If both the organism and the environment follow classical statistics, then the total uncertainty in the system will increase exponentially with time and no definite species can emerge. If the organism follows classical statistics and the environment obeys quantum statistics, then there is a theoretical inconsistency in evolution. Evolution is possible only when both the organism and the environment are quantum theoretic systems, but that also entails design and purpose. The purpose creates a design—i.e. relations—and the relations select the states; this is the typical process by which we can explain the origin of species. Of course, in some cases, the state can select the relation, and the purpose is therefore subordinated. These correspond to the cases where the goal selects a reality vs. the case where reality selects a goal. We can say that sometimes our desires are the causes of reality, and sometimes they are caused by reality. In all cases, emotion exists—either as a cause or an effect—but it stands apart from the material objects and their mutual interrelations.

The Theory of Balance

If a man always goes out to drink beer with his male friends, his woman will probably go out with her friends to shop. Over time, the preference to be in a state—e.g. to drink or shop—will break the bond between the two. To retain the bond, one must *balance* the different states and relationships. This means that different relationships (and hence different states) are instantiated at different times. The choice that selects a relationship (and state) acts as the *balancer* in order to keep the potentiality for other states open *in the future*. This is the essence of the probabilities that all the states will occur over time because they are being "balanced" against each other, although the exact time of their occurrence is unpredictable. A higher or lower probability for a relation or state just entails that the balance is tilted towards a particular relation or state, in order to fulfill different purposes. Therefore, a different probability distribution can be attributed to a different purpose.

Probability means that if a man has dined out with the woman a few times, he is now more likely to go for a drink at a bar with his male friends—if he still wants to retain his relationship with them. The exact dates and times of dining and drinking can vary, but on average all relationships can be balanced. Probability is not an indicator of an uncertainty in the system. It is rather an indicator that a person tries to *balance* many relationships.

That balancing is the outcome of a *purpose*—i.e. what one *wants*. If they did not value a state, they could remove some relations, eliminate some possibilities, and change the probability distribution. There is hence a subtle but important difference between *possibility* and *probability*. The relations change the probabilities, but not the possibilities. Thus, if a relation with a shopping partner is terminated, the *possibility* of shopping is unchanged, but the probability is reduced. The possibility has a low probability and it becomes unconscious. It can spring into the conscious when a new relation is established. Thus, interaction with the world creates new thoughts in us and empiricists are therefore fond of thinking that all ideas come to us from the outside world because they were invoked in our minds by their presence. The fact is that all these ideas were *possible* inside us but had a low *probability* because the probability is defined by a system's interaction with other systems. As a new interaction is created, the probability increases, the will desires it, and the combination of the possibility, relation, and will manifests it.

What we call 'balance' is giving equal priorities to alternatives. Conversely, imbalance is giving a high priority to some states and relations, while neglecting others. Under an imbalance, many functions in a part stop working, as the relations that instantiate that function have been deprioritized. In human life, it can lead to stunted behaviors. In biology, it leads to a diseased body. A healthy body is characterized by a good balance between all the possible states of each part, which keeps the part fully functional in all respects. Under an imbalance, some functions in the body stop working because the relations to other parts—which instantiated those functions—have been broken. Keeping the body in balance requires one to establish a routine such that all body parts go through all their states at an appointed time. A good routine is one that keeps an almost equal focus on all states and relationships, in order to keep all possibilities likely (probable) to happen in the future. This routine is produced by our purpose, and following the routine creates emotional stability because when all the parts are functional, there is equal amount of focus on each of the activities, relationships, and states.

When the routine is broken, or the routine is stunted towards fewer states, an emotional imbalance naturally follows, some parts of the body stop working, some relationships are naturally broken, and life goes through turmoil. The preliminary stages of a healthy life in *yoga* therefore are called *yama* and *niyama*. *Yama* means terminating some unwanted states and relationships. *Niyama* means doing the remaining desirable activities in a routine. Anyone who wants to lead an emotionally stable life must therefore establish a routine. We can empirically test this thesis by doing it ourselves. The above explanation provides the theoretical background for understanding it.

The idea of a routine seems "boring". We like to think that to be happy, we need novelty, innovation, and thrill, which means establishing new relationships, breaking old ones, and continuously iterating this change to seek novelties, innovations, and thrills. This idea further stems from the notion that time moves "forward" so there must be continuous progress in life; in fact, being bound to a routine would seem like spinning one's wheels while remaining at the same place. There are two problems in this criticism of routine which I will discuss in the following paragraphs one by one.

The first problem is the probability of states in a closed system. If time moves forward linearly then each state has a minuscule probability of recurring because the state is never repeated, and all states have the same probability because they are visited once. Finite probabilities—indicating event recurrence—on the other hand, entail that the same states and relationships are instantiated again. The probabilities might be less or more, which would mean that we spend less or more time on different states, but the fact that the state has a finite probability means that it must be repeated, cyclically. The real rationale for this outcome is that the system is closed and in any isolated system, the possible states of the system are bounded. Continuous movement in such a system entails that the same states must be repeated cyclically.

The second problem is that systems are not always closed, and forward movement occurs when the system evolves from one state to another, which changes the possible states, and the routine. The system jumps from one routine to another, creating a forward movement, although that movement is not *linear*. If we combined the cyclic and the forward movements, we will arrive at a *spiral* in which stability is created by the routine, and change is produced by a shift in the routine. If the system was linear, there would be no stability. And if there were only stability, there would be no progress. The spiral movement produces both stability and progress, which remains consistent with the idea that a system exists in a state of possibility of being many states, and the idea that a system progresses from one stability to another.

The idea of 'balance' involves cyclic change, but it is disturbed by forward movement until the system settles into a new cycle. There are hence—ideally—short periods of instability (as a system settles into a new cycle) followed by longer periods of routine. Typically, if a system is unable to settle into a new periodicity after a change, the system appears to be chaotic[20] because the previous possibilities are no longer attainable, and the new possibilities haven't yet been sequenced in a periodic order. To an extent, the order of states in a system depends on the order of states in other systems; for example, most people tend to work during the day and sleep during the night, so if you had to interact with those people you would do it during the day. However, recall that state instantiation is a *mutual* problem, and others cannot do their work if you are not available for an interaction. Each person thus has some control over finding a mutually agreeable periodic order, although no one is completely free to define their cycle. A chaotic state is the outcome of the fact that a system is yet to find alignment with other systems.

An isolated quantum system will be chaotic. However, as this system is related to orderly systems, it acquires order as the systems align with each other (to be related) and that entails mutually compatible periodicities. This is the basis on which quantum theorists consider decoherence as the mechanism by which the classical stable world emerges from quantum uncertainty. Of course, the problem is that decoherence doesn't define *which* two systems have to decohere together, given that there are infinite possible relations.

A person in society loses a disorderly life due to relations to others because the others enforce an order. Conversely, if a person is always disorderly, he or she would make the lives of others (who relate to him or her) disorderedly or would become incompatible with the orderly lives of others and break the relationship between them. An ordered system thus brings order to other systems, and a disordered system spreads this disorder to other systems or becomes independent of the other systems. The outcome of an interaction between ordered and disordered systems entirely depends on the relative the 'strength' of the order or disorder and that of the relation between them. If the order and the relation are strong, a disorderly system will be put into order. If the disorder and relation are strong then an orderly system will be made disordered. If order and disorder are strong but the relation is weak, the relation would be broken to create independent systems. The succession of states is time, and time is produced by purpose. Therefore the 'strength' of order or disorder is the relative dominance of purpose in a person. A person with a strong sense of purpose and order will bring order into other's lives, and a person without a purpose can make other's lives disorderly.

Without a purpose, there are only probabilities, and the world appears to be random although within limits. With a purpose, the probability becomes a periodicity, and with periodicity the behavior becomes predictable; the chaos is over. Quantum probabilities are indicators of the fact that the system doesn't have a purpose, due to which the states are not periodic, and hence unpredictable. A purpose can thus be given a very precise definition: it is that which settles a system into a new periodicity. Note that given a set of possible states, the *sequence* of states has many alternatives, all consistent with the probabilities. A purpose is the *choice* of a periodicity in order to bring stability. Of course, purpose may not necessarily entail a periodicity if a person jumps from one state to another randomly—by choice—but such a system remains unstable, and without a good balance becomes emotionally disturbed and the outcome of that disturbance is even more randomness. Even though choice may be involved even in random decisions (because the person is confused due to emotional disturbance) this disturbed state cannot be called purposeful. Purpose entails balance and stability, and that in turn entails a periodic iteration through the possibilities—i.e. a routine.

A periodic system works like a clock. We see purpose in a clock because it is periodic. If the clock worked randomly, we would not consider it a designed system. Thus, mechanism is not contrary to purpose because all periodic systems have rejected chaos and settled into an order, and that order is itself caused by purpose. But there is another sense in which we speak of purpose—namely moving forward from one cycle to another—quite like linear motion. To determine the next state of the cycle, again we must choose from among many possible cycles (defined in relation to other systems). That choice can only be made by another purpose as opposed to randomness. A system that randomly jumps from one cycle to another is also chaotic although in a different sense than a system that just never settles into a cycle[21].

We can therefore distinguish between the linear and cyclic forms of purpose: the cyclic form creates stability and the linear form creates progress. But this appearance of linearity is generally an illusion, created by looking at a very small segment of a cycle, where the circle appears to be a straight line. The fact is that our purposes also change over time in a cyclic manner. This means that the linear form is also cyclic, which would mean that there is a cycle embedded inside another cycle: the system cyclically jumps from one periodicity to another. In fact, now we can envision a hierarchy of cycles, produced from a hierarchy of purposes, with each purpose only aiming for stability rather than progress. The universe as a whole can be described as the repetition of cycles inside cycles. Such a universe is not progressive as it never comes to an end; in fact, the purpose of stability produces an eternally repeating universe. A progressive universe would be one that ends and never begins again. Human life can be progressive in this sense because it can jump from one cycle to another, and never return to the previous cycles.

The key point is that there is a new way to describe stability and progress—as purposes—which create cyclic vs. progressive times. Time can be called progressive only if moves across states in order to end the cycle of repetitions. Accordingly, our life is progressive only if we are ending the cycle of birth and death. Our life is cyclic if that repetition is continued. Thus, only some people are living in progressive time—those who end the cycle. Most people are living in cyclic time. The demand for stability entails that there must be routine. But the demand for progress means that the higher-level purpose must be progressive rather than stable. The higher-level purpose creates a slower evolution and routines can therefore be slowly evolved: there would be much higher periodicity at the lowest level, somewhat lesser periodicity at the intermediate level, and only progress at the highest level. In simple terms, it would mean that the body follows a periodic routine, the mind gradually evolves from one idea-set to another, and the soul continuously progresses—overcoming its coverings of fears and desires. Hence, there can be slow spiritual progress, overlaid on a more-or-less repetitive bodily life, with an intermediate level of mental evolution in the middle.

The body cannot handle rapid progress; it must be stable and periodic. Similarly, the soul cannot remain stagnant in a routine; it must progress. For the body and soul to remain together there must be bodily periodicity and spiritual progress. This is the path of *yoga*—routine at the bodily level, and progress at the level of the soul, with a moderate rate of mental and intellectual development. Ultimately, the body and the mind can change their routine only as fast as the soul evolves. If the soul is evolving fast—discarding its fear and desire—then the mental development and the bodily changes can be rapid too. Thus, an advanced soul doesn't need to follow a routine, but a practicing soul must be disciplined. A body and a mind that change too fast—without a concomitant spiritual advancement—will be disconnected and either the body will perish, or the mind will be afflicted by madness. Therefore, a balance is only meant to maintain the body-mind and the soul together.

The Process of Life and Death

The body is created as a combination of *guna* and *karma*; we also call these two nature and nurture. At the time of birth, the soul's conceptual abilities—physical, sensual, mental, intellectual, individuality, and morality—are underdeveloped; most people acquire these ideas through the combination of nature and nurture. However, in rare cases, the conceptual abilities may be well developed too; thus, some children are more capable than others at birth. They are also naturally inclined—due to *guna* or nature—toward certain types of pleasures. However, their *memory* of the past is generally gone due to which they cannot explain why they like certain things, why some are more capable than others, and why some are luckier than others.

The memory is always cognitive: it exists in us as a part of the intellect which comprises the beliefs that we consider *true*. By default, if you remember something, you believe it happened and therefore it is true. At the point of death, the intellect is generally wiped clean, and hence our beliefs of true and false are gone. However, the ego (our sense of good and bad) and morality (the sense of right and wrong) are always persistent. In that sense, the soul's material body is not fully destroyed even at the point of death because at least two bodily instruments—the ego and the moral sense—persist beyond death. The moral sense is the cause of *karma* (the judgment of right and wrong) and the ego represents our desires and purposes—the *guna*. Both *guna* and *karma* survive death, and the ego and morality are thus reborn.

However, since our sense of true and false is reset at death, we cannot explain why some things are right and wrong, good or bad. We intuitively do those things due to the moral sense and the ego, until we are educated about the nature of truth. Since a subset of truths is good, and a subset of good is right, by teaching the appropriate truths, we can also change a person's ego and morality. This education can be carried out through the intellect, but it also informs the ego and the moral sense. Effectively, the mind is not *tabula rasa* or a blank slate at birth as far as our moral sense and ego are concerned. But it is generally a blank slate as far as knowledge and truth are concerned. The knowledge is created by the combination of all the opportunities created by *karma* and the selection of these opportunities by the *guna*. Thus, some people will become well-informed while others will remain ignorant.

In some cases, parts of the intellect, mind, and senses, may not be wiped. These people thus have strong beliefs right at birth, and sometimes even remember past life events. Thus, some children naturally have the ability for art and music, others have native leadership capacity, while some are very creative and imaginative storytellers: we call such people *talented* and sometimes when extraordinary talent is displayed—*savants*. Others may not be born talented but they can acquire their talent through the combination of effort and opportunities, and be as good as others who were born talented. Some successful musicians—e.g. Pink Floyd—have openly admitted that when they started, they could not play anything, but they *wanted* to be musicians and got the *opportunities*. Malcolm Gladwell[22], in his book *Outliers*[23], even tries to quantify the effort required to be world-class to 10,000 hours of dedicated effort. The exact quantum of time is not important, because it also hinges on how strongly you desire and pay attention to the activity, besides the quality of the opportunity itself. The key point is that if you are not born talented, you can acquire talent. That acquisition may not entail *success*—because success requires a combination of other people liking your work, and you having encounters with those people. But you can still become talented. The key point is that the talent once acquired can remain persistent across lives.

When the memory of previous knowledge is wiped, the effort in acquiring that knowledge is wasted, and one must start all over again. The nature of material energy is that our effort is constantly being wasted, because the concepts acquired through that effort are lost. In modern science, we call this the *Second Law of Thermodynamics*[24] by which order is destroyed and replaced by disorder. However, science today doesn't understand how order is recreated by the combination of *guna* and *karma*, essentially because science doesn't study purpose and choice, and it doesn't understand why an object only interacts with specific objects, both of which contribute to the production of new order. As a result, many people postulate that if order is being destroyed, then overall the universe must head towards disorder—the "Heat Death" scenario[25] in which all matter and energy are uniformly dispersed.

Death signifies the destruction of order, but this order is not merely the body, but also deeper conceptual abilities in the senses, the mind, and the intellect, due to which we forget the past life and start all over again. However, in rare cases, this order may not be destroyed, and while the body is changed, the senses, mind, and intellect, may retain some of their former capabilities into the new life. Clearly, new order is created by *guna* and *karma* combining, so the question then is: Why is the order created, why is it preserved for some duration, and what causes the destruction of the order?

All order exists as a tree, which has higher and lower nodes. Specifically, order is the existence of higher nodes, which organize the lower nodes in the tree. We have seen that the higher nodes are longer lived, and they are abstract—i.e. they cover more possibilities and hence a greater amount of conceptual space. The destruction of order is the cessation of the higher node; the order exists only so long as the higher node organizes the lower node. In that sense, order exists because each node has an associated *lifetime*.

The lifetime of an idea is conditional upon its *truth*. The truer ideas are longer lived, while the false ideas are shorter lived. Perfectly true ideas are eternal. To the extent that we know the truth, it will persist across lives, and to the extent that our ideas pertain to the falsities, they will also be temporary. The reason we forget most of the previous encounters after death is that most of the ideas acquired in the previous lives were false. On the other hand, those who acquire true knowledge in this life will also remember it innately in subsequent lives. Of course, sometimes, even false knowledge may persist across lives because it was acquired late in life, and the time of its existence hasn't yet expired. Typically, this happens for those who die due to catastrophes, accidents, or homicide, and studies on reincarnation[26] have noted that about 2/3rd of the cases of past life memories are seen in such cases.

But we also know that the pursuit of truth continues across lifetimes, and whatever truth is acquired in a life is not forgotten in future lives. In this regard, there is a famous story about king Bharata who renounces his kingdom to pursue spiritual realization but becomes attached to a deer in the forest. When the deer dies, the king also dies out of sadness, and in the next life he is born as a deer. But he remembers the realizations from earlier lives. The key point is that false knowledge is forgotten because it has a lifespan determined by the life of a person, but true knowledge crosses lifetimes, and the perfect truth once acquired is never forgotten, even in subsequent lives.

The Role of the Life Force

The tree of knowledge is created by a connection between nodes of the tree, and when the connection is destroyed, the concept is lost, and the lower nodes of the tree disintegrate because their organizing principle is lost. Matter itself is not destroyed, although the *organization* is changed. This change underlies numerous forms of decay described by the *Second Law of Thermodynamics*, including, but not limited to the disintegration of molecules. The nodes of the tree are held together by *prāna* (sometimes called the "life force") but if the *prāna* leaves, the higher nodes are disconnected from the lower nodes. Thus, death is sometimes described as *prāna* leaving the body, which is a way of saying that the higher nodes (the senses, mind, intellect, ego, and the moral sense) have detached from the lower nodes (the body).

Prāna is the agency that connects the nodes within each of the three trees—relations, emotions, and concepts—and the agency that connects the nodes of one tree to those of the other two trees. In that sense, *prāna* is described as the most important agency in the body because it is responsible for creating the body (by connecting the higher and lower nodes), maintaining the body (by keeping the connection intact), and then destroying it (by disconnecting the nodes). Once disconnected, the nodes are also connected to other nodes, thus creating a new body. The system of *aśtanga-yoga* is based on the control of *prāna*. This control has three parts—*pūraka* or breathing in which leads to creation, *kumbhaka* or holding the breath which results in the sustaining of the body, and *rechaka* which is exhalation that excretes the toxins. The *pūraka* function is important to absorb the creative power, and the *rechaka* is important to excrete the waste out of the body. But ultimately, to make the body long-lived, to recognize the nature of the truth, and to remain aware of this acquired truth at all times, one needs *kumbhaka*, which is the power that produces steadiness, and is obtained by holding the breath. The breath can also be held inside or outside the body, which are ways of learning about what the truth is (inside) and what the falsities are (outside).

The advanced *yogi* can hold the breath for hours, and in the *aśtanga-yoga* system, the *yogi* progresses from the *pranayama* stage (the fourth stage of the practice) to the *pratyāhāra* stage (the fifth stage) when he is able to hold the breath for three hours[27]. In the *pratyāhāra* stage one's consciousness is fixed, and one starts concentrating on the nature of the truth; this is the beginning of the so-called 'meditation', which is a very advanced state only followed by very long breath control. If we cannot hold that breath, then even if we acquire some truth, it is easily forgotten and meditation becomes another temporary activity (we can meditate for some time, but we cannot 'enter' the meditative state permanently). Attaining that state is not easy, and the *yoga* exercises are meant to facilitate the breath control, and even the exercises are properly performed only when one regulates the life through *yama* (things that one should not do) and *niyama* (things that one should do regularly). At present, of course, all these steps of *yoga* have been neglected and as a result one cannot hold the breath, which means they cannot meditate, which also means that they cannot fulfill the ultimate aim—truth and eternity. If one cannot obtain the truth, the lifespan cannot be extended, and whatever one acquires within this life is also temporary and transitory.

Breath control is the route to emotional stability. When the breath is rapid, the mind is unstable—thoughts pass fleetingly. If the breath is held, then the mind quietens and concentrates. As the mind is fixed on a purpose, one can apply their energy to the attainment of that purpose—which should ideally be the truth—because, ultimately, only the truth is stable and eternal. If one pursues the false, the results are temporary, which produces a disturbed mind, and the person moves from one purpose to another, creating instability. Therefore, *yoga* is successful only when dovetailed to the pursuit of truth, although many people use it at present to obtain falsities. In their practice, they can certainly obtain more peace of mind to concentrate on a chosen purpose, but ultimately the results of such attainment will be temporary, which means that they would not be able to prolong their focus.

The Classification of Species

In the early days of modern biology, species were classified based on their physical traits—the *phenotype*[28]. Jean-Baptiste Lamarck[29] postulated that the physical traits acquired during the life of a member of the species is passed to its offspring—kind of like saying that a bodybuilder's son would have a muscular body. Gregor Mendel[30] proved this wrong based on experiments on peas, showing that many acquired phenotypes were never inherited. Mendel also suggested that some genetic material was involved in inheritance, and that this material existed in *pairs*—taken from the mating parents. This gave rise to the distinction between the *genotype* and the *phenotype*, and to the problem of how to explain the phenotype from the genotype.

The problem has proved difficult because minor genotypic differences can lead to major phenotypic variations—e.g. humans and chimpanzees have 99% similar genes but many phenotypic variations. While the attempts to bridge the genotype-phenotype gaps were being pursued in biology, biologists also found out that most of the genetic material is never *expressed* and lies dormant. For example, just because you have the genes for a particular type of cancer doesn't mean that you will get it. The genes only indicate a higher possibility of a phenotype, but that possibility has to be selected by some *epigenetic*[31] factors, which can be influenced by a person's mental state (e.g. emotions) or environmental conditions.

Biology has now come full circle beginning with Lamarck in whose theory the environment significantly influenced biological traits, which were then inherited, to Mendelian genetics where the environment may play a role in acquiring new phenotypes but the acquired traits would not be transmitted because inheritance was caused only by the genes, to the modern view on inheritance where the environment plays a role in changing the epigenetic controllers of gene expression and these controllers once changed can be transmitted to offspring, thereby changing the gene expression.

The DNA indicates not a fixed set of traits, but possibilities which remain dormant unless selected by a combination of environmental and emotional factors. Of these two, biologists have a better understanding of the environment—in so far as it can be modeled as a set of chemical compounds—but the influence of mental and emotional states on epigenetics presents a much harder problem given that the chemical basis of emotions is itself not very well explained. Of no less importance is the impact this has on genetic determinism, the belief that genes control your life. Because if emotions control epigenetics, which then change gene expression then you can control your gene expression by changing your thoughts, emotions, and the environment. Cancers are known to go into remission by changes to the mental state[32]. The ability to control the genetic mechanisms via thoughts and feelings points to the fact that the mind is a causal agent in its own right—not reduced and not produced by the DNA alone, although the DNA does indicate higher and lower probabilities of certain types of phenotypic traits occurring.

The dilemmas in the understanding of inheritance—and genetic expression into physical traits—can be demystified by the tripartite model of reality I have described. The genes in this model are the atomic reality, which exists as a *possibility*. One among the many possible states is selected by an encounter with the environment. But the encounters with the environment can be selected by emotions. The genetic expression is a combination of the possible states, the relations to the environment that select one among the many possible states, and the choice of the relation through a purpose. The DNA is not itself the reality. Rather, a reality is produced from the combination of possibility, relation, and purpose. If we could change our purpose, then we could alter the relation, which will then express alternative possibilities. The problem of genetic expression is therefore no different than the problem of quantum indeterminism—as seen from the above tripartite model of reality.

The expression of life therefore also must be based on three factors: (1) the native abilities of a species, (2) which abilities are expressed or repressed by the encounter with specific factors within the environment, and (3) how one's emotions select specific parts of the available environment.

In Vedic philosophy, the encounters with the world is called *karma*, and it lies dormant. The desires of selecting among the possible relations are called *guna* and they too lie dormant. Under the influence of time, both *guna* and *karma* are manifest, which means that the soul experiences the desire for encounters, and the soul finds the possibilities of encounters. When the possibility of an encounter is combined with the desire of that encounter an experience is created—e.g. that of eating food—which then builds the body. We can say that the *guna* are one's *nature* and the encounter with the world produced by *karma* is one's *nurture*. The body is produced by the combination of nature and nurture. Changes to the body are modeled by the same process as that of the body's creation. When the soul enters the womb of a mother, he brings his *guna* and *karma*. The *karma* is the cause of the soul being placed in a certain mother's womb, and the *guna* selects and rejects from the alternatives that are possible in the mother's womb. The situation doesn't change after the soul is born—the alternatives and their selection continue.

Hence, the species are classified by *guna* and *karma*, although this is neither genotype nor phenotype. The phenotype is produced from the combination of *guna*, *karma*, and time, as much as the genotype. In other words, both the body and the genes are *phenomena*, but these are produced from something unobservable. Our desires can't be observed until after they are manifest and when they manifest you only see a phenomenon, not the desire for it. Similarly, we cannot observe that many encounters were possible before an interaction. What we observe is the specific encounter that was selected. Once an encounter is selected by a desire, some material energy is transferred. The energy is eternal—i.e. neither created nor destroyed—but its association with a soul (e.g. making up their bodies) is temporary.

Since the soul can have many types of bodies, which body the soul acquires is due to their *guna* and *karma*, and the key ingredients employed for classifying the species are also *guna* and *karma*. In one sense, we are not classifying the bodies; we are classifying the souls by their *guna* and *karma* which *cause* the soul to acquire a body. The body is the visible phenomena, and modern biology studies these phenomena, but not their cause. We can thus distinguish between the phenomenal and the noumenal methods of classification—the former classifies the types of bodies, and the latter the types of souls. The soul is not type-casted eternally by *guna* and *karma* because these keep changing, leading to the succession of bodies. The classification is temporary and at the time of birth. Even if the soul changes its *guna* and *karma* during its life, it continues to live in the opportunities afforded by the *karma* although it might now make different choices due to changing *guna*.

Emotions play an important role in the classification of souls because these create the desires by which the soul selects an alternative from the environment which then builds the body. If a different set of alternatives were picked, the body would also turn out to be different. And even when the body has been built, matter exists in an indeterministic state, and that state can be chosen by the environment which can be selected by the emotional state.

To a large extent, the body is determined by the womb of the mother in which the soul is placed, and that placement is caused by *guna*. For example, if a soul desires to eat flesh, it would be placed in the womb of a carnivore mother, which determines their species. However, there are many possible mothers within that species and the selection of the particular mother in the species—which results in their inherited traits in the species—is caused by *karma*. Thus, *guna* is the broad classification of living entities into species and *karma* is the detailed classification within a particular species. Some mothers will nurture the soul into a strong and healthy body while others will pass them diseases. Whether the mother nurtures the body or passes diseases to it is based on *karma*. Thus, we can say that we choose the species of our birth, but we cannot choose the specific parents we are born to. Our choice of parental species is *guna* and the choice of specific parents is *karma*. The soul still has the option to enjoy its life according to the species, which naturally affords it certain kinds of pleasures, but the options are limited by *karma*.

Thus, the broad classification of DNA based on species is due to *chit* by which we can distinguish between a tiger and a deer. This is called genetics in modern science. However, the genes of a species are not always expressed. Rather, some genes are suppressed while others are enhanced. This is called *epigenetics* in modern science. The epigenetic expression is due to the environment and emotional states. Therefore, the genes are merely existing as a possibility of expression. They are like the *abilities* in a person. Furthermore, these abilities are enhanced or suppressed by our emotional state, and the opportunities, which we call nature and nurture in ordinary language, and are called *guna* and *karma* in Vedic philosophy. The *guna* and *karma* convert the possibilities encoded in the DNA into a reality. The manifest cause of the inherited traits is the parental genes, but why a soul enters the womb of a certain type of mother is due to *guna* and *karma* because the soul could have potentially been placed in other wombs where it would have inherited a different set of possibilities from their parents. The key explanation for the inherited traits is not parental traits but the causes that make the parent selection. Unless we see how the soul is placed in a mother's womb, we will keep thinking that inheritance is caused by the parental genes when the real cause is the selection of an appropriate parent according to *guna* and *karma*.

The broad biological classification of species—e.g. dogs, cats, giraffes, elephants, tigers, humans, etc.—is based on the material ingredients originating from *chit*. However, the reason that the soul enters a specific type of species is due to *guna* and *karma*. The *guna* are the kinds of pleasures we want to enjoy, and *karma* is the environment in which these species are placed—which may be suited or unsuited for the given situation. If the traits are suited, the living entity enjoys life, but if they are unsuited then the living entity suffers. There is no such thing as selection by the environment based on "fit" between the environment and the species because if all living entities were going toward greater "fit" then they should be naturally enjoying their lives more, and the world as a whole would be moving toward greater happiness. Whether an organism is fit or unfit in the environment is given by *karma*—some organisms will be more fit, and those souls which deserve a better life will be born to these parents. Conversely, some organisms will be less fit and those souls which are destined to suffer their *karma* will be born to such parents. The fit, therefore, don't necessarily survive longer and the unfit don't necessarily perish because one can keep surviving and keep suffering.

Of course, it is possible that if the soul suffers too much in a species it will develop a distaste for it and desire another form of life that seems better suited for the type of pleasure they wish to enjoy. As humans, for example, we sometimes look at the sky and see birds flying and if our life seems too unhappy, we might think that it would so much better to be like a bird—no professional responsibilities! Suffering makes us desire a different life form and the souls are hurtling from one form to another—getting frustrated with one form after another and returning to the same form because the previous form seems comparatively better. Due to this transmigration, some species may disappear in some places and appear in others, and the change of environment is due to *karma* but the choice of the species itself is due to *guna*.

It is difficult to pinpoint the cause of a lifeform to *guna* or *karma* because what was forced circumstance for one soul might be the preferred alternative for another. As an example, some people hate their life of riches and aspire for a life of carefree abandon even if relatively poor, while some poor people may love to trade their life of carefree abandon with riches even if it comes with a lot of responsibility. You cannot be sure if the person leading a life of simple abandon has chosen this life because they love it or were forced into it by situations out of their control. In the same way, the preferred choice for one person may be the forced alternative for another, and the same effect may therefore be produced either by *guna* or by *karma*. There is no point, hence, in *correlating* a particular trait to either a particular type of *guna* or *karma* because these correlations will eventually turn out to be random.

The methods of genotype and phenotype correlation are not false, because there is indeed material inheritance from the parents which determines the species. However, this causation cannot work without *guna* and *karma* because the same outcome may be determined by many combinations of the two. Thus, some souls enjoy a situation and others crave to get out of it. Those who enjoy the situation have the *guna* that desires it, and the fact that the situation is available to them is due to their good *karma*. Conversely, those who crave to exit the situation have the *guna* that hates the situation, but they are put into the situation due to their bad *karma*. The real cause of the situation can therefore be explained only in the first-person way— depending on whether you enjoy or suffer it—and if we know whether we are enjoying or suffering then we can know whether the situation is caused by bad or good *karma*. In this way, the causal explanation can be obtained by knowing the first-person situation but not by the third-person situation.

5

The Emotional Basis of Society

Six Kinds of Emotions

The Vedic texts describe six kinds of emotions called *kāma* (lust or desire), *krodha* (anger), *mada* (pride or egotism), *lobha* (greed), *matsar* (envy or competition), and *moha* (confusion or lack of clarity). The first five of the six help us make decisions, but the sixth (confusion) prevents decision-making. The world is perceived cognitively as a possibility and emotions select one of the possibilities. Under lust, anger, pride, greed, and envy, we can make the decisions, but confusion is that emotional state in which we see the possibilities, but we cannot decide which one to choose. Confusion is the gateway to depression, and it arises because we are unsure of what we want, or the things that we are sure of are unavailable under the circumstances at present. When we are unsure, we don't decide, we don't create the reality out of the possibilities, we don't enjoy the act of creating that reality, the sense of happiness goes out of life, which makes us even more uncertain.

All the six emotions above can be caused by fear. As we have discussed previously, the soul is constrained by material nature and that constraint creates a fear, which then leads to desire and other emotions. Thus, even when we desire things, we fear not fulfilling the desire; the desire excites us, and the fear makes us anxious; every desire has both anticipation of fulfillment and anxiety of frustration. Therefore, desire by itself is not happiness because it is accompanied by fear. Under anger, we have the fear of losing what we had or could attain, and anger arises when the chances of loss surpass the hope of attainment. Under pride, that fear is superficially suppressed, but every pride is easily insulted because the fear of not being recognized for achievement is latent. Greed manifests because one is fearful—you are not satisfied by owning something as you fear losing it eventually, and thus you want to accumulate more of it in order to mitigate the fear. Finally, confusion is not just an intellectual indecision about which alternative to choose; it is produced from the fear that if you make a choice, you would preempt other alternatives and the fear of losing the alternative makes us indecisive because the choices appear to be mutually exclusive.

Happiness is the freedom from the six emotions emerging out of fear; hope entails freedom from fear. The same six emotions can also be caused by hope. For instance, desire becomes the pursuit of happiness accompanied by the hope of success and without the fear of loss. There can be anger at not achieving the desired results, but because there is no inherent fear of failure, the anger propels a person toward a greater effort, rather than being directed against causes of that hurdle. There is pride arising from the satisfaction that one has achieved their goals through effort, but the pride is not easily hurt because there is an innate optimism about one's ability and ridicule doesn't hurt the pride but drives one even stronger toward their goal. Greed is produced to increase pleasure, not because one is fearful of losing what was previously accumulated (and accumulates more in order to avoid a collapse). There can be envy of others purely in the sense of competitiveness, which propels one forward to greater achievement, rather than working to bring others down, because there is innate belief in one's own capacity. There can be confusion as to which choice is better—or which choice maximizes the happiness—not which choice minimizes the pain.

Our emotional life is markedly distinguished by the ideologies of hope vs. fear. Desire, anger, pride, greed, envy, or confusion, are not themselves evil emotions. They can be, instead, great propellers for forward movement in life if there is *hope*. The greatest people whose stories we narrate again and again also had desires, anger, pride, competitiveness, greed, and confusion, but without fear. Their emotions drove them toward greater achievements because they fundamentally replaced their fear of failure with the hope of success. This hope is a very deep notion about the world we hold—i.e. whether the world is ultimately righteous, good, and truthful. We can call this the belief in the ultimate goodness of life vs. the ultimate meaninglessness of existence. If you have hope, then all the emotions—desire, anger, pride, greed, envy, and confusion—will propel you forward and fulfill the faith in hopefulness. If, instead, you believe that life is hopeless, the same emotions will propel you toward fear, anxiety, nervousness, depression, and collapse.

Both hope and fear are self-fulfilling prophecies. Under hope, we believe that the world is just and moral, that we are endowed with the power and ability to pursue happiness and we might have temporary setbacks but ultimately everyone gets what they deserve. If you have hope, every failure is a challenge to get up and play the odds again, every hurdle is only a contest that will sweeten the success, and every rejection is a motivator toward a new struggle. But if you are afraid, then every setback appears final, people get not what they deserve but what they steal from others, every failure is an insult that humiliates us, every challenge ridicules our capacity, and every rejection produces a deep-seated hurt and desire to exact future revenge.

The same six types of emotions can be produced from either hope or fear. Depending on the source, their effects are radically different. Therefore, we cannot study emotional life comprising lust, anger, greed, pride, envy, and confusion unless we also understand their basic origin from hope or fear. In fact, the underlying philosophies of hope or fear become the most important determinant of our subsequent emotions and help us understand them.

To make someone happy, give them hope; their hope will change the flavor of all the other emotions. If you want to make someone unhappy, give them fear, and all their emotional life will naturally be unhappy. The greatest service to humanity is not giving them food, shelter, education, or jobs. It is rather giving them hope in the goodness of life itself. Once they have the hope, they will automatically strive toward a happy life themselves. If they are afraid instead, they will drive themselves toward unhappiness.

It is well-known that children who grow up in an environment of hope have a far greater chance of leading a happy life than those who have grown up under fear. In fact, fearful encounters in early childhood predispose people towards a fearful response to every other encounter in life—which indicates that the ideologies of hope and fear are often acquired early in life. This is not to say that these ideologies can't be changed later in life. It is only to indicate how important the ideology of hope vs. fear is relative to everything else. Those who have experienced love, care, and hope in early childhood turn out to be more confident and optimistic about their future. Conversely, those who have been hurt, rejected, or left uncared for during childhood are also generally prone to pessimism and negativity in life. Everyone experiences desire, anger, pride, greed, envy, and confusion, but these can be tinged either with hope or fear depending on one's childhood experiences.

Hope, Fear, and Detachment

The sense of hope in life is called *rajo-guna* or *rajas* in Vedic philosophy. The sense of fear is similarly called *tamo-guna* or *tamas*. Finally, there is a sense of detachment called *sato-guna* or *sattva*. Corresponding to these roots of emotional life is a cognitive worldview that creates hope, fear, or detachment. In the worldview of hope, one gets what they deserve, and the world is just. To become happy, therefore, one has to strive and struggle. The results will be temporary, but one can attain what they desire. It leads to competition and honest work, which is also called *dharma* or performing one's duties. In the worldview of fear and despair, the world is unjust. To become happy, therefore, one has to cheat and lie because there is no point in doing honest work as the results are not guaranteed, and one would only trade the unhappiness of struggle with the even greater unhappiness of failure. This leads to a life of deception, laziness, and dishonesty, which is also called *adharma*. Finally, the worldview of detachment concludes that even if one honestly performs their duties, the results are only temporary, just as if one cheats their way to success. One must thus be detached from both hope and fear.

The worldview of hope creates satisfaction, and the worldview of fear leads to suffering. But both outcomes are temporary and hence entail a life of continuous struggle. How can one become happy if they are always struggling to attain what they desire, and protect what they have obtained after struggle? The worldview of detachment concludes that the lives of desire—under hope or fear—are both breeding grounds for unhappiness. One must therefore discard the fulfillment of desires and quietly exit the world.

The universe is thus divided—in Vedic philosophy—into three parts. The upper part is the life of hope—working honestly to obtain the pleasures of life through effort. The lower part is the life of fear—laziness, deception, and dishonesty to obtain the pleasures of life. The middle part is the mixture of fear and hope, and humans are one of the several species that live under the influence of a combination of *rajas* and *tamas*. Their ability to see the futility of hope and fear (i.e. that happiness produced out of either path is temporary) makes them qualified to pursue a life of detachment from both, which is not available in the upper and lower parts of the universe. In the ultimate analysis, the life of detachment is the final destination of life. But the life of hope and honest work is better than that of fear and dishonesty.

The division between hope, fear, and detachment is entrenched in every society due to which the increase in hope is called 'rising up' and the increase in fear is called 'falling down'. They are also compared to good and evil, such that goodness is upward, and evil is downward. The land of hope is bright, open, and free, but the land of evil is dark, closed, and bound. They are also contrasted as heaven and hell in most cultures. This division of the world is not based on physical objects (although the worlds are physically different). The division is rather based on a deep sense of emotional difference between the types of pleasure or happiness they enjoy based on their worldview of hope or fear. The difference is also based on the cognitive worldviews that accompany the lives of hope and fear—we call them 'positive' and 'negative' views of life. The 'positive' view says that there is natural justice in life and by doing the right thing we will obtain the happiness we desire. The 'negative' view is cynical; it claims that life is unjust, and happiness is not a result of honest hard work but gained by grabbing and snatching from others.

It's noteworthy that if your worldview is one of hope and honesty, you will get along with others who are also hopeful and honest—both will understand the philosophy and ideology of performing their respective duties and enjoying their life as an outcome of their work. Conversely, people with the worldview of fear cannot get along even with others who have a similar worldview because they fear and distrust everyone. Of course, the fearful perceive the existence of fear in others much better, and they can therefore understand those who are fearful much better. But despite the ability to read each other better, they don't necessarily trust each other because the very nature of fear perception is that you must remain fearful of others.

Similarly, those who are honest can understand others who are honest, and they develop close bonds of trust with their honest counterparts. The ideology of fear, however, only invites more distrust and fear of others— whether they are fearful or hopeful—but the ideology of hope builds trust with those who have hope and distrusts those who are fearful. This is a crucial difference because those who live in hope can find trust with like-minded hopeful people but those who live in fear only find distrust in others, whether they are hopeful or fearful. Thus, the honest collaborate with the honest and find a bond. But the thieves always distrust even the other thieves. Finally, the thieves are always distrusted by the honest. Ultimately, the thieves end up the most lonely and fearful, while the honest find more hope in life.

The Basis of Social Order

A person living under the worldview of hope desires greater power to act freely and owns up to the responsibilities that come with that freedom. Their pleasure in life is derived from having the freedom and using it appropriately. A person living under the worldview of fear dislikes freedom and choice because they are afraid of making mistakes. They desire to be guided by rules, but they also resent those who make them. Their pleasure in life is using the crutch of rules to not execute their responsibilities or finding ways to complain about the rules and try to break them in different ways.

You can enjoy the fact that you have considerable freedom to decide but you always decide responsibly curtailing temptations of frivolity. You can also enjoy the fact that you have limited freedom, but you employ your intellect to find the loopholes for acting frivolously within those rules, or by breaking the rules. There is happiness in being powerful and responsible, and there is happiness in being weak but mischievous. The responsible person understands the intent behind rules and enjoys fulfilling it. The mischievous only obey the rules and enjoy violating the intents that created those rules.

The upper part of the universe can be graded by increasing freedom and responsibility accompanied by fewer rules and laws to be followed, while the lower part of the universe can be graded by decreasing freedom and responsibility accompanied by increasing rules and laws to be obeyed. The pleasure in the upper part of the universe is how to maintain honesty given enormous freedom and relative lack of guidance by rules. The pleasure in the lower part of the universe is how to become dishonest even though one is bound by so many rules and regulations. Thus, as one rises in the universe, there are lesser rules and greater freedom to choose while maintaining responsibility, and as one falls in the universe there is lesser freedom afforded by the multitude of rules and regulations because the living entities are dishonest and seek loopholes. There is self-imposed regulation in the honest, and there are externally enforced regulations on the dishonest. The honest lead a life of hope that their honesty despite freedom entitles them to a life of greater freedom and honesty, while the dishonest lead a life of fear that their dishonesty in spite of rules will push them towards lesser alternatives to choose from.

As the rules increase, life becomes more mechanized. One feels not in control because all their decisions are controlled by those who enact the rules. The powerful in this part of the universe use their power to control the mischievous from their tendency for mischief. As the mischievous indulge in greater mischief, the rulers create even more devious rules to prevent their mischief, causing greater fear of breaking the laws. Conversely, in the upper part of the universe, as the rules are reduced, there is a concomitant fear that any irresponsible behavior would naturally reduce their freedom.

There is, hence, fear—of being demoted on acting irresponsibly—even in the highest echelons of the universe. There is similarly hope—of being promoted on acting responsibly—even in the lowest depths of the universe. Hope and fear are relative terms in these cases, and no one is completely devoid of hope or fear in any part of the universe. By irresponsible action, the righteous can fall, and by responsibly obeying rules even the devious can rise. The enlightened therefore realize that this existence controlled by hope and fear—of following or breaking rules—is not the ultimate goal of life. They desire freedom from both hope and fear; they don't desire the power that could make one fearful due to ensuing responsibility, and they don't desire the control by rules that could make one hopeful through obedience.

Our present lives are a mixture of freedom and rules. As society acts more responsibly, fewer rules are needed. As people become irresponsible, more rules must be enacted, there is more surveillance and monitoring of everyone's actions, greater power used by the rulers to enforce compliance to rules, life becomes more mechanized, and people always live in fear of being punished for breaking the law. The oppression of the law causes them to retaliate, which only brings into existence even more laws and forced compliance and the only pleasure in life is when one can break the rules and feel free. However, breaking those rules is not the answer; becoming more responsible is the answer because that leads to a voluntary reduction in rules. Moral cultivation is the only legitimate route to happiness, even to lead a life of hope. As morality goes down, the rules begin to increase, one feels lesser control over their life, and loses the hope arising from freedom of choice.

Evolution of the Modern State

Modern society is decidedly shifting from more responsibility toward more rules. Formerly, nations were governed by a single ruler with a very small government, and a military force only large enough to defend their borders from aggressors. There was a very limited need to use that military for internal policing because the citizens mostly acted responsibly. The responsible action was in turn grounded on moral principles, and that morality, in turn, rested on a religious viewpoint about the goodness of life itself.

Once we remove religion as the grounds for morality, people act less responsibly. The ruler is now replaced by a 'state' which creates more and more rules to restrict irresponsible behaviors. To enforce those rules you need to monitor people, detect violators, try them for their rule-breaking, punish them for their indiscretions, which requires ever-growing government machinery, needing increasing amounts of funding to sustain, which results in growing taxes, and the net result is that people end up with less money, more taxes, and more rules. As the people are oppressed by state rules, they look for ways to violate them. That doesn't help the situation overall. It only leads to more rules, more machinery to enforce the rules, more taxes to maintain the machinery, and eventually even less money in the hands of people plus more rules. The activity of making more rules is also prone to manipulation and there is the tendency to overturn previous rules and create new ones. These are outcomes of the replacement of moral responsibility with rules.

Yes, I'm with the right-wing political class that argues for the reduction in government, followed by the tax reduction. But that is possible when people act responsibly toward the rest of society, something the right-wing doesn't believe in. The right-wing doesn't see that government machinery comes from rules, which follow lesser moral responsibility. They only see the need for more choices and fewer regulations, but don't understand that these choices are possible only when there is greater moral accountability.

I'm also with the left-wing political class which argues for greater moral accountability, but if they practiced that accountability, there would be lesser rules, followed by the reduction in government. The left-wing doesn't see that moral accountability and reduced government go hand-in-hand. In fact, they see the unseating of religions as the ground of moral principles as the founding principle on which equality in society can be further advanced.

Left-wing and right-wing political classes are two sides of the same coin. The left-wing dismantles religion and argues for a new basis of moral accountability, but if you dismantle religion you have less morality, more rules, bigger government, more taxes, and less freedom. The right-wing dismantles government without acting responsibly, which leads to more irresponsible action, which must be controlled by increasing the rules and surveillance, increasing taxes and decreasing freedom. Once the basic principle of society—moral responsibility—is missed, government spending to maintain order is inevitable. Neither the left nor the right wings argue for a greater moral conduct followed by lesser government. They either argue for greater responsibility with a greater government, or lesser responsibility with a lesser government. One must look closer to see the contradiction in their views.

The argument for lesser government at present is the argument for greater theft: if there is lesser government, there would be fewer rules inhibiting our choices, there would be lesser machinery to enforce rules, and the violators would get away with their immorality. The argument for greater government is the argument of replacing the God-given morality with people-defined relativized government rules. Once you relativize the rules, then there is no moral good and the law of the land places morality, and to enforce that law of the land, one requires a very large government apparatus.

Once the principle of morality is ignored, the present world begins to resemble the lower parts of the universe. The pleasure of freedom and accountability is gone. Only the pleasure of mischief created by violating rules remains. But more mischief leads to more rules, or to complete chaos. To prevent that chaos more people employed by the government live off the work of the common people—controlling and surveilling them. Society can never be happy in this way because it loses the hope emerging from freedom and harbors the fear of being caught while breaking rules. Ultimately, there is a limit to how many rules you can foist upon the population while still taxing them to maintain that rule-enforcement system. Once that limit is reached, there is not enough money to maintain the machinery, the population is already rebellious due to sustained control, and when immorality outweighs the controlling machinery, society decays into relentless chaos.

In former times, the king was considered the *representation* of God. He enforced moral rules and educated society to remain moral. Society was also hierarchical with the people with greater morality given a higher place in the social order. When the people are moral, there is less crime, lesser need for rules, lesser government machinery, lesser monitoring and control, and finally there are reduced taxes. The modern state replaces the moral representation of God with a man-made state constituted through the rules created by politicians whose main aim is to protect their position of power. The central problem in this replacement is that society talks about choice but doesn't preach responsibility. The responsibility is replaced by rules, but nobody wants to follow the rules because there is no *moral incentive* to do so.

The basic paradox of choice lies in the accompanying responsibility. If you forego responsibility, then you must lose choice too—through greater taxes, more rules, and more people chasing you to follow the rules, paid for by your earnings. Conversely, if you maintain responsibility, then you regain choice—through reduced taxes, lesser rules, and fewer people asking you to follow rules by taking your wealth. In short, there is no choice without responsibility. Greater responsibility brings greater choice, and lesser responsibility reduces the choice. As Ben Parker[1] in the movie Spider-Man[2] says: "With great choice comes great responsibility". If only this idea was understood, society would teach responsibility before it teaches choice.

The Laws of Morality

The connection between choice and responsibility is called *karma* in Vedic philosophy. The idea is simple: with greater responsibility comes greater freedom, and with irresponsible action freedom is reduced. We can call this the tradeoff between more responsibilities vs. more rules. The upper part of the universe enables more freedom and responsibility while in the lower part of the universe there is less accountability and more rules. The law is universal, but its application is contextual because what constitutes responsibility depends on a person's *role*, the capacity to perform the role, and the time, place, and circumstances under which the action is being performed.

The law of *karma* is a natural law, which means that no government is needed to enforce the retribution for irresponsible action and rule violation. The rules are also not created by a "democratically elected" government; they are all natural, and their enforcement is also natural. The government only exists to educate the people about these rules, and their enforcement should be seen as education. But the government is fallible, and the ruler can make mistakes. Nature doesn't rely on the good or bad rulers to create and enforce the rules of behavior. Nature is independent of the rulers, but the rulers can follow nature's rules, educating people to follow them, and discouraging them from violation. Taking the position of a ruler also implicates the rulers in the law of *karma* if they don't use their position of responsibility according to natural laws. The rulers are therefore not free from the laws of choice and responsibility. Under the law of *karma*, a government is a proxy for nature's laws. Nature's laws will act regardless of the ruler or government. The question is only whether the government is a good proxy or a misleading one.

The job of the government is to balance the worldview of hope, fear, and detachment. It must advocate hope by reducing government machinery and laws, giving people more freedom. For those who act irresponsibly, the government is required to provide fast and furious justice. Above all, the rulers must provide the moral education on being responsible, and act responsibly themselves. The rulers must realize that they are also under the control of the law of *karma*. Their position of power comes with a responsibility and accountability and neglecting that responsibility doesn't mean that they will get off scot-free from the laws of nature, just because they control the government. The laws of nature are aware of a person's position in society and they act contextually according to the person's *role*. Thus, there are different choices and different responsibilities for each role. While a role cannot be seen as an object via the senses, it can be perceived through the mind.

Recall that nature is comprised of objects, functions, and purposes. We see the objects sensually, but the objects exist—prior to sensation—as possibilities. One among the many possibilities is selected by *relating* two or more objects in a context. But which objects would be related at which point in time depends on the purpose. A person's role is their relation to the other person, under the control of a choice driven by a purpose. The action is created by the choice and purpose, but the action is in *relation* to other persons, and the choices can be *judged* to be right and wrong based on whether the action is their duty in a relation. The fact that the world exists as possibility only affords us freedom. This freedom can be used through a choice. But the choice can be judged based on the fact that it is enacted in a specific role.

The law of *karma* is a natural law because the material ontology comprises possibilities, relations, and choices. In the classical material worldview, nature is only objects and no possibilities. The objects interact with all other objects simultaneously so we cannot talk about a role. And because the world is governed by deterministic laws, there is absolutely no room for choices. The moral worldview is eliminated from science by postulating fixed objects that interact with all other objects at once under deterministic laws because that thesis removes *role* and *goal* from the description of nature. Reinstating the moral view, therefore, requires a revision of the material ontology.

Every choice has a consequence because choice creates an action in relation to a specific object, selecting a possibility, and we can ask if the action was appropriate—i.e. if it was done at the right time, between the right kinds of roles, and by the right person. Note how the questions of morality are also questions of time (when an action is performed), space (the roles involved in the action), and object (the capabilities of the persons who are involved in the action). And yet, we have rephrased the nature of time, space, and object as purpose, relation, and possibility—essentially changing the nature of science. In this new worldview, moral responsibility becomes scientific.

The laws of modern science are mathematical formulae, which exist in a Platonic world of ideas, and how these ideas govern the world remains unknown today (see, for example, Eugene Wigner's[3] article The Unreasonable Effectiveness of Mathematics in Modern Science[4]). The law of *karma* doesn't exist in a Platonic world. It exists in the *relation* between the objects that define their roles. The law of *karma* is also not always fixed for all persons. It rather evolves with time—as the role, capacities, and situations of the person change with time. Any person who enters that role is expected to behave according to the role. However, this behavior is only an *expectation* not a reality, quite like material objects are only possibilities and not reality. Quite specifically, a person has the *choice* to not act according to expectations. As a result, the expectation is *normative* and not *descriptive*—a person *should* act in a particular way but is not guaranteed to act in that stipulated manner. Just as we define probabilities for object states, there are also expectations of behavior. We can model them as probabilities but that's not the important point. The important fact is that some of these possibilities are *right* while the others are *wrong*—regardless of which one is more or less *probable*.

Like objects are described as probabilities which indicate the likelihood of an outcome, roles must be described as *expectations* that indicate the rightness of the action. Morality is nothing but the *expected* action. Fact may violate the expectation, and that would entail consequences. The essence of the law of *karma* is that each relationship has to be defined in terms of *expectations*—i.e. what actions are *expected* to occur. If the action exceeds or falls short of expectations, good or bad consequences may be created. These consequences then place one in a new role where the expectations are different. As one acts responsibly, he or she is placed in roles that increase freedom and responsibility. Conversely, as a person acts irresponsibly, he or she is bound by rules that he can't overcome. The law of *karma*, therefore, begins in defining a role as expectation, the subsequent actions conform to or violate the expectations, and the resulting consequences place the person into new roles.

The entire process can be described scientifically and naturally, provided we can reconceive nature as possibility, relationship, and purpose.

Quantum probabilities are sometimes called "expectation values"[5] because they are expected to happen. But by expectation I don't mean here that something is likely to happen. Instead, I mean that something *should* happen, not that it *will* happen. The abilities in the body are what *could* be used but the mandates of the role indicate what *should* happen. There are hence two ways in which the same possibility is described—*could* (for abilities) and *should* (for expectations)—if we treat the world semantically. If we remove the meaning, they are just probabilities. If the quantum probability indicated something that is more *righteous* rather than something more *likely*, then we could build a law that completes the quantum indeterminism by saying that the righteous is not always likely, but the outcome that is unrighteous entails consequences. In short, the current quantum law—described by Schrodinger's Equation[6]—would be incomplete because it doesn't describe the consequences when the righteous alternative isn't the most likely option and is hence not chosen at the right time in the right relation as the right action.

It is not enough to describe how *likely* an event is. It is more important to describe what the *expected* action is. But that expectation is not likelihood. In current science, the expected behavior is treated as the likely behavior, which means that we reduce the moral imperative to the actual outcome, when the actual outcome may not actually be moral action. As a result, we are unable to formulate a new law that would determine the outcome of a discrepancy between moral expectation and actual outcome. Such a law involves an interaction between the prior expectation and the present outcome, which presents a problem of reverse causation—from the present (outcome) to the past (expectation). This problem can be solved if the consequence of the action is created at the point of choice—if the expected alternative within the present relation is not chosen. Choice is therefore not about radical uncertainty in science. It is about another kind of law—of responsibility—that results from violating the expected behaviors. This consequence then acts to create a new role and situation, where the person gets to exercise choice once again. This new kind of law—the law of morality—is outside science unless we see the world as good and bad, right and wrong, beyond truth and falsities.

Our choices are not entirely free. They are often governed by the innate ideologies of hope and fear. Under the hope that we can achieve our desired goals, or under the fear that we might not fulfill the intended purpose, we don't choose the ideal alternative and thereby create *karma*. The ideal alternatives are always chosen under the ideology of detachment—i.e. freedom from both hope and fear. This type of action is called *karma-yoga* under which we are not performing action that exceeds expectations with the hope of fulfilling our incessant desires, nor are we neglecting our duties because we fear an adverse outcome. We do what we are expected to do ideally under the circumstances. *Karma-yoga* leads to freedom from *karma*—i.e. good or bad consequences—because the law of *karma* creates consequences only when actions exceed expectations or fall short of the expectations. Thus while a ruler punishes the actions of fear and rewards the actions of hope, he must also educate everyone about the ideology of detachment from hope and fear because only by such detachment can we cease the creation of *karma*.

Detachment and Compassion

Choices are made under the influence of emotions, and to make the right choices, we must understand the right kinds of emotions. We normally think that detachment is not an emotion, and to be detached is to be emotionless. This is not true. Just as hope and fear create emotions, detachment also creates the same emotions—desire, anger, greed, pride, envy, and confusion—but they are now not in relation to the self, but in relation to others. Detachment means that I don't care for my well-being, but still care for others' well-being—which we call *compassion*. Detachment that appears to be emotionless is most often a lack of empathy for others. That is not true detachment because the person is indeed attached to their own happiness, might harbor an ideology of hope or fear, which drives them to make choices. Complete emotionlessness would mean a lack of purpose, which ends in a lack of choice, and without a choice there can be no experience. If experiences exist, there must be emotion, although it can be based on compassion for others.

Compassion is the highest form of emotion in the material world. Under compassion, desire manifests as the will to do good to others. Anger appears if the others aren't choosing what is good for them. Greed manifests as the feeling to push others toward their own good. Pride manifests as the happiness when others are successful and happy. Envy becomes the competitiveness to excel more than others in serving the greater good. And confusion appears in the indecision on which alternative will help others more, just in case there are more than one alternative paths to choose from.

It is therefore false to think that if a person becomes detached, he or she also becomes disconnected from the world, feels no happiness, desire, greed, pride, or anger. The truly detached do not cease to engage with the world, although they don't engage due to their hope or fear. The truly detached person is also truly fearless because their personal injury or insult doesn't disturb them. The detached person is free of material hopes because they have no personal desires and ambitions left to fulfill. A detached person still engages with the world—as much as those under hope and fear do—but due to compassion for other living beings. Emotion therefore never ceases; under detachment it becomes purer. That desire to serve others, the anger when they don't accept their good, the greed to spread the good to more people, the competition to do better than other helpful people, the pride in the achievements of those whom they have helped, and the confusion on how to find the best path for those who might be stuck in a helpless situation, is pure.

It is natural for everyone to be hopeful. We don't have to teach a lot of hope in this world, we must just remove the conditions that create fear, and everyone will be hopeful themselves. But it is not easy to practice compassion, kindness, and concern while dedicating your life to the well-being of others. It is possible to practice *karma-yoga* in which one performs their prescribed duties in a detached manner. But what is a person's prescribed duty? If you are a tailor, carpenter, plumber, or mechanic, you have a duty toward your family by which you earn and provide for them. Doing these duties without desire for recognition or ridicule is *karma-yoga*. You become free from the frustration of hope, or the fear of failure, and that freedom is happiness. However, it is not *great* happiness because you only give them food, clothing, and shelter. Millions of people have these and are still unhappy. Therefore, doing your prescribed duties might bring you relief from suffering, but it doesn't necessarily make anyone else happy because they continue to suffer from the problems created by their own hopes and fears. A greater happiness is not when one makes oneself happy, but also makes others happier.

Psychologists study happiness as the pursuit of success with hope. They also study the unhappiness arising from fear. But they have no idea of the happiness that comes from altruism, after one has conquered their fear, and had enough success that they no longer find it great happiness. The pursuit of happiness begins with the overcoming of fear, followed by the search for success and hope, it then proceeds into personal detachment from both hope and fear and finally is reinvigorated into the quest of bringing happiness to others. A society that destroys fear is good. A society that brings hope is even better. A society of people who perform their duties without hope and fear is even preferred. But a society where people live for the benefit of other's happiness is the best. This idea is very counterintuitive because people think that happiness means making oneself happy. If they fail to find that happiness persistently, they might get detached from the outcomes of their actions. But these are all incrementally improving forms of selfishness. They are better as compared to hope and fear, but not comparable to making others happy. Removing fear from the minds of others, giving them hope, making them detached, and finally making them altruistic constitutes progressive altruism.

Altruism is described as the ability to help others after sacrificing one's happiness. Seldom is altruism presented as the highest form of happiness—even for the self. As a result, society has been built on the ideology of everyone seeking their happiness, which in the best-case scenario is a worldview of hope, and under the worst-case scenario—where everyone competes with others to grab the most resources, and only the fittest survive—is a worldview of fear. The selfish pursuit of happiness is the lowest form of pleasure because you recognize that everyone else is selfish and they would not mind cutting you if they needed to fulfill their desires. You can't help but feel fear in such a society. A higher form of happiness is based on the ideology of hope—that everyone gets what they deserve—which means that nobody can take away your happiness even if they wanted to. Detachment builds on this form of happiness because you realize that even if you temporarily lost something due to the consequences of past action, the loss is immaterial. Finally, altruism builds on detachment because it teaches people that giving away something that makes others hopeful or detached is even greater.

Modern society teaches the lowest form of happiness—arising from fear—as 'natural'. We have forgotten that the law of *karma* gives us hope because we get what we deserve, and nobody can take away what is due to us. We have forgotten the philosophy of *karma-yoga* or detachment from desire—because no matter what you do, you will not get more than your due owing to previous *karma*. And we have completely ignored the highest form of happiness produced by making others happier. If society is formed to make us collectively happy, but it only teaches fear, then how can it ever succeed in its goals? Furthermore, how can the social structure created from the worldview of fear be the correct form of social organization for happiness?

Cooperation vs. Competition

Economists and social theorists advance the idea of competition based on selfish interest. However, if everyone is acting selfishly, then there can be no society, and every man would be an island unto himself. To constitute society, we must also cooperate, which leads to exchange and trade, governed by fair practices. Competition alone leads to anarchy but combining competition with cooperation leads to a conceptual contradiction. For example: when should we cooperate and when should we compete? What limits demarcate their application? Every socio-economic-political system can be characterized as a different take on how the contradiction between cooperation and competition must be resolved. Those who argue for more competition fall on the right side of the political spectrum and those who advocate more cooperation lie on the left side. But given this dichotomy, political theory is beset with a fundamentally unresolvable contradiction from the outset: we don't expect to find perfectly satisfactory answers to political questions so long as we keep thinking within the confines of these contradictory extremes.

The problem with cooperation and competition is that you expect to cooperate within some man-made boundary and compete outside that boundary but it's not clear how you draw the boundary. In the limiting case where the boundary is drawn around an individual, there can be no cooperation because everyone else becomes a competitor. Similarly, when the boundary includes everyone in the world, there can be no competition between them.

In the ideology of fear, there is no cooperation because the fearful do not trust anyone. Even if they pretend to cooperate, they are creating competitive plans in the background, because for them the boundary of cooperation ends with the individual. Under fear, nobody can be trusted, and hence nobody should collaborate. When there is no cooperation and only competition, each individual lives a lonely life of fear and retribution where he or she is threatened by others, finds no support and validation from others, is afraid to provide support to others for dread of their empathy not being reciprocated, and faces continuous self-doubt because competitors tend to always criticize each other. The ideology of the fearful justifies this viewpoint by the claim that if there was no fear then everyone would be lazy and the lazy would live off the hard work of the honest people. The fearful don't want to share their earnings with others because they are afraid that if something is given away it will never come back. They remain overly attached to the limited things they have, and they advocate fear to bring the lazy into action. The problem is that fear is applied not just to the lazy but also to the less competent, those who might be unable to work due to sickness, lack of education, disability, or other reasons. These people need compassion rather than fear, but the ideology of fear is unable to distinguish between the lazy and the unfortunate.

Cooperation begins with the ideology of hope because the hopeful can trust other hopeful people, and distrust the fearful. Typically, this cooperation works in smaller pockets of similar people, who have similar language, culture, beliefs, social status, hopes, and aspirations. Differences naturally lead to distrust, and they end the cooperation. The ideology of hope extends the competitive boundary from the individual to a group—e.g. a family, an organization, a city, a country, or a race. Everything beyond that boundary is the domain of competition as the differences cannot be trusted, and lack of trust leads to fear, which leads to competition. People within that boundary are trusted and form the domain of cooperation. This ideology of hope—in which cooperation exists in smaller boundaries and people outside are distrusted—is today widely known as "free market economy"[7] in which people gather to form unions and communities in order to compete with other groupings. There is a shared sense of belonging and validation inside the cooperation. But there is fear and ruthless criticism outside that boundary of belonging.

As the boundary gets smaller, the belonging decreases and fear increases. For example, with urban nuclear families, the unit of belonging is getting smaller and the competition and fear of others is increasing. To remain more hopeful, you must find the safety of a bigger group—e.g. a larger company to work for, a bigger country to live in, a greater circle of friends to move into, or a larger number of relatives to talk to. The reason is that smaller groups provide lesser validation and present greater threats of responsibility. To feel more secure and hopeful, therefore, you will join a larger group, which provides greater validation and a shared responsibility. Conversely, if you seek the thrill of fear, you will pursue more individualistic pursuits, and that means you will work and play alone, rather than in groups of people.

The ideology of hope is better than the ideology of fear because there is more cooperation. But you can also see that the fear and the hope are expressed in the relative sizes of the cohesive groups. Those who enjoy fear and competitiveness work in smaller groups. But those who relish the safety of larger validation live in larger communities. A classic example of this behavior is working in a start-up company with few people vs. a large established corporation with thousands of employees. It is unfortunate that modern society eulogizes competitiveness and criticizes cooperation. It is not uncommon, for example, to call those who cooperate more with others 'sheep' who refuse to think for themselves, as compared to the 'wolves' who always think only about themselves. The fact is that if people stopped cooperating, there would only be fear and no hope. Greater cooperation— among like-minded people—is better. This cooperation doesn't imply laziness, although we do find that large groups tend to get lazy and fear is needed to bring them into action.

The laziness in large groups is the effect of the fearful joining large groups. While the hopeful are competing externally and cooperating internally, the fearful create distrust inside the group and compete against the members of the group internally. The internal competition converts the hopeful—who would like to compete externally—into those who are fearful and compete with each other. Over time, the focus shifts from external to internal competition, and the boundary of the organization becomes meaningless, because it is now every individual for themselves. The result is chaos and anarchy, and the fear of survival halts group progress. Those who were working sincerely find that the results they produce are snatched by the competitive people which means that, over time, they stop contributing to the organization. Such organizations are prone to rapid destruction from within.

Many organizations encourage this internal competition, thinking that competition is the basis of social organization and the result is that the organization is fractured into groups who behave as if they were competitors outside the organization. Energy is wasted in trying to win against one's colleagues and the organization loses its focus of competing against outsiders. Such organizations are destroyed both from external and internal competition because they lack the benefits of uniting their forces against a common competitor. Data on companies shows[8] that the average life of a Fortune 500 company has now shrunk from 75 to 15 years, over fifty years. Most companies are dying—and much faster than before. Researchers blame these changes on a variety of factors such as "market transitions", "economic downturns", "inability to keep pace", etc. But they are unable to explain why other companies navigate such challenges far better. Ultimately, the difference comes down to the organizational culture—cooperation vs. competition.

Those who cooperate grow the best talent, have the best leaders, and create the most sustainable organizations. Those who compete internally forcibly push the best talent and leaders out of the organization, and ultimately self-destruct. Internal competition forces people to make decisions not in the best interest of the group; they keep choosing what is best for themselves.

Therefore, the ideologies of hope and fear cannot mix because while the hopeful are cooperating the fearful are undercutting them. The psychology of fear converts the hopeful into the fearful, and the organization is destroyed from within. A successful organization carefully and conscientiously weeds out those who play on fear instead of hope—even if the fearful seem to bring success temporarily. No organization can survive internal competition, and what works between competing groups must be rejected within a group.

Given that it is difficult to isolate the hopeful and fearful people, all social groups tend to be temporary. In a marriage for instance if one partner thinks about the good of the family while the other only thinks about their own good then over time both partners will only think about their own good, leading to separation. For the family to continue both partners must cooperate and think about the good of the family—even if it means sometimes sacrificing their individual desires. That sacrifice is what keeps the family going strong. Inherent in all cooperation is therefore a sense of sacrifice, which the weak, fearful, and selfish are incapable of precisely because of their innate fears.

The psychology of hope, however, is not truly altruistic. The hopeful sacrifice because they believe that it gives them something in return, not because they inherently care about the person for whom they sacrifice. Cooperation is therefore also selfish, but the ambit of selfishness is extended to a grouping where one agrees to cooperate for their mutual good. Thus, even in hope there is an inherent fear that sacrifice may not be reciprocated, and the hopeful may change into the fearful over time—giving up their altruistic and sacrificing nature. The truly altruistic person is one who doesn't expect reciprocation as he or she considers all reciprocation or selfishness to be temporary. A person who lives in the hope of happiness is disturbed by the selfishness of others and reacts in a tit-for-tat manner, thus perpetuating the cycle where selfishness is only reciprocated by another selfish encounter.

The fact is that the moral laws compel us into situations where our work is not reciprocated—because we did not reciprocate in the past. There is an understanding of *karma* involved in the psychology of hope: that if I sacrifice for others, others will sacrifice for me. But this belief is lost in the face of selfishness. To keep that faith, one must graduate to true altruism where selfishness is reciprocated by sacrifice. The fact that we meet selfish people is because we have been selfish earlier. To end the encounters with selfishness we must remain altruistic even with the selfish. As the *karma* of selfishness is over, only the altruistic encounters remain, whereupon all fear disappears.

That practice of altruism in the face of selfishness is *karma-yoga* where we don't end our cooperation although others compete with us. It is based on a much fuller understanding of *karma*, namely that good returns good, but also that any bad encounter is caused by our past bad deeds. We don't attribute the bad action to the person who is acting selfishly. We rather attribute it to our own bad actions which have caused an *encounter* with the selfish person. If we did not have prior bad deeds, the selfish person would still exist, but we will not encounter them. Their existence is hence not the problem; the problem is that we encounter them, and that encounter is caused by our actions. This understanding of *karma* leads us to detachment: we continue to cooperate regardless of whether the others cooperate or compete. Such action ultimately destroys all encounters with competition; we are now left only with actions of cooperation—and we eventually become happy.

The clash between cooperation and competition creates contradicting ideologies about social organization—the socialists promulgate cooperation, but internal competition makes society stagnant, while the capitalists advocate competition but that only brings more fear and uncertainty into life. Cooperation is not the enemy. The enemy is competition—overt or covert. The ideology of cooperation, however, is not based on laziness and living off the work of others. It is rather based on sacrifice and altruism where one willingly foregoes the desire for reciprocation in order to enter a world where they only encounter those who have no expectation of reciprocation.

Once we understand the moral law of nature, then we can at least theoretically understand how cooperation trumps competition—both as a better way to compete between groups and to give up all competition to find those encounters where there is only cooperation and no competition. If this practice is perfected, we can envision a new type of competition in which people want to rival each other's sacrifices. Unlike the selfish competition which makes even the cooperative people selfish, the rivalry of making bigger sacrifices doesn't make others selfish. Rather, it increases their desire to magnify their level of altruism. This is the only stable form of society as it never reverses the behavior whether one is cooperating or competing because the competition is to increase the cooperation. Every other form of society—including those that only compete, and those that mix competition and cooperation—is unstable and temporary. Social stability is deeply connected to emotions because the ideologies of hope and fear create instability, but the ideology of detachment, compassion, and altruism creates stability.

The Spiritual Basis of Compassion

The description of social stability based on cooperation is incomplete without defining cooperation because cooperating with a murderer to kill more innocent people cannot be the basis of a stable society. Yes, cooperation alone can bring stability, but cooperation also must extend to broader well-being. A murderer may cooperate with others to kill more people, but that doesn't bode well for those who are killed because his concept of cooperation is very narrow. In fact, cooperating to murder is a good counterexample of why cooperative societies that desire to compete with others economically, militarily, or racially, are highly prone to instability because any competition—which is designed to *harm* others—can only bring instability. Only competition meant to help others can create a stable society because the dichotomy between cooperation and competition is imminently dissolved.

This realization is sometimes called *vasudhaiva kutumbakam*, or that the whole world is my family—that you don't compete within the family, or you only compete to make others happier. The love confined within a boundary is imperfect love. True love is that which spreads to everything—you don't aim to help a person while hurting others; you aim to help someone without hurting anyone. This is the origin of the idea of *non-violence* in all religions, but it is also incomplete because it doesn't address the problem of cooperating with the uncooperative—e.g. punishing a murderer. What should one do to those killers who only believe in helping themselves, by hurting others? Should a non-violent person not defend himself against unjust violence? And should a non-violent ruler not protect his people from violent aggressors?

The theory of *karma* enlightens us by giving answers to these dilemmas. The answer is that killing an evil person is an act of compassion because it prevents him from committing more evil which would otherwise elongate their own duration of future suffering. Killing the evil is obviously compassionate to the people who are being hurt, but the surprise is that it is compassionate even to the evildoers because it pauses or halts their evil actions. Indeed, not killing them would be more painful to both those who suffer and those who cause the suffering, so there is no contradiction between violence to protect one from the evil, and non-violence to not commit evil.

Violence and compassion are thus not contradictory; in fact, violence against the evil is compassion. However, the killing of the evil must be performed compassionately—i.e. no torture and pain. The ruler is justified in killing the killers, by employing the method that causes the least suffering to those being killed because the goal is to terminate their evil actions—an act of compassion. Of course, death is very painful to every living being, and therefore death even to the evildoers must be chosen only if there is no alternative reformation. This choice is based on the understanding of the evildoer's emotional state—e.g. was the killer motivated by justified revenge or unjustifiable rage to just hurt other people? The job of the person who awards such justice is not easy because it is not merely based on observable facts; it is rather based on the assessment of the emotional state of the evildoer.

The sense of justice is also based on the idea that the soul is eternal and by killing the body we only take away the current opportunities to commit evil but we don't end the future potential for good or evil actions as the soul will be reborn into a new body to enjoy or suffer the consequences of their previous actions, and make new evil or good choices. If the soul is not eternal, and life is limited to this body (as the atheists like to believe), then everyone is entitled to live as long as possible and there should be no death penalty even for the most heinous crimes. Some people even complain that capital punishment is retribution and not justice and we cannot preach non-violence by committing the highest type of violence. All these claims are flawed when we take *karma* into account because (1) non-violence and killing are not contradictory, (2) if the ruler doesn't punish the extremely violent, he is doing injustice to those affected, (3) killing the criminal is even kind to the criminal himself, provided there was no room for reformation in the present body and the person must be awarded a different body to vent his violent tendencies. In short, the person is not fit to live as a human but is fit to live in another species of life where violence is the norm and not unexpected behavior.

Those who complain against the death penalty for a human being won't complain against killing a man-eating tiger because nature has an arrangement of reward and retribution, but certain types of prizes and punishments are not meant for humans. Humans who exhibit the behaviors of animals and cannot be reformed are fit to enter animal life, and taking them out of human society is an act of compassion because the retribution for animal behavior in human life is far greater than in animal life. Nobody will fault a tiger for killing because that is natural. Those who want to kill, therefore, can kill in a tiger's body without creating the retribution of humans—this satisfies their desire to kill, it protects human society from unwanted suffering, and it ensures that the tiger can enjoy its natural tendencies without any moral consequences. This is compassionate because it is good for everyone; the compassion is not limited to those who are being hurt, but even to the person who is hurting others. However, to practice this compassion we must see that the soul in the tiger and the human being is qualitatively similar—i.e. both have the *sat, chit,* and *ananda* tendencies—although these tendencies only appropriately fulfilled by different roles, bodies, and pleasures.

Just as cooperation and competition are not contradictory ideas under an altruistic conception of society, similarly, violence and non-violence are not contradictory under a compassionate understanding of nature's laws. Both altruism and compassion are based on the idea that life is spiritual; the bodily capacities, the worldly opportunities, and the carnal desires are material modifications of the soul's abilities, relations, and pleasure. Nature has an arrangement for both killers and the killed in other species that we don't need to bring it into human life. But if such tendencies have crept into human society, then they must also be pushed out into the animal life.

Ultimately, a soul's choices depend on their conception of happiness. A certain type of pleasure can be afforded—without punishment—in a certain type of species. And in that species, one can enjoy their chosen form of pleasure only in certain relations—e.g. tigers eating deer. This is a compassionate arrangement because all types of pleasure are afforded, the soul is accorded a body to enjoy that pleasure, but the restriction is that you can't enjoy it with everyone. The tiger will eat flesh, but it will not chew grass; the deer will chew grass but not flesh. Their respective desires are being fulfilled as they pay for the consequences of their previous actions—essentially to teach them competitive life entails a fearful existence and to be happy one must learn to cooperate. Increasing competition creates an unstable society with unhappy people, but increasing cooperation makes society stable and happy.

Morality for Diverse Species

To understand and implement these ideals we must extend the concept of society from humans to all species of life. We need to recognize that just as there is desire in humans, there are also emotions in the other species. And yet, one species is the food of another; certain behaviors are acceptable in some species but unacceptable in others. How do we know what is allowed or disallowed for a species? The answer depends on natural laws based on *roles*. Yes, human society is in a role in relation to the other species of life. Furthermore, individual humans have a role in relation to other humans and animals. The role affords us choices but there is always a best choice—the ideal and right choice—and many inferior and incorrect choices, naturally.

It is morally acceptable for a lion to habitually maul and kill for survival. We don't expect lions to till the land, grow their food, and cook it before eating. But we expect humans to do so. This expectation is not due to the human taste buds or proclivity to eat grains. This is also nature's law which we can understand if we see that a human is not just a type of body, but also a type of role in relation to other roles. The body gives us abilities to act, but just because we can act as an animal doesn't mean we *should* because the bodily activity and our desire are not the only reality—there are also moral imperatives of a role. Animal killing, for example, is *possible* with the human body, but it is not the best choice available in the human role. When we indulge in imperfect choices, we demonstrate that we are incapable of handling a role appropriately. That's when nature arranges a transfer into another kind of body where the misuse of free will is curtailed by taking out the prohibited options and allowing only those options that are suited to a soul's proclivities.

Once the body is decided, it is placed in roles with other bodies where it can reap the consequences of past actions. The soul with the proclivities of a hunter gets a body where hunting is natural, but that body is also hunted by others. Thus, the soul gets an opportunity to fulfill its desire for hunting, and yet pays for the actions previously performed—in the form that it desires. Nature thus indulges in both compassion and retribution. By compassion, it gives the soul a body that it well-suited for hunting. And by retribution it forces that body in situations where it also becomes hunted by other bodies. There is both choice and responsibility—the soul is free to desire anything, but once it has been accorded a body to fulfill that desire, it must act according to the dictates of that type of body and role, to avoid adverse *karma*.

Morality, therefore, is not universal. It is rather contextual to a type of body, and the role in which the body is situated, and the time and place. In Vedic philosophy, this morality is called *dharma*, which is incorrectly translated as "religion"; while most "religions" try to universalize their behaviors, *dharma* is always contextual to the specific type of body and role. *Dharma* is not religion. It is one's duties—or those which will free the person from *karma* because once the consequences of actions have ceased, the soul is free from the repetitive cycle of birth and death, enjoyment and suffering.

Dharma is a social system of duties in a person's current role. But this role is not just toward one's family, occupation, or nation. The role in question rather relates the soul to the rest of the universe, and every living being in their respective roles. The role is the soul's position in relation to the rest of the universe. And the norms of acceptable behavior are dictated by that position and the moral law of consequences is based on that position. However, since this position is defined hierarchically, we can conceive of many kinds of *dharma*—in relation to the different hierarchical levels. Generally, if a lower level *dharma* is violated in order to fulfill a higher-level *dharma*, the violation of the lower-level *dharma* doesn't create a moral consequence. Conversely, when some lower-level *dharma* is fulfilled while violating a higher-level *dharma*, an adverse moral consequence is produced. As a result, one doesn't become free of *karma* unless the hierarchy of roles is fully understood, and actions are always in accordance with the highest *dharma*.

The highest *dharma* is called *sanātana dharma* or the eternal duty. If everyone is aware of their eternal duty, then even the lower-level duties are correctly performed because there is consistency of duty at all levels of the hierarchy. However, if one is unaware of the higher-level duties, then they perform their lower-level duties correctly but break the higher principles. "I am just doing my job" is not an excuse for breaking the higher moral principles because each person is expected to be aware of the entire hierarchy and being unaware or deliberately ignoring those principles—while conforming to the lower level duties—doesn't absolve the soul of the consequences of its actions. The moral law of consequences is therefore a natural law: it acts whether or not you know about it. If a government creates a secret law and doesn't notify the citizens, ignorance of the law cannot be a crime. But everyone is expected to inquire about the nature's laws, which don't change with time (as government laws) although they are contextual to each person.

My *dharma* is different from yours and finding that *dharma* and acting according to it is the essential function of human life. Animals don't have the mental, intellectual, and moral advancement to understand their *dharma*, or that there are many levels of *dharma*. They act according to their proclivities. That is sufficient for the animal body and role, but it is insufficient in the human body and role. As a result, if humans act like animals, there are serious consequences for humans, although there are no consequences for the animals. This is because the morality and *dharma* for different species vary.

Morality and duty are defined by one's position on the tree of roles. In the animal form of life, the role and the body are nearly identical in the sense that the body can do only what the role demands, and the role doesn't demand what the body can't do. In the human form, the body can do far more than what the role demands, and sometimes the role demands what the body is incapable of. Therefore, humans have to sometimes stretch (when the body is incapable of the roles) and sometimes curtail (when the body can do far more than the role's demands). This stretching and curtailing are not expected of the animals, but it is an essential feature of the human form of life.

In short, every form of life has a *dharma* but by and large their body and their role are almost identically matched due to which just being in the body itself fulfills their *dharma*, and because they don't deviate from their duties, they don't create *karma*—although they have to reap the results of previously created *karma* (good or bad). The human life is very unique, not because it is the highest type of role, but because it involves stretching and curtailing because the body and the role are not ideally matched. That demand in turn forces the person to inquire about the nature of *dharma* in relation to the entire hierarchy because there is a necessity. In other species of life—including higher species than the humans—there is no stretching and curtailing because your duty is closely matched with what you desire to do, and therefore just doing what you desire itself constitutes *dharma*. The body and the role are so similar that we cannot distinguish between them, and there are few discrepancies between bodily abilities, desires, and the role's demands.

In most species of life, the *sat, chit,* and *ananda* are aligned due to which their bodily abilities (*chit*) are matched to their role (*sat*) and their desires (*ananda*). The soul identifies with its body, and its situation, and considers that body and situation itself to be its desire—i.e. one is satisfied with their body and situation. The condition in the human life is different as our relations, bodily ability, and desires are not fully matched, and as a result we remain dissatisfied. Sometimes we enter situations that we don't desire, and at other times we find ourselves not having the ability to deal with the situation. That struggle for existence is caused by the *conflict* between *sat, chit,* and *ananda* and that conflict forces us to inquire into the nature of reality.

Without that conflict, there is no need to inquire into the nature of reality because what you want is what you are capable of, and what the situation affords you. Why would anyone inquire into reality if you can get what you want because the situation and the abilities fulfill it? In that sense, the human form of life is far superior to the others because there is inherent dissatisfaction in this form of life which can lead to a much better understanding—if we inquire into the nature of reality—and, consequently, liberation.

The human *dharma* begins with the understanding of the nature of reality[9], unlike other species where this discovery is unnecessary—the desire, ability, and opportunity are matched such that the soul will not desire what is beyond its ability, and the soul will not frequently face situations that it can't handle by its ability. There is still birth and death in all species of life, so the ability, opportunity, and desire are not perfectly matched in any species. However, the gaps between the three tend to get greater in human life, and those gaps are the wake-up call for the soul to inquire into the nature of reality. If the body can tolerate a lot of pain, even painful situations don't create a problem. If the soul doesn't desire certain things, the inability to find those things doesn't result in an existential crisis. And if the soul doesn't face situations that require upskilling and doesn't have desires that need upskilling, the fact that it isn't upskilling doesn't cause a disturbance. In that sense, life has to undergo contradictions between opportunity, ability, and desire and these kinds of crises are possible only in the human form of life. We are superior because we can be troubled to a far greater extent than others.

The animals too suffer pain, but their ability to tolerate it is greater than us. Even when they are hurt, the pain doesn't create an existential crisis. In the animal body, the soul doesn't desire what the body cannot provide. There is a limited need for upskilling in the animal life. And most animals live in their natural conditions where their bodily abilities are sufficient to handle the situations they encounter, and their desires are matched with the pleasures afforded in that situation. The point is that the conflict between ability, desire, and opportunity is minimized in other species of life, and hence there is no necessity to inquire into the nature of reality because such an inquiry becomes imperative only when we are faced with severe contradictions.

It is well known that humans turn to philosophy triggered by an existential crisis. The Buddha was triggered into inquiring about the meaning of life only when He saw the pain of old age, death, and disease. Philosophy in the West was invented during Greek times to answer basic questions about the meaning of life. In fact, the word "philosophy" means the "love of wisdom" but only those who are troubled by life's situations seek that wisdom, and philosophy has therefore been associated for millennia with sadness, resignation, angst, and desperation to find answers. Over time, of course, this inquiry turned from the love of wisdom to the solution of practical problems by bridging the gaps between ability, desire, and opportunity. For instance, humans have invented machines to do things that their bodies cannot do: airplanes fly, cars help us move faster, telephones allow us to communicate over great distances, and medicines help us fight the diseases that the body cannot fight on its own. Humans continually invent new technology to expand and fulfill new desires. We are not satisfied by what the body can obtain easily, and what the opportunities afford us simply. We rather want to create new abilities and opportunities to satisfy the ever-expanding desires. In short, we first create a contradiction between desire and ability or opportunity and then fight the battle to overcome that gap. We are trying to harmonize ability, desire, and opportunity, after creating a contradiction between them.

But in this effort, we miss the prominent point of human life, which is that these three are conflicted in every form of life, to a lesser or greater extent. Human life is the opportunity not to expand the gaps and then bridge them to attain a life like the other species, but to recognize that these can never be perfectly harmonized in the material world, unless we accept our eternal duties, learn to perform these duties, and become free of *karma*.

6

Emotion and Relationships

Nature and Nurture

We have seen the distinction between *sat* which creates relationships and *ananda* which creates emotions. The relationship dictates the sense of right and wrong—i.e. our sense of duty and responsibility in a role. The emotion determines whether we enjoy or suffer in the given role—our sense of good and bad. We have also seen that relationships (like material objects) are *possibilities*—i.e. we can take different roles and form relations to objects. And we have noted that everything we see is a combination of *sat*, *chit*, and *ananda*, which means that even the material body, the senses, the mind, the intellect, the ego, and the moral sense combine the ability to perceive and create concepts (*chit*), relationships (*sat*), and pleasure (*ananda*).

Each of these three can be the decision-making authorities. These decisions are represented by dominant-subordinate relations between the three. When emotion dominates and becomes the decision-making authority, then it selects the relationship and the ability to create an action, so that it can enjoy the outcome. In a simple sense, we select from available relationships and abilities to become happy, but of course, it is entirely possible that abilities and relations that would make us happy are not available to us. In such cases, the relation may be the decision-making authority and it would present itself as circumstances that we cannot avoid. The cognition forced by the circumstance and the resulting emotion are subordinate to the circumstance.

The relations available to us are due to *karma*, and the choices of those relations are due to *guna*. By the combination of relations and choices (*karma* and *guna*), certain concepts—morals, the sense of self, beliefs about truths, language and ideas, sensual capabilities, and finally the material body—become dominant, while others are suppressed. The ability to think about and understand alternative morals, have a different sense of self, believe in different truths, speak different languages and know different ideas, have alternative sensual capabilities, and, finally, the material body, exists with all souls. Finally, sometimes, our cognitive and conative abilities themselves may be the dominant force, and what we can perceive and do would determine whether we can establish a relation and enjoy the outcomes. For instance, if someone is deaf, the lack of ability to hear would restrict the formation of relations to musical instruments or sources of sound, and the resulting pleasure. Conversely, a heightened sense of hearing would draw their ears toward sounds that others could not have heard even if they were listening.

The experience, however, generally always begins in either relation or emotion. For instance, we either desire to see something and then establish a relation to that thing, before we see it. Or, the thing we see is thrust in our vision, which then leads to a cognition, which might then be a pleasant surprise or a painful experience. Once this initial experience has occurred, then our relational abilities may draw us further into the experience. For example, if we hear a beautiful sound accidentally, then our cognitive ability to understand its nuances would create a sense of curiosity in us, which will drive us to focus our attention on that sound by excluding other things from the perception. Eventually, if we like what we hear, then the curiosity converts into pleasure, and we move even closer to listen more carefully.

The key point is that each of these three tendencies can rapidly go dominant or subordinate. And yet, the cognitive and conative ability of the *chit* only acts to restrict what we can achieve through a relation or an emotion. The driver of these experiences is relation or emotion. The cognitive and conative abilities are like tools; they don't initiate the experience, although they can be used for experiences, and the tools can restrict what we can experience. The material body is a tool; you can study it objectively, and yet the tool is useless without purpose and relation to something where the potentiality is converted into a reality. The most important determinants of how a tool is used are opportunities and desires. In order to use the tool, there must be something on which to do it—this constitutes the relation or opportunity. Similarly, to use the tool, we must want to do it for a goal—this is the purpose and emotion. Emotions are frustrated when there is no relationship because one is unable to apply their motives onto another person. Emotions are also frustrated when one has the relationship but lacks the ability. For instance, a person may be in love, but may not have the money and power to fulfill the desires of the person he or she loves. Emotional fulfillment, therefore, depends on the abilities to give and take, and these abilities can enhance or restrict our experiences, but the abilities don't drive the creation of experiences.

The emotive ability is called *guna* and the opportunities are created by *karma*. These two are the dominant drivers of all experiences. The tools of perception either limit or enhance the experience, but they don't drive it.

There are many kinds of emotions created from different relationships. These are the pleasures of childhood (when one depends on parents for fulfillment), friendship (when one relies on a friend on a platform of equality and mutual support), marriage (where one enjoys sexual love together with the sense of shared destiny), parenthood (where one cherishes nurturing children, fulfilling their fancies, and seeing them grow into adults), and appreciation of others (where one is not in a close relationship but still feels gratitude and indebtedness to the other person). There is also happiness in detachment from these relationships, where one becomes situated in the relation to the self—loving and fulfilling oneself rather than others. Unhappiness only results when one tries to have a relationship, but is unable to do so, or lacks the ability to act according to the needs of the role, jeopardizing the relation.

Self-relationship is the most fundamental of all relationships, but it is also the least understood. At one end it seems: How could one not have a relation to the self? At the other, you can ask: What could be the value of the self-relationship? The relationship to the self is the need to be alone and enjoy solitude. If you have a good self-relation, then you would be comfortable with solitude because you have yourself for company. This is an indication that you can live with people who are just like you. Conversely, if you are uncomfortable in solitude it means that you won't be able to live with others who are just like you. You will, instead, seek people who are different from you, because you don't like who you are, and you neglect your awareness of yourself by becoming aware of others—where you can either blame others for what they are (remaining ignorant of the faults in yourself) or you will appreciate others (remaining unaware of the good qualities within yourself).

The ability to live in solitude indicates that you are comfortable with yourself—if you are *happy* in solitude. That comfort is essential to form other relationships because those who are uncomfortable with themselves fear losing the relationships (as they would be forced to live by themselves). However, every relationship creates new problems: (1) if the other person is happy with themselves it makes you insecure since it highlights that you are unhappy with yourself, and (2) if they are unhappy with themselves, they cannot make you happy, and the attempt to escape from self-consciousness leads to another person who is also disinterested and averse to self-consciousness. Everyone likes to be around a happy person—one who is happy by themselves. But a self-contented person makes a self-discontented person unhappy. Hence, there is no scenario in which a self-discontented person can be happy. To be happy, one must be self-contented before relating to others.

It is possible that a person who enjoys solitude may not enjoy others' company because they don't have the traits the solitary person considers essential for happiness. But if you don't like solitude then you are both unhappy with yourself and unable to make others happy. The ability for solitude is a good indication that you have a purposeful life; that you have attained what you expect from yourself, and at least you are able to love yourself and enjoy your own company. Only when one finds self-contentment can one have good relationships. Self-relationship is thus the foundation for all other relationships, and if the foundation is weak, all other relations will be weak too. If one becomes content and satisfied with oneself, he or she can be happy with others (provided they have the qualities the contented person appreciates).

All meditative traditions, therefore, encourage practitioners to practice solitude. When one can live in solitude, he or she has reached the platform where they are comfortable with who they are, and they can relate to others who are similarly comfortable. In Vedic philosophy, this self-contentment is called 'liberation'. It is not an end but a stepping stone to fruitful relations with others because, as noted above, a person who is unhappy with themselves cannot make others happy, and also cannot be happy in the company of other happy people. One has to first find contentment within the self, and once such contentment has been attained, the relation to others—provided they have shared interests and desires—will also become useful and happy. The preliminary form of meditation is therefore just silence, ending the mental buzz, and being able to sit in a comfortable posture by yourself. There are higher forms of meditation that build upon the self-satisfied state.

Six Types of Relationships

In Vedic philosophy, the above-mentioned six types of relationships have both spiritual and material counterparts. The relationships have a hierarchy, but the higher and lower positions in that hierarchy depend on whether the relationship is material or spiritual. In the case of spiritual relationships, at the bottom of the hierarchy is the relation to the self; the soul seeks happiness for the self, and through the relation to self. The soul doesn't desire to please others, and it also doesn't want to use others for its happiness. The soul simply exists in and of itself, neither interacting with others nor using them for its happiness. This stage of existence is sometimes called *Brahman*. There is pleasure in the understanding of the self, but it is considered inferior to the other relations that create even higher types of happiness.

Spiritually, the relationship of appreciation and gratitude is higher than the self-relation; here, one expresses thankfulness for what has received, but the relation ends with appreciation. The grateful person in the relation of gratitude doesn't repay the favor by serving the person from whom he received the favor. The servitor relationship is higher than that of gratitude because now a person grows beyond feeling gratitude and decides to do something about it—i.e. repaying the person from whom he has previously received the favor. Of course, to repay the debt, the person must know how to repay, but the servitor does not know how to satisfy the master for whom he feels the gratitude. The servitor asks the master about what he can do to repay the debt, and the decision of what the servitor will provide depends on the master. Note that this 'service' is voluntary—i.e. driven by gratitude—different from the material master-servant relationship where the master may use the servant against the servant's desire and the servant may have no choice but to fulfill the demand. While the master-servant relation is imbued with material connotations of exploitation, it is only because we don't see the hierarchy, namely that this servitude follows a deep appreciation and gratitude and is performed because the grateful ask to give something.

The relation of friendship is higher than that of servitude because the friend doesn't just ask the other person what is required; he voluntarily offers advice and action. Besides, a friend doesn't consider himself obliged to do what his friend asks; he might also sometimes overrule the friend's ask because he considers it inappropriate for the friend's interest. There can be a difference of opinion between friends, even regarding what is good for the other person. This difference is based on a deep knowledge of the friend's needs, and a judgment of what makes them happy, in the given situation. For instance, a friend will do things for a friend even without being asked to do so, and sometimes even after being told not to take the trouble in doing it. Unlike the servant who does things that are asked for, a friend does things that were not asked for because he knows that the friend would not ask for those favors if he considers that activity an inconvenience to his friend.

The parental relation is higher than friendship because the hesitation from the perceived inconvenience caused to a friend is replaced by entitlement to demand an action from others. The child, for instance, feels entitled to demand from the parent, and the parent feels entitled to force action on the child. The proximity of the relation is such that one doesn't feel embarrassed to ask for something, or that asking the other person may result in an inconvenience. Nevertheless, the parent-child relationship involves a 'generation gap' due to which neither party shares their deepest feelings with the other. They are closer to each other than friends, but there is still a distance between the two due to which they hold back their innermost feelings.

The conjugal relationship is higher than the parental relation because the distance created by a 'generation gap' is gone. The partners in a conjugal relationship don't feel the need to hold back anything from each other. They are prepared to share their deepest desires, feelings, goals, and purposes, and seek fulfillment from the other party. They are emotionally 'naked' for each other because there is nothing to hide, as the innermost feelings are openly disclosed in the utmost confidence. One generally doesn't become emotionally 'naked' in the relation toward parents, friends, servants, or distant appreciators. In that sense, there is nothing higher than the conjugal relationship.

The material relationships are perverted reflections of the above spiritual counterparts. The perversion is that one is primarily in the relationship to the self, and everything else is seen as the way to fulfill one's own happiness. In the spiritual relation, the relation to the other grows out of the self-relation due to *love*—i.e. a person feels greater happiness in doing something for the other than in doing the same thing for oneself. The material relation also grows out of the self-relation but due to *selfishness*—i.e. a person feels that nothing could be better than doing something for fulfilling oneself.

Thus, in the material relationships, those who appreciate others do not truly feel indebted for what they have received; they like what they have received, but they want more of it, and their appreciation is contingent on the continued receipt of what lead to the gratitude. If that reception is stopped, the gratitude disappears as one doesn't feel eternally obliged for the past.

Similarly, the servant works for a master, but not because he truly wants to serve; the service is because the servant is compensated for his service, and if the compensation stops, the service also ends. The friends ask each other for favors even if inconvenient for the other person to fulfill, but they themselves don't take the inconvenience for the others. There is not enough hesitation in asking, but if a hesitant friend has breached that hesitation, their unsympathetic friend may easily deny the request not realizing how hard it was to even ask for a favor. The parents also don't care enough about the children, especially if it is inconvenient or hard on themselves. Most parents, for example, do not risk their financial future for the sake of their children; they don't sacrifice their personal careers even when it might be beneficial to their children; many parents leave their children to their fate in order to find 'love'. Finally, in the conjugal relationships most couples hesitate to tell their innermost secrets to their partners because it makes them vulnerable. They are also not prepared to go the extra mile to make each other happy; marriages are mostly 'agreements' of what one will give in order to take something else, and couples often 'calculate' what they have taken and given.

Owing to these facts, the self-relationship is considered the highest among the material relationships because it is the least selfish of all—a person is satisfied with the self, and although he doesn't contribute to anyone else, he also doesn't use anyone else for their ulterior purposes. All successive relations involve a sense of entitlement to receive but not a commensurate loving responsibility to reciprocate, or gratitude for having received.

Thus, people become more demanding of each other, but if their demands are unfulfilled, they remain sullen about their disappointments, unwilling to consider the happiness of the other person in the fear that their kindness would likely be exploited by the unscrupulous. The greater the proximity of the relation, the greater tends to be the dissatisfaction. For instance, one wouldn't mind losing some fans or silent appreciators. One is somewhat unhappy on losing an employee or servant, but these are easily replaced. One is relatively unhappier on losing a friend, but friends can be replaced by other companions even if they are not true friends. The breakaway from parents or children causes greater pain—especially when one is very young or very old—and although the pain might linger throughout one's life, its intensity declines with distance. The break in one's marriage causes the greatest pain of all because each person in the relationship has been very vulnerable, and disappointment after one has exposed oneself to the other is hurtful because it constitutes the deepest form of breach in trust and faith.

The spiritual and material relationships are inverted because the former is founded on gratitude while the latter is based on selfishness. The relationship to the self exists between the two and it is considered spiritual, but only in a narrow sense. The soul originally exists in this state—having a relation to the self which creates self-awareness—but not involved in neither gratitude nor selfishness. The self-relation is eternal because we never forget our existence, nor do we ever truly stop thinking about our own happiness and interest. However, the commitment to gratitude or selfishness can change—i.e. a person may decide to serve others or exploit others for their happiness.

Equality is a False Idea

Every relationship has two sides. In the master-servant relation, the two roles are master and servant. In a marriage, the roles are husband and wife. In a parental relation there is parent and child. The relation is something that exists *in between* two persons, and it creates a *pair* of roles; we cannot define a child without a parent, a husband without a wife. These are co-created and must co-exist; if one of them disappears, the other disappears as well.

This is important in the study of relations because generally we never think of *objects* as being connected in this way. The fact is that even material properties are defined relationally. For instance, 'red' is defined only in relation to 'yellow' and 'blue'; 'bitter' is defined through its contrast to 'sweet' and 'sour'; 'morning' is defined through its distinction from 'afternoon' and 'night'. You cannot call something 'hot' without calling something else 'cold', and in that sense, you can never define properties individually. To study relationships, we must first understand this new way of thinking about material properties in which nothing exists just by itself, but only through a conceptual distinction to the other. We can recall the tree hierarchy to understand the nature of these connections. In the case of material properties, the individual properties are like the leaves connected to a branch. For example, 'red' and 'blue' are connected through a higher property 'color'; 'bitter' and 'sweet' are related through a higher property 'taste'. The higher property is necessarily more abstract than the properties it connects. Similarly, 'husband' and 'wife' are related via a 'marriage', while 'master' and 'servant' are linked via 'employment'. Thus, we can speak about a relationship—e.g. 'marriage' as a single entity, while 'husband' and 'wife' as two aspects of that relation, such that if the 'marriage' is dissolved, then the 'husband' and 'wife' disappear.

A relationship is therefore one thing or many things, depending on how one looks at the tree hierarchy. It is one thing if we look at the higher-level reality in the tree hierarchy, and many things if we see lower reality. And yet the lower reality is only defined collectively rather than individually because they are related by a higher reality, which constitutes their relation. This is not a unique fact about human relations, it is not even just a fact about ordinary concepts. Rather, all these are consequences of the tree hierarchy, which means that the individuals don't just 'enter' a relationship; they are also *defined* by that relation, and their nature is altered by a relation change.

This idea seems problematic because we think of 'husband' and 'wife' as real things, but we never see 'marriage' as a real material entity—i.e. per-ceivable through the senses. And yet, if you could not postulate the reality of 'gender' and 'marriage', then you could not also employ concepts such as 'man', 'woman', 'husband', and 'wife'. Therefore, 'gender', 'man', and 'woman' are either simultaneously real or not at all. Likewise, 'marriage', 'husband' and 'wife' are either real at once or not all. The 'marriage' is *higher* than both 'husband' and 'wife', and 'gender' is higher than both 'man' and 'woman' even though we cannot perceive them by the senses; they have to be perceived by the mind, their truth judged by the intellect, their pleasure enjoyed by the ego, and the respective responsibilities understood by the moral sense.

When we count things in a tree hierarchy, we must decide which leaf or branch to count ahead of the other. For instance, if a twig has two leaves, which leaf should we call *first* vs. *second*? Whichever leaf is ordered ahead of the other, also acquires a *higher* position in the tree, even though the higher position is defined relationally to the *lower* position. This seems counterintu-itive because in forming a relation, we tend to think that the related entities are at the same *level*. But, factually, we must solve two problems— (1) that they are defined mutually by a relation, and (2) they must be distinguished, ordered, and finally counted. These two are however not distinct problems, although they appear to be distinct if we begin in the notion of independent objects, which are then related, and which can then be counted in arbi-trary orders equally well. If instead we begin with the understanding that the objects are conceptual, their relations are mutually defined via a hierar-chy, then we can also see why the entities connected through a relation can-not be at the same level. Rather, just as the relation 'employment' is higher than 'employer' and 'employed', similarly, one of the two— 'employer' or 'employed'—must be higher, if we must distinguish, order, and count them.

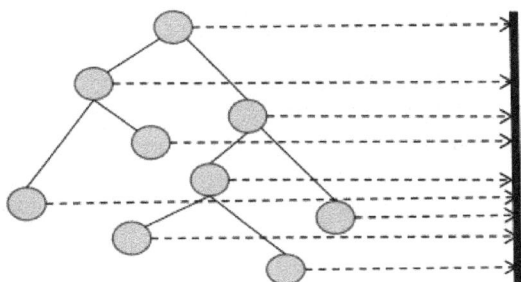

Figure-4 Linear Hierarchy in an Inverted Tree

In other words, no two branches, twigs, or leaves in a tree are at the same *level*. Always, one branch is higher than the other, even though they are produced from the same root, and therefore 'children' of the root. We can say that no two children are the same; always one child will be older than the other children (even if they are 'twins'). The older child is logically prior relative to the younger children in the act of counting the progeny; hence, while counting the children, we will always count in the order they were born.

This fact is important to understand the issues in modern egalitarian societies, which treat all people as being equal. The fact is that no two people are equal; always one person is higher than the other, and it is due to this higher position that we can count them in order, and that order reflects a *natural* and *objective* property. The supposed equality is contrary to natural principles of organization, because we still have to count people, but we have no natural way of counting them. Thus, each person—if he begins the counting—would also begin from themselves, and count others who are 'closer' to him ahead of those who are 'farther' than him. Effectively, there are as many *reference frames*[1] of counting as there are observers, and each person's counting is true just for themselves because the others cannot agree, and society must rely only on the principle of relativism and agreeing to disagree. Since we cannot truly organize anything if everyone disagrees with each other, the need arises to obtain majoritarian opinions and views, which are then enforced upon the rest of the population—even if they disagree.

This is the essence of the contradiction in modern society where we articulate each person's individuality and freedom to think however they like, but then we subjugate that individuality to majority opinion. Ultimately, most people must either think like the majority or be forced to do so by the majoritarian thinking. In the limiting case, everyone must think in the same way—which creates the universal reference frame by which everything has to be counted. We cannot effectively organize society via a relative viewpoint. Even if we acknowledge relativism, we must adopt a majoritarian view, which then grows larger and larger until it eliminates all contrarian views, unless of course, it is overthrown by yet another universalizing viewpoint.

The question is never between individual vs. universal because there is always a universal. The question is whether we chose that universal correctly or incorrectly. In other words, each person is entitled to count with themselves as the origin, but that counting is not necessarily real and objective, although there must be a starting point in some observer which produces the objective count. There is hence universalism only because there is a unique observer from whose viewpoint the universe must be described ideally and objectively. Other relative viewpoints can exist, but they are only subjective illusions if they disagree with the ideal and universal viewpoint about reality. Universal and individual are therefore reconciled when the universal view is produced by the vision of a specific individual—the highest individual—and the other individuals accept that universal viewpoint as the truth.

This fact has specific implications for all relationships, namely that there is no relationship of equality. In every relationship, there must be a higher and a lower. All relations are different forms of the master-servant association; although the difference between the two can keep decreasing, it can never be zero to create equality, because that means we lose the ability to order, count, and know the truth. If each person counts with themselves as the origin, then we can never reconcile between different viewpoints. Different perspectives can only be reconciled if there is indeed a hierarchal tree defined from the perspective of a root, and the various trunks, branches, twigs, and leaves count the reality by becoming aware of the tree's root. Their individuality is that they are situated on a specific branch or leaf and see the tree from their specific viewpoint, but their perspective is fully in accord with the universal perspective, including their own position on the tree.

The supposed equality between men, or between men and women, is an illusion that results from not recognizing that there is a universal hierarchy, and everyone has a position on that hierarchy. By rejecting that hierarchy and producing diverging versions of truth we produce conflicting accounts of reality, and as long as that conflict exists, there cannot be emotionally satisfying relationships because each person considers themselves the origin of their world, and they cannot agree on the real origin, because no one wants to accept that they are situated lower down in the universal hierarchy.

The Origin of Male and Female

We have seen the nature of three trees, rooted in the soul's capacity for *sat*, *chit*, and *ananda*. But there are many individual souls, who are also parts of a universal tree, which is different from the tree of material reality. Vedic philosophy describes that there are three dominant types of trees or branches of a single encompassing tree— (1) the material world, (2) the spiritual world, and (3) the souls. Since the souls are distinct from both matter and spirit, they can either overlap with the material or spiritual worlds or stay apart from both. We can imagine this overlap like leaves from two separate tree branches coming in proximity of each other. The soul by itself can only know itself, and this self-knowledge is called *Brahman*, which lies midway between the spiritual and material worlds, where the soul can also know other souls. In that sense, the soul is not 'spirit', which is defined as the eternal knowledge and pleasure obtained by knowing others. The soul can, however, be situated in the spiritual world, quite like in the material world.

All the branches of the universal tree comprising matter, spirit, and soul, are emanated from a root, which is also called the Supreme Soul, or God. God is also a soul, and He also has the three properties—*sat*, *chit*, and *ananda*. His *sat* is His relationship to Himself which leads to His self-awareness. Through this awareness, He comes to know of His nature, and this nature is the original six concepts namely knowledge, beauty, power, fame, wealth, and renunciation. There are many beautiful objects in this world, but there is also the idea of Beauty Itself. Similarly, there are many instances of wealth and power, but there is also the idea of Wealth Itself, and Power Itself. God is these original ideas, which constitute His *chit*. Through His awareness—*sat*—He discovers the *chit*—or the nature of the original concepts. And through this awareness, He enjoys His self-knowledge—the original *ananda*.

Vedic philosophy, at this point, draws a distinction between two aspects of God—which are designated as *male* and *female*. The female is called His *śakti* and becomes the basis of His experience. In the case of *sat*, the *śakti* is called *bhūti-śakti* or the power of Being, by which He becomes aware of Himself and experiences His own existence. The *kriya-śakti* is His power of understanding and action, which we perceive as the senses of knowledge and action, and it leads to conceptual knowledge of the six original concepts. There are, hence, those original concepts, and then there is the experience of the concepts. Finally, *māyā-śakti* is the desire for something, which creates happiness. The *male* aspect of God is the person, concept, and pleasure capacity, but the *female* aspect of God is the power of awareness, the power of understanding and action, and the power of desire. God is an individual (*sat*) with six original qualities—knowledge, beauty, power, fame, wealth, and renunciation (*chit*). And He has the capacity to enjoy (*ananda*). But the existence of a person with qualities and the capacity to enjoy doesn't entail self-awareness, knowledge, and pleasure, because the power of awareness, understanding, and desire is His *śakti*—separate from God. When God meets His *śakti*, the person combines with the power of awareness to become self-aware. The concept combines with the power of knowledge to create cognition. The potential for action combines with the power of action to create activity. And the ability to enjoy combines with desire to create pleasure.

In this way, the *sat*, *chit*, and *ananda* of the soul is divided into male and female components, where the male is the object of awareness, knowledge, and pleasure, and the female is the power by which He is aware, knows, acts, and enjoys. Both male and female are thus described as *sat-chit-ananda*, but they are two components that combine to create *experience*. The experience comprises of an object, and the power of knowing that object. The object is male, and the power is female. God is therefore both male and female, because His experience is created from the combination of male and female. The male and the female are in one sense individuals and therefore separate. And yet, they are always combined as powerful and power to create the experience. We can also say that the experience is produced from the male-female combination, although the powerful and the power are distinct persons.

Vedic philosophy describes the origin of sexuality in which God and His power mate to create experience. The spiritual and material worlds, along with the souls, are byproducts of this mating—i.e. they are parts of God's experience. The original male and female are the two cotyledons of a seed—joined and yet separate. But when they combine, the seed produces a tree of matter, spirit, and soul. Every part of this tree carries the same twin cotyledons by which the tree expands into further branches, twigs, and leaves.

We have seen previously that the tree develops due to *prāna* where the higher node connects the lower nodes (if these already existed). The *prāna* also creates the lower nodes (if they did not already exist). We have also seen how *prāna* is responsible for creating the trees of *sat, chit,* and *ananda*. In other words, to create the tree, we need two things—a root, and the *prāna* which expands the root into its child nodes. This *prāna* is God's *śakti* and it can be understood in two ways. First, the *śakti* creates child nodes of the tree. Second, the *śakti* creates the experience. God's experience is His 'children'. God is the father—the original object—and the child is the experience of this object, created by His power of awareness. The notable thing here is that God is not becoming aware of a pre-existing reality. Rather, by His power, He *creates* this reality. Therefore, the creation is sometimes called His "dream" or "imagination". The father and the child are connected by the *śakti*—who is said to be the 'mother' responsible for creating the child from the father. For the most part, the *śakti* is sufficient to explain the manifest world, because the *śakti* is the primary cause for the successive expansions of the root. God becomes important when we speak of the origin or root prior to this manifestation. The soul too is a 'creation' from the Supreme Soul, although the creation is eternal and therefore, we cannot find a time in the past in which the soul did not exist, or a point in the future when it will cease to be. In that sense, the soul is the 'child' of God—he was created as God's experience.

The *śakti* available to God to create His self-awareness, knowledge, and pleasure is also available to the soul, by which he creates his own experience—mind, and body. Therefore, we can say that the soul too combines with the *śakti*—as male and female—to create his experience. Owing to this fact, the soul is sometimes called a *puruṣa* or "man" and material energy is described as *prakriti* or "creatrix". The fact is that the power available to the soul—called *prakriti*—is not the soul's power. It is rather God's power, delegated to the soul for his awareness, creativity, and pleasure. Ideally, the soul must employ this power for God's awareness, knowledge, and pleasure, and this ideal situation is called the *spiritual world*. When the soul presumes that the power delegated to him by God is now his own, and can therefore be utilized for his awareness, knowledge, and pleasure, the situation is called the *material world*. In between these extremes is the situation in which the soul neither uses the power for God's pleasure nor his own pleasure. In a sense, the power lies dormant and unutilized; we can say that the two cotyledons of the seed exist side by side, but they do not combine to create experience.

Therefore, the soul is not to be referred as a "he", regardless of the gender of the mind-body, because the mind-body is the "she" of the soul. We can say that the soul is the master of the mind-body and uses the mind-body to know and enjoy the world. In another sense, however, the soul can be referred to as a "she" (regardless of the gender of the mind-body) because the ideal expectation of the soul is to use God's *śakti* for God's awareness, knowledge, and pleasure, thus acting as the *śakti* acts in relation to God. Thus, in the spiritual world, the soul is a "female" (regardless of the mind-body gender) and in the material world the soul acts as a "male" (again, regardless of the mind-body gender). Depending on the context, the soul can be referred to either as "he" or "she", indicating the non-ideal and ideal behaviors.

In self-knowledge, the male and the female and hence the forms of God which are absorbed in their own self-realization are described as male-female combinations. However, when the male wants to know or create something other than his self, he still relies on the *śakti* or the female, because the *śakti* is the ability or the power to relate, know, act, and enjoy.

When a soul has a predominantly 'known' tendency, he has a masculine nature, whereby he wants to expand aspects of his self into children created in his image. But when a soul has a dominantly 'knower' tendency, it has a feminine tendency, by which she selects aspects of the male to be created in his image. The fact is that no soul is purely male or female because originally the soul is created in God's image although by a mother—the *śakti*. Nevertheless, there can be a difference of emphasis—in either spirit or matter—in which either the male defines which aspects of the self are known, or the female determines which aspects of the male she wants to be known. The difference between the two is subtle because both choices determine what becomes visible and what remains hidden, but they are made from the view of the knower or the known. Thus, the Original Being is attracted to the self and by that attraction is divided into two—one male and the other female.

The 'created' soul is always subordinate to the Supreme Soul and His *śakti* and can never become independent of the two because the soul doesn't have his own *śakti*—he only has the delegated power of the Supreme Soul. The enjoyment of the soul, therefore, depends on God's will by which His *śakti* is available to the soul to relate, know, act, and enjoy. If this *śakti* is not available, despite being the known, the soul cannot become the knower. If the *śakti* is withdrawn from the soul, all experiences cease to exist. In most religions, the soul is said to be the 'child' of God, who is considered the 'father' of the soul, but these religions do not acknowledge the importance of a 'mother'. This is a unique facet of Vedic philosophy, which constitutes a personalist theory of creation—both matter and spirit—in which God is both male, and yet His *śakti* is female, both are together the cause of everything else. The soul becomes successful in his endeavors when he surrenders to God because by that surrender, he obtains the necessary *śakti* to be successful.

The Internal vs. External Distinction

The power of relating, knowing, acting, and enjoying is divided into two parts—the 'internal' and 'external' *śakti*. The 'internal' *śakti* is that by which God (and all the souls) relate to themselves, know themselves, serve themselves, and enjoy themselves. The 'external' *śakti* is that by which a soul relates to other souls, knows about the others, serves them, and enjoys that experience. When God focuses on His self-awareness, the original form of *puruṣa* and *prakriti* are called *Kṛṣṇa* and *Hara*. Similarly, when God focuses on the awareness of the other, the original form of *puruṣa* and *prakriti* are called *Rāma* and *Ramā*. In the material creation, similarly, *Narayana* and *Lakshmi* are the *puruṣa* and *prakriti* of self-awareness, while *Shiva* and *Pārvati* are the *puruṣa* and *prakriti* of external experience. Vedic texts provide a detailed theology of why God manifests in many forms; its essence is that God is satisfied in Himself due to his 'internal' *śakti* of self-awareness. However, He creates the world—the awareness of the 'other'—through His 'external' energy.

The difference between the 'internal' and the 'external' experiences is like a creative person who first imagines a reality in his own image, creating the pleasure of this imagination. He might then decide to express this imagination into an external reality as his representation. The externalization of the ideas follows the ideas, and the external experience is created after the internal one. Consequently, *Kṛṣṇa* and *Hara* are the primordial forms of God Who create an internal experience and *Rāma* and *Ramā* externalize this experience. Thus, what is seen internally also becomes externally visible.

There is considerable confusion in the use of the words 'internal' and 'external' among the different preceptors and commentators on Vedic texts because there are two kinds of meanings associated with them. The first meaning of 'internal' and 'external' is *self* and *other*; the knowledge of the self is 'internal' because it is obtained through first-person experience, while the knowledge of the other is 'external' and obtained through third-person experience. The second meaning of 'internal' and 'external' is assertion and negation—or what something *is* and what it is *not*. What something *is* constitutes the meaning of 'internal', but what it is *not* embodies all that lies 'external' to that thing. If the assertion is that the soul is eternal, knowledgeable, and happy, then the negation would be that it is temporary, ignorant, or unhappy. The second distinction creates the material vs. spiritual worlds. The material world, for instance, is said to be a bad dream for *Narayana*. The 'dream' is temporary, what is dreamt is false, and since the dream is bad, the experience is not pleasing. Thus, the temporary, ignorant, and unhappy world is created by negating the world of truth, eternity, and happiness. We can say that the former type of world is 'internal', while the later type of world is 'external'.

There is hence an 'internal' vs. 'external' distinction that demarcates the spiritual truth, right, and good, from the material temporariness, falsities, and suffering. There is also an 'internal' vs. 'external' that demarcates the self from the other. A school of Vedanta—called *Advaita* philosophy—confuses these two kinds of distinctions and claims that the rejection of material temporariness, falsity, and suffering is also the rejection of the other, which means that there is nothing besides the self. The self is true, right, and good, but anything besides the self is temporary, false, and painful. Other Vedanta schools—called *Vaishnava* philosophy—maintain the distinction between true vs. false, and the self vs. other. In this philosophy, there are two worlds—based on true and false—which have two kinds of experiences: the self and the other. The rejection of the material world doesn't mean the dissolution of the soul's individuality—i.e. the distinction between the self and the other.

But the picture is not yet complete because there is yet another meaning of 'internal' vs. 'external'—selfishness vs. love. The selfishness is 'internal' and love is 'external'. Thus, given a relation, you can either seek your pleasure, or the pleasure of the other. There can be selfish pleasure even with truth and eternity, just as there can be love with temporary falsities. For instance, material love is based on temporary and false ideas—e.g. the skin-deep beauty of a person—just as there is spiritual love based on the eternal truths about the soul's nature. Similarly, there is material selfishness based on temporary and false ideas—e.g. using the other person's skin-deep beauty for sense plea-sure—just as there is spiritual selfishness based on the soul's true nature, by which the soul chooses the relationship and activity to make oneself happy (rather than serving to make someone else happy).

The contrast between the material and spiritual selfishness is subtle but can be described by an example. If you are not yet married, you will seek a partner who is most compatible to your needs, and at this time the focus is not making the prospective partner happy, but on making yourself happy. If you think that a given partner will not make you happy, you will seek another partner. But if you are married, you are expected to discard that selfishness—where you prioritized your happiness—and adopt a loving atti-tude where you must do things that makes the partner happy. Before the marriage, you are expected to be selfish and find the right partner that fits your needs. But after the marriage you are expected to be loving and meet the needs of the partner, sacrificing your happiness. If the fit between the part-ners is perfect, even the selfish need to seek one's own happiness would still produce happiness. The problem only emerges if one person changes their desires, which then produces a relationship mismatch, at which point either the relationship must break down or result in unhappiness. Such changes are the primary reason for a soul's fall from the spiritual world—because the relation was chosen based on a selfish need, and there was no willingness to compromise. It is like a marriage that seems perfectly compatible at the start, but over time the partners develop different interests or viewpoints and the marriage breaks apart. Conversely, in the unselfish relation, both partners are willing to compromise on change, and make the other person happy. This creates infinitely greater stability—if both sides are equally compromising—and the possibility of a breakaway (e.g. a fall) is minimized considerably.

While the material and spiritual worlds are created by assertion and nega-tion of *sat*, *chit*, and *ananda*, and the different parts of these worlds are meant for self-awareness and other-awareness, the inhabitants of these worlds—the souls—are created from the differences in their respective desires for pleasure through self-interest or loving-care. This split can also be call 'internal' (self-ish) and 'external' (love), but if the selfish vs. loving dichotomy is equated with the false vs. truth, or the self vs. other dichotomies, then one arrives at the false conclusion that spirituality is being selfish (loving oneself) because only the self is the truth, and that truth is eternal. The fact is that self-experi-ence is selfish, although it can be true and eternal. There is also the experience of others—with a selfish aim—which may be true and eternal. Finally, there is the loving experience of the other which can be true and eternal, in which one sacrifices their selfishness to serve others.

The 'internal' vs. 'external' distinction therefore has three kinds of meanings— (1) true vs. false, eternal vs. temporary, and happiness vs. suffering, (2) self vs. other, and (3) selfish vs. altruistic. The last two seem similar, but they are not, because one can be selfish even in relationship to others (i.e. using them for one's ends), and one can be altruistic even in self-absorption (i.e. remaining self-satisfied and allowing others to take away what was rightfully yours). By knowing these distinctions, we can see how a single self creates variety by desiring to know itself and the others, by knowing oneself as one is and as one is not, and by enjoying the selfish or altruistic pleasures.

The above distinctions are employed in Vedic philosophy to construct a cosmology based on divisions of conscious experience. At the highest level is the distinction between material and spiritual realms; the material realm is that which is temporary, false, and painful, while the spiritual realm is that which is eternal, true, and happy. Within this material realm are two parts, comprising of self-knowledge and other-knowledge. What we call the 'material world' is the realm of other-knowledge, and it is false because it is *inconsistent*—you cannot create harmony in this world due to *duality* or oppositions. The other part of the material realm is self-knowledge, in which only I exist, only I know myself, and only I can enjoy with myself—this is called *Brahman*. This is also false realization because it is *incomplete* although not *inconsistent* because it fails to recognize the existence of other souls and the Supreme Soul. Once we cross these two types of knowledge, we arrive at the realm of truth, eternity, and happiness, in which there is both consistency and completeness—namely, you can see yourself, see other souls, and see the Supreme Soul, and all these living entities exist in mutual harmony with each other. However, now, there is a further division inside this realm based on selfishness and altruism. The 'liberated' realm called *Vaikuṇṭha* is the realm of selfish spirituality—i.e. happiness for the self—in which the soul chooses the right type of relation and activity in order to fit its innate need for happiness. The 'devoted' realm called *Goloka* is that of altruistic spirituality—i.e. happiness for the other—the soul doesn't pick its own relation and activity and does what will make the others happy in the relation they desire.

This type of cosmology is not based on empirical observation. It is rather based on the understanding of the soul and its various proclivities. All the varieties of places, times, circumstances, objects, activities, and pleasures are simply consequences of the fact that the soul's tendencies of *sat, chit,* and *ananda* divide and combine infinitely, thereby creating infinite variety, although that variety can still be logically *classified* into different realms. In that sense, the material world has infinite possibilities and yet it is distinct from other infinite worlds. These infinities are logical realms and hence they don't overlap or run into each other, although the soul can 'move' from one realm to the other, crossing over from one infinity to another. We cannot understand how the soul moves in this way until we understand the nature of the soul, and why the types of worlds are created simply from the proclivities of the Supreme Soul and satisfy the varied proclivities in the individual souls.

The Original Personality Archetypes

Kṛṣṇa is the original narcissistic soul[2] and *Hara* is His energy—She is the power by which *Kṛṣṇa* becomes aware of Himself, knows Himself, and enjoys Himself. *Kṛṣṇa's* attraction to Himself is His narcissism—He is so confident about His attractiveness that He doesn't need anyone else, and yet He attracts everyone by His self-love. Even in the present world the most attractive people are generally narcissists—they are charming and self-confident, and they become the center of attraction with the opposite sex. They are overrepresented where being the center of attraction is important, such as entertainment and politics. Women are inexorably drawn to narcissistic men because they imagine that if he is so satisfied in himself then he must be worth loving. The self-absorbed man appears to be hiding something precious; others can't figure out how someone could love themselves so much—which makes him a worthy treasure hunt. Such men, while very charming, are also hard to get, and the hardship in owning them makes the pursuit exhilarating.

Hara is the embodiment of the love of a self-absorbed *Kṛṣṇa.* While *Kṛṣṇa* is very attractive, it is enhanced by his narcissism, and since that self-love is *Hara,* She makes *Kṛṣṇa* seem more attractive. We might say that *Kṛṣṇa* appears most attractive because the most discerning woman is so inexorably attracted to Him, and Her love makes everyone want Him even more. This idea is well-known even in the present world where many women are drawn to a man if a very attractive woman chooses that man first. The thinking is that if such an attractive and loving woman wants to be with some man, then he must indeed be worthy of that love and attention. Thus, the attraction of a beautiful woman toward a man attracts other beautiful women. Conversely, if a man sees another man—more attractive than himself—pursuing a woman, he discards the pursuit because he doesn't want to be second best.

Thus, men and women behave differently—an attractive woman's love attracts other women to the same man (even if they are less attractive), but an attractive man's love repels other men from that woman (if they are less attractive). If an attractive woman loves a man, a lot of women gather around that man. But if an attractive man loves a woman, all the other men leave that man alone. Thus, all the women are attracted to *Kṛṣṇa* because *Hara* loves Him so much. But when the other men see *Kṛṣṇa* in love with *Hara*, they leave Him alone. As a result, *Kṛṣṇa* is surrounded by many women because the other women are attracted to *Kṛṣṇa* due to *Hara*'s love while the other men have already left[3] due to the nature of men described above. *Kṛṣṇa* and *Hara* are inseparable because He is the self and She is the love of that self.

A woman enjoys the fact that her man is incredibly attractive to other women, and yet resents it if the man is also attracted to those women. This contradiction underlies the feminine psychology in which a woman wants to "show off" her man but doesn't want him to look at anyone else. A man, on the other hand, will be immediately upset if another man looks at his woman. Thus, after all the men have left an attractive man to be with many women, a new dynamic between women is created—they compete for a man's attention and resent the presence of other women, while concurrently loving the fact that other women are also equally attracted to the same man.

This competitive-cooperative dynamic is the basis of the pastimes between *Kṛṣṇa* and the *gopis* who are in competition with each other and yet their attraction to *Kṛṣṇa* grows because of the attraction of the other *gopis*. Even though *Kṛṣṇa* is with many women, no woman wants to leave Him, and yet they compete for *Kṛṣṇa*'s attention. Every woman's love enhances the other women's love—this constitutes their cooperation. However, once that love has been enhanced, they also crave for *Kṛṣṇa* attention—this is their competition. This bitter-sweet relationship between *Kṛṣṇa* and the *gopis* is the pinnacle of spiritual understanding in *Gaudīya Vaishnava Vedanta*[4].

Rāma (also called Balarama) is the original compassionate person who loves others, and *Ramā* is His energy—She fulfills all *Rāma*'s compassionate desires because She loves the fact that *Rāma* loves others so much that He is not hesitant to give away what He has. Many women are attracted to the charitable, giving, altruistic, and compassionate men because it is obvious that they have such bounty that they are not afraid or reluctant to give it to others. In fact, *Ramā* assists *Rāma* by giving away all His bounties and is hence the charitable, compassionate, and altruistic energy of *Rāma*. *Ramā* enjoys the fact that the bounty of *Rāma* is so unlimited that no matter how much She distributes it, it will never end. Her man is unlimitedly resourceful, and She can therefore be infinitely charitable and loving toward the other.

The Role of the Male and the Female

The manipulative man portrays his narcissistic and kindhearted personality alternately. He first gains the attention of a woman by appearing to be resourceful, kind, and giving, but having obtained the woman's attention, he pretends to be self-absorbed, busy, and narcissistic. The man's self-love drives the woman crazy, and getting the woman is no longer a man's project; in fact, getting the man is the woman's prerogative. Conversely, a manipulative woman pretends to be narcissistic and spends time making herself attractive and plays very hard to get. But once she has gotten the attention of the man she wants, she pretends to be resourceful, kind and giving, to hold the man she wants. The blend of narcissism and generosity is hard to resist for both men and women, but it plays in opposite ways for each of them.

Kṛṣṇa is also an expert manipulator. He first garners the attention of women by performing chivalrous deeds and acting in a protective and generous manner. But once He has obtained that attention, He pretends to be self-absorbed and busy, driving the *gopis* mad in His love. The *gopis* similarly appear to be narcissistic and spend great endeavors in dressing up and making themselves attractive, pretending to be busy with their girlfriends and objecting to all kinds of overtures of love from *Kṛṣṇa*, often complaining to His parents about how *Kṛṣṇa* behaves in indecent and provocative ways towards them. But once they have obtained *Kṛṣṇa*'s attention, they become very loving toward Him, generously offering him all that He might desire.

Kṛṣṇa and *Hara* are not the creators of the spiritual world, because they are primarily absorbed in the selfish pursuit of self-love. The spiritual world is created by *Rāma* and *Ramā*, who are the compassionate givers of unlimited bounty. Similarly, *Narayana* and *Lakshmi* are not the creators of the material world; they are rather absorbed in their self-love produced out of temporary and imaginary austerity. The material world is created by *Shiva* and *Pārvati*. As a result, Vedic philosophy is often misunderstood because it emphasizes different forms—sometimes male and other times female, sometimes *Narayana* and other times *Shiva*, sometimes *Vishnu* (who expands from *Rāma*) and at other times *Kṛṣṇa*. These are not contradictory descriptions because ultimately there is only one reality from which the distinction between true and false, self and other, selfish and altruistic, produces many varieties.

Since there are three kinds of trees, the *śakti* is sometimes divided into three parts—called *bhūti-śakti* (the power of awareness which produces the souls from God), *kriya-śakti* (the power of cognition and activity which creates the body of the soul), and *māyā-śakti* (the power of pleasure which produces a personality of the soul). The three *śakti* produce the three trees, which are the causes of all experience—object, awareness, and pleasure. We can say that the soul has three 'mothers' because of its three properties of eternity, cognition, and happiness. But we can also say that there is one 'mother' who has the above three properties. This 'mother' is, in an everyday sense, that power by which we become aware, know the world, and enjoy the knowledge of reality. In another sense, this 'mother' connects us to the original 'father'—God. Accordingly, the same 'mother' is the cause of all that we can see, as well as the process and path by which to realize God.

The relationship between the original 'father' and 'mother' is the source of all subsequent relations; the cognition and activity in that relationship is the source of all further concepts and actions; the pleasure enjoyed in that relation is the source of all subsequent types of enjoyments. Ultimately, therefore, everything that exists can be understood by the relationship, knowledge, activity, and pleasure of this 'couple'. This is not an ordinary couple, and yet, their relationship, exchanges, and happiness, can be described like an ordinary man-woman couple. This is a distinctive aspect of Vedic philosophy because in it, God is not the creator. Rather, the manifest reality is produced by the mother, but the mother connects this reality to the father as His 'children'.

Numerous types of subsequent varieties in the creation are manifest through a relative difference in the emphasis of male and female. For instance, if the male wants to demonstrate his knowledge, but the female prefers to emphasize wealth, the result will be knowledge about wealth. Conversely, if the male wants to emphasize wealth, and the female prefers knowledge, their combination will result in wealth through knowledge. In this way, both male and female are satisfied, even if their desires are different because they know how to fulfill their desires as well as the other's desires. Still, the male's desire is the first choice, and the female makes the second choice: the male decides *what* he wants, and the female *how* he gets it.

The existence of these six qualities is the basis of the attraction between them: the 'male' wants to be sought based on these qualities, and the 'female' seeks these qualities. The male desires the female's attention by virtue of possessing these qualities, and the female desires the male's attention so that she can associate with someone who has these qualities. The male is the Supreme Object, and the female is the Supreme Knower. The object is incomplete if there is no knower, and the knower is incomplete if there is no object to be known. In that sense, the male and the female are bound together by their mutual need for each other; that need is their attraction and love.

The Material Reflection of Spiritual Archetypes

The *Hara* tendency is manifest in women before they are married—they seek the narcissistic self-absorbed man who would be a prize catch because he is the center of attraction everywhere. The *Ramā* tendency is manifest in women when they have children—they want their man to be resourceful and provide for her children unlimitedly. No woman wants a narcissistic self-absorbed man once she has children. Similarly, women become disinterested in men if they would not be prospectively attractive to other women.

Marriage between men and women becomes problematic because both men and women are expected to be narcissistic before marriage (i.e. looking for the ideal partner for their satisfaction) but altruistic after marriage (i.e. seeking to please their partner more than themselves). Women fall in love with narcissistic, self-absorbed, and hard-to-get men before marriage, but they expect the man to be compassionate and charitable afterward. This expectation proves disappointing because the narcissistic men don't become charitable just because they got married to a woman, while the charitable men don't become narcissistic upon getting married. The beauty in the love of *Kṛṣṇa* and the *gopis* is imperfectly reflected in the men-women relationships in the material world because both men and women don't know how to shift between being self-absorbed and kind-hearted. They know how to do one thing well, but the perfection of love requires the existence of both.

As a result, a couple who falls in love based on their narcissism finds after marriage that their partners expect them to be kind, giving, and tolerant, but that would require a personality change. Similarly, those who get married because the partner is resourceful, kind, and responsible, start seeking romance, but you can't expect a person who isn't absorbed in self-love to appear attractive. Thus, men and women seek the thrill of attraction outside their marriage. The key point is that both men and women seek a combination of narcissism for the person to appear attractive from a distance, and then generosity for the relationship to be enjoyable at proximity. If there is only narcissism, the relation of proximity doesn't work. But if there is only generosity then the attraction to the person dissipates and disappears.

Romantic life is represented by *Kṛṣṇa* and *Hara* while married life is represented by *Rāma* and *Ramā*. *Kṛṣṇa* is dominantly narcissistic and rarely resourceful. *Rāma* is mostly resourceful and rarely narcissistic. *Kṛṣṇa's* resourcefulness is meant only to attract women, but once He has attracted them, the attraction of other women propels His (and other's) love affairs. Conversely, *Rāma's* self-absorption is only to attract women, but once He has attracted the women, then His resourcefulness propels His (and others') love affairs. Both *Kṛṣṇa* and *Rāma* are capable of the same activities but they differ in their relative emphasis. This ability to shift between narcissism and kindness is generally missing in human relationships besides the obvious limitations in their resourcefulness and narcissism. When a man is very resourceful in keeping a woman happy, she likes the things that the man provides, but she craves for a self-absorbed narcissistic man. But when a man is always self-absorbed and doesn't fulfill the woman's needs, she seeks a resourceful man. To sustain a relationship, from a woman's viewpoint, a man must be both resourceful and self-absorbed—at the appropriate times that she needs him to provide and when she seeks romance. But this is practically impossible for any man to achieve. Most men tend to be either always self-absorbed or always generous. Regardless of which extreme the man lives on, it makes the woman unhappy. Anyone who wants both romance and security in a marriage is asking for serious trouble because the selfish person appears attractive but is unable to fulfill other's needs, while the selfless person performs all their duties but still doesn't seem attractive. Yet, people don't get tired of thinking that they will obtain romance within marriage itself, while also leading a life of security, stability, success, and prosperity.

This is due to the latent understanding of divine love in each soul. But instead of seeking that love in relation to *Rāma* or *Kṛṣṇa*, the soul tries to find that love independently, not realizing that we can either excel at narcissism or generosity, not both. The practical needs of day-to-day life require resourceful partners. But the desire for romance requires a person to be impulsive. The impulsive hate the idea of being responsible and resourceful; they like to live life for themselves and not for others. Conversely, the responsible people hate the idea of being impulsive; they like to lead a life of responsibility and accountability, taking care of their family. As a result, you can either obtain a resourceful partner, with little romance, which leads to a marriage in which everyone has all the things they need, but little love in life. Or you can find romantic love, but you might lack the necessities of life.

The Man-Woman Relationship

Typically, every woman seeks the six godly qualities in a man: the man must be attractive (beauty), intelligent (knowledge), powerful (healthy, virile, and protective), famous (well-known and desired by others), generous (kind due to his detachment from things—i.e. ready to give away what he has), and rich (able to provide whatever the woman wants just by asking for it).

Clearly, that list is long, and most men find it unachievable. Since men don't already have what the woman wants, they spend time acquiring knowledge, wealth, fame, power, and beauty, but the pursuit of these attributes takes time away from the woman which frustrates her because she interprets man's pursuit of desirable qualities as lack of interest in her. The man is also frustrated because he was trying to make the woman happy but the pursuit of the things that make her happy makes the woman feel she is not getting the man's attention. The woman may also feel insecure that, as the man becomes rich, powerful, famous, wealthy, and knowledgeable, he is attractive to other women. When a woman feels frustrated (due to lack of attention) and jealous (due to the feeling of insecurity), the man is confused and unhappy. Now he focuses greater time in the pursuit of manly attributes, but the outcome is the opposite: it makes the woman even more frustrated (because more time is spent away from her) and jealous (because the man now seems ever more attractive due to his improving desirability).

If the man doesn't have beauty, power, wealth, fame, and knowledge, then he is not desirable to the woman. But if he spends time in the acquisition of these attributes, he still manages to make the woman feel isolated and jealous. This is the root of most tensions between men and women, and their discord. There is essentially no answer to this problem except that the man must already be powerful, famous, rich, knowledgeable, generous, and beautiful, so that he can spend all his time satisfying the woman, without spending time in the pursuit of such goals. Typically, therefore, a woman is attracted to those who are already successful, rather than those who might be successful in the future, because the woman wishes not to compromise her needs.

Of course, if a woman feels that she cannot easily get a successful man, she often looks for 'potentials' who can, *in the future*, fulfill her needs. This calls into action her 'motherly' instincts and she adopts the prospective man as a 'project' to be completed through encouragement and nurturing. The woman expects that her adopted 'son' will eventually grow up and become a real man, but the son must obey the mother in order for her to grow him into the person she wants him to be. This has given rise to the often-abused adage— "behind every successful man there is a woman". The woman in such cases is a mother figure who nurtures and pampers a man—her 'son'.

If a man is competent to be successful on his own, he will resent a woman 'mothering' him, while the woman feels compelled to control him because she considers him incapable of success without her help. This also leads to discord between the two because the woman tries to control the man—in her imagination, for his own good—while the man resents this control because he considers himself capable and views the woman's control as disrespect and feels unloved for what he is at present. Alternately, the man might be nurtured by the woman for a while, while internally resenting her control, and he either becomes accustomed to the ways of the controlling woman or waits for the right opportunity to find another woman who doesn't mother him— typically after he has already used the 'mother' to be successful.

A growing number of women—*feminists*—have thus decided to relinquish the traditional womanly roles: they don't want to *seek* a man for his wealth, knowledge, fame, power, and knowledge; instead, they want to be just like the man in terms of his traditional attributes. This, however, leads to two kinds of problems. First, the man feels less desired by the woman, so he has even less desire to pursue the qualities that would make him attractive; he feels depressed and unmotivated, and his life languishes in the shame and anger of being unworthy and unloved. Second, the women compete with the men in order to acquire all those desirable attributes, but their success makes the man even less interested in the woman because he already may have many of the things the woman has acquired and wants to be loved for his success, rather than celebrating the woman's success to be his equal.

The woman feels disrespected by this neglect, because in her mind if something made the man desirable then the same thing should make a woman attractive. The man also feels unloved by the woman's success because in his mind she pursues all these goals independently only because he is unable to fulfill them. Feminism, therefore, drives both men and women away from each other. A man seeks those women who will cherish him, but as the women become more successful, they tend to cherish a man much less because they consider themselves equals. Alternately, the men begin to use the women because the man is now unmotivated while the woman is becoming more successful. When the woman realizes that she is being used, she loses respect for the man, because despite her success she expects the man to be *manly*—i.e. more successful, powerful, famous, knowledgeable, and wealthy.

There can never be happiness between man and woman unless the woman realizes that the man she seeks is not the Supreme Object of love, and the man understands that the woman's love is not the Supreme Desire for him. The man cannot—due to his deficiencies—become the perfection in knowledge, beauty, power, fame, and wealth, while also remaining perfectly charitable, kind, and renounced. Similarly, even if the man were to excel in some of these attributes, the woman would find something lacking and not love him adequately. Feminism is not the answer either, because the more a woman is successful, the less she is inclined to respect a man, which means that the man would quit the relation and seek another woman who respects him more. The recipe for happiness is that once a man-woman relationship is made, the woman loves and respects the man regardless of his position, which motivates the man to be more successful in order to keep winning her love and respect, which can then become a self-fulfilling prophecy. This love is not a 'mother' adopting a man-child to grow him into something useful to the woman in the future, because sooner or later the man-child will grow tired of the 'mother' (if he is successful) or become a parasite on the 'mother' (if he is unsuccessful despite the 'mother's' best efforts). The first alternative pushes the man to leave the woman, and the second option forces the woman to leave the man after spending much time on him. Similarly, the man must recognize that a woman seeks a man for his good qualities and unless he becomes a suitable object, he should not expect a woman's love. There is no unrequited love between man and woman; the woman's love is conditional on the man being desirable, and the man's effort toward being that object depends on obtaining the woman's love. If a woman doesn't love her man, she drives the man toward depression. Similarly, if the man doesn't become the object of a woman's desires, he drives a woman toward fear and sadness.

The love of a man and that of a woman are very different—the man is the object of love, and the woman is the seeker of the object. When a woman loves strongly, she desires the man intensely for what he is. When a man loves a woman strongly, he tries to become the object of her desires. If a woman doesn't love and cherish her man after he has provided her with most of what she desires, the woman is cheating the man, and that lack of reciprocation will break the man away from the relationship. Similarly, if a man doesn't provide what the woman desires after she has given him the love and respect he needed, the woman will very likely break away from him.

Relationships and Fate

The real test of a relationship comes when a man is limited by his destiny or *karma* to provide what the woman desires, despite his best efforts. That is the point at which the woman must realize that the man she chose is not the ideal man she wanted, and she should accept her destiny and attempt to love the man to the best of her ability. Both men and women have desires which they can try to fulfill for each other, but these desires may go beyond what a person *deserves* to get in life due to the consequences of their past actions. For a woman to disrespect and not love her man because he is unable to provide what she wants is tantamount to hating or rejecting her own destiny and blaming her fate on the inability of the man. Similarly, for a man to leave a woman because she is dissatisfied with him amounts to hating the woman for his destiny where he is not deserving of the woman's love.

The match between man and woman is not made in heaven. It is made by their *karma* as the consequences of their own past actions. Ideally, a man should provide what a woman wants, but if destiny limits that success, then the woman must recognize it as their collective destiny and continue to cherish her man. Likewise, even if a woman doesn't cherish and love her man, the man should continue to provide her what she needs to the best of his ability. If both men and women are sincere in their efforts, the man-woman relationship will be happy and safe. If either one becomes insincere and expects more than what their own destiny can provide, they will jeopardize the relationship, although they cannot obtain anything more even in a new relationship. The fact is that a woman can uplift a man's condition if she is deserving of a good life, but the man isn't, and a man can uplift a woman even if she was undeserving of a good life, but the man has the ability to provide the good life. Only when both are undeserving, they will share their sorry fate.

There is, hence, no condition under which the relationship should break down if both man and woman are sincere and understanding of each other's limitations, including the limits exerted by their respective fates. The relation breaks when either one of them thinks that they are deserving of something better than what they can get. The guidance for a happy relation is for the woman to reduce her desires and expectations of a man. Similarly, the man must not attempt very hard to fulfill the desires of a woman. Having high expectations is sure to meet failure and trying too hard to achieve the unachievable will surely result in frustration and disappointment. Happy relationships are possible with contentment on the part of the woman and, on the part of the man, detachment from being the object of the woman's love.

This is contrary to the 'romantic' ideology that society perpetrates on the hapless generations, even though the previous generations were consistently unable to find love. We might note that the romantic ideology is inspired by the love of the Divine Couple because the Supreme Male has knowledge, beauty, power, wealth, fame, and renunciation in full, and the Supreme Female has an intense and unmitigated desire for these attributes. Male-female romance tries to mimic the Divine Couple although the males cannot get anywhere close to the perfection of knowledge, beauty, power, wealth, fame, and renunciation, while the females cannot get anywhere close to the intensity of desire for the above-mentioned perfection.

When a man becomes too intellectual, women consider him boring; they would rather prefer someone who is funny, even to the point of being stupid sometimes. If the man is too famous, the woman will consider it infringing her privacy; if the man is not famous, the woman will consider him not respected in society. If the man is too renounced, she will consider him not aggressive enough; if he is not generous enough, she will consider him selfish. If a man has enormous power, a woman will often find him cruel; if he doesn't have enough power, she will consider him weak and timid. If the man has too much beauty, the woman will consider him not rugged enough; if, however, he is too rugged, then he would be considered ugly. If the man has too much wealth, the women will find him snotty; if he doesn't have enough money, he would be considered a pauper. No situation can be considered perfect.

Being perfect and loving the perfect are both difficult in different ways: being perfect requires too much effort, and loving that perfection means seeing oneself as being devoid of perfection. A woman may desire a successful man, but if the man is successful, she will also resent that success because she looks comparatively inferior to him. To love that successful man, the woman must have the capacity to handle the greatness—i.e. the humility that she is relatively inferior. Loving follows humility because without that humility proximity to greatness—and the fact that everyone loves greatness—leads to resentment. The key point is that just as success brings greatness, one must also be humble in order to love that greatness because greatness when seen closely leads to resentment as the lover looks inferior in comparison.

The soul falls from the association of greatness due to this resentment because he or she is unable to handle that greatness. Being great and loving the great are not easy, and this holds true even in the present world. For a woman to push a man to be great is as detrimental to her (if she is unable to ultimately handle that greatness) as it is for a man to expect a woman to desire him intensely for becoming great (if he is unable to handle the pressure of becoming great). The desire between man and woman is futile if they don't have the respective capacities of greatness and humility. It is thus a folly for a woman to imagine that she would love a man if only he was great; the fact is that his greatness could even make the woman very uneasy and resentful. Similarly, it is a mistake for a man to think that he would only become great if a woman desires that greatness—greatness to find a woman's love—because he might find that he doesn't get the love because his greatness is limited.

The secret to success in a relationship is that a man's greatness is matched by a woman's love; that, as a man becomes more successful, she can increasingly love the man, and not resent his success. If the woman is insecure, then she should be matched with a man who is less successful because through that match she will feel less threatened by her man's success. If the woman is very loving and secure, she should be matched to a successful man. This is a natural balance in relationships where the amount of success one obtains as a couple is proportional to the success they can handle as a couple.

Man-Woman Oscillations

A man oscillates between pursuing greatness and then letting go of that pressure of obtaining greatness in order to just relax, be pampered, and comforted. A woman also oscillates between being a lover and a mother. As a lover, she expects to be pampered by a man, but as a mother she is in control of the children and nurtures and protects them from any kind of danger.

A woman who doesn't have children of her own will try to mother a man. If a woman with children doesn't have a man, she will project manly expectations on her children, asking them to be successful, driven, educated, and unrelenting in their life. For a woman to be happy, ideally, she must express her motherly instincts on her children, and her lover instincts on her man. That is, she must expect her man to be successful and driven while she protects and nurtures her children. But these proclivities are distorted when a woman lacks either a man or children. A woman who has neither a man nor children often hops between relationships, sometimes seeking a great man, and at other times going in the opposite direction—falling for a man that she has to mother. It seems paradoxical but it is very natural for a woman to achieve fulfillment by both being a lover and a mother. If these proclivities are unsatisfied, they will most likely be vectored into the available avenues.

A man who doesn't have greatness will fall prey to depression, addiction, and crime because his desire for greatness is not fulfilled in the acceptable ways and he must therefore find alternative expression of his desire for greatness. But a man who is not pampered and comforted by a woman drives himself into overwork, trying to achieve even more greatness, imagining that the shortage of rest, love, and relaxation is due to his shortfall in greatness. Then again, a man who has neither greatness nor love in his life oscillates between depression and sloth vs. overwork and burnout, sometimes compensating for the lack of love and at other times the lack of greatness. For a man to be happy, ideally, he must have success and greatness through his work and then relaxing, pampering, comforting by a woman at home.

Many of these things might appear to be stereotypical in modern society where women tend to pursue individual greatness and many men are satisfied while living under the protection of other men (or women). You can call me sexist or gender-biased but I don't believe in the new gender roles for the reasons that I mentioned above—feminism drives men and women away from each other because the men are emasculated by feminine control, and lose their pursuit of greatness in life. These men then start using the women for their ends rather than being their heroes, protectors, and providers.

Women who are blinded by their newfound power in society don't realize that men are now going to prey on them rather than protect them. For example, as men become demotivated and work less, they also earn less, and the women must now bear a larger share of the work that brings money. The men they contact will leave them with children and since the woman is the main breadwinner, she also gets to support her children for life. The man gets away scot-free—enjoying the woman's body without responsibility.

A working woman might want to avoid useless men and seek only those men who are successful and responsible, but the fact is that the truly successful men are not seeking the feminists. They are more comfortable with the traditional roles of man and woman, which means that the feminist women will not find good, successful men. In their quest for love, these women would be mostly left with the uncaring and unsuccessful men—who they have to mother even for a future prospect—after which the reckless man might still leave them. The key point is that women changing by themselves cannot bring a difference in society unless men change too—e.g. the successful men should now be seeking successful women. But why does a successful man need to go after an equally successful woman when his innate emotional need is for love and respect from a woman, not competition from a successful woman (which he already has enough of through other men and women)?

Even if we set aside the emotional needs of men and women, the practical reality of life is that the traditional gender roles of men and women have far more advantage due to division of responsibility than a feminist woman who must either focus on work and forego her emotional needs with a man and children, or bear the burden of both working and raising children by contacting an irresponsible man. The fact is that most responsible men seek traditional roles while the irresponsible men have no aspirations for greatness and only use the woman for pleasure and then leave her with children.

The feminist woman is left with no choice other than to find love with fickle men and raise his children by working harder or live without the emotional benefits of a responsible and successful man and children. If society trickles toward greater feminism—and I'm not denying that it could—then the result will be either a dramatic decline in the social structure because nobody would desire children, or many unwanted children, who are already too damaged during their childhood to lead any kind of meaningful life.

The only alternative to such depredation is that as women seek equality with men—and usurp the traditional men roles—the men will now aspire for the traditional womanly roles and provide the nurturing for children that was previously the forte of women. That too is not impossible, except for the fact that women would not be emotionally satisfied with such men—they are more likely to keep pushing the men to be more successful because the woman expects a man to be *manly*. Therefore, even if such a role reversal occurs in society, even women would be unhappy with the men, let alone the men who would not be satisfying their traditional aspirations for worldly greatness.

There is simply no scenario in which men can satisfy their emotional need for greatness and recognition, while the women fulfill their need for loving and mothering, without maintaining the traditional gender roles. This is only based on the understanding of the emotional needs of both men and women and founded on the perfection of love in the Divine Couple. The traditional gender roles have not only existed for a very long time in history, but they are the only roles compatible with the emotional needs of men and women, as well as a healthy and productive society. If society overturns these roles, then not only will the society fail to understand the nature of true love, but also fail to find true emotional satisfaction in their lives (in both men and women), while producing a profoundly broken and fractured progeny.

7

The Symbols of Emotion

Matter as a Symbol

The body is the symbol of the mind and by knowing the bodily states, we can know the mental states—whenever they are expressed in the body. Thus, for instance, when a person lies, instruments can detect the higher pulse rate and blood pressure, indicating their deceit. However, it is also possible to beat lie detector tests, which means that the lie exists in the mind but may not be expressed in the body and lie detector tests are not considered adequate evidence in many courts of law. The relationship between the body and the mind is like that between meaning and a symbol of that meaning. The symbol expresses the meaning, but that symbol is not the meaning because the meaning may sometimes not be expressed or expressed incorrectly.

Our emotions can be expressed through physical objects, which then become the symbols of the mind, and by reading those symbols we can deduce the mental state. Our body language, pulse rate, blood pressure, and facial expressions can all be good indicators of the mental state. But beyond the body, the emotions can also be expressed through stories, art, music, politics, economics, and even scientific theories. All these are symbols of the mind. To read these symbols, they must be interpreted through a language like physical states which are interpreted through measuring instruments. The difference between physical measurements and linguistic interpretations is that languages can be contextual, while physical instruments are universal. That is, you can use the same instrument everywhere, but you cannot use the same language in all cases. By language, I mean the social conventions, the culture of a group of people, the history of events, the goals a group aims for, and the personality of the person who exaggerates or suppresses expressions.

Since emotions are caused by our purposes, we frequently derive a person's purpose—i.e. the direction in which he or she is headed—by reading the bodily language into their emotional states, and then by treating the emotions as the symbols of purposes. If you, for example, don't like the hurdles being faced toward your goal, you may likely express your displeasure and anger on encountering those hurdles. By observing the unhappiness one can know your purposes. If, on the other hand, you wanted to hide your purposes, you will also have to hide your true emotions—either not expressing them at all or showing your emotions in an exaggerated or suppressed manner. Of course, we don't feel the emotions felt by others, we only *deduce* them from the bodily symbols. In such deduction, we *read* the body like a book—i.e. treating the bodily expression as symbols of the meanings that lie hidden.

There are three kinds of meanings we can derive from the body: the purpose, the concepts, and the references; these correspond to the *ananda*, *chit*, and *sat* of the soul. Thus, when you say that "the sun is bright", the word "sun" is a reference to an object to which we can establish a relationship in order to know its properties. When you say that "nectarines are sweet fruits", you use "nectarine" as a concept, which has other conceptual parts and properties such as sweetness. Finally, when we say that "a clear direction will make life easy" we are using the word "direction" as the goal to be fulfilled.

Any word can be interpreted as either a concept, a reference, or a goal[1]. In fact, every observable is produced from the combination of the three factors, but only the context reveals the true meaning. For example, if you say that "a clear direction will make life easy" you may be stating it as a fact or implying sarcastically that goals are not clear. The emotional state experienced in the two cases is different because the manifest portion of the sentence is that goals are important for success, but the subtle unstated claim may be to imply incompetence and ineptitude. The cognitive component of the statement is therefore unclear unless the emotional state underlying that statement is also clear. To read sarcasm in a sentence we must know the speaker's emotions, which will then alter the cognitive meaning implied by the statement. The three types of meanings derived from a sentence have an internal hierarchy between them—i.e. they can be dominant or subordinate. Sometimes, the dominant factor is the emotion, but it remains hidden, while only the facts are stated. At other times, the facts are the dominant factor, but they remain subordinate while the expression seems emotional. To know the meaning of an utterance, we must decode not just the individual concept, reference, and goal, but also which one is dominant or subordinate.

Clearly, this is an indeterministic problem, because there are many interpretations of the same observation, and the meanings cannot be reduced to the words—there are many concepts, references, and goals consistent with the same words. Since the same state combines the relation, purpose, and concept, by knowing the state we can *read* each of the three from the state, but we are frequently mistaken in this reading if we don't fully know the context, we don't understand a person's nature, or we just don't have the perceptive and interpretive abilities to transform a symbol into its meaning.

With this background about interpreting and judging, how it is dominated by concept, relation, or emotion, how the dominant-subordinate structure produces different types, and how these types correctly judge similar types but misjudge and confront the other types, we can now turn toward the various expressions of the mind, intellect, ego, and the moral sense into the worldly symbols. I will cover, in this chapter, a few dominant types of expression—literature, music, art, economy, politics, and science. This list is by no means exhaustive, and the aim is not completeness. The aim is only to apply these principles to a broad enough set of expressions to demonstrate how the model works, so the reader can understand its relevance.

I will also try to use this opportunity to highlight the different ways emotions affect expression. In literature, we will see how the story plot is decided by an emotional theme—e.g. victory of good over evil. In music, the composition is based on the emotionality associated with a time of day or month of the year—e.g. chirpy music for a bright morning and morose sounds for a dark night, depiction of love during spring, and depiction of loss for the autumn season. Every observation is created not just by the facts, but also by the observer's emotional state by which he or she picks out some chosen facets of reality—expressing them into art—which raises the question: What *should be* our emotional state to observe the world such that we are depicting it in art in the most appropriate way? This question marks a departure from viewing art as simply an expression of free will and choice, to what is the *ideal* and *responsible* use of that choice. Now, the artist's choices—and hence emotional states—come into focus, because the ideologies of hope and fear (as we have seen) are not the ideal emotional backgrounds. Rather, the artist must adopt the ideology of compassionate detachment to even portray the world in art, because reality is perfectly depicted only in this view.

The question of ideal emotional states takes us into subsequent implications of emotional behavior in the context of economics and politics. In economics, the simple question of what constitutes 'economic value'—i.e. the *price* for a product or service—is based on our emotional response called "demand", which is often manipulated by marketers to raise prices and profit from it. There are two related questions that we can ponder. First, is monetary value just based on our desire, or is there real value in something? Second, is the emotional manipulation to alter this value an ethical activity?

Our desires and emotions are not the final arbiters of judging the ethical nature of an action. As we have seen earlier, the moral sense is superior to the ego, because the judgment of right and wrong is higher than that of good and bad. Society therefore should not be organized based on making people happy by fulfilling their desires, but by engaging in ethical actions. Modern political systems involving democratic selection are pointless because they only rely on individual choices, which are all based on what each person considers 'good' for them, not what is 'right'. The importance we give to a sense of happiness has to be subordinated to the importance that we must give to ethical action. That is then the basis on which we can speak about a political culture that looks at happiness as the end goal, rather than the *means*. The means to happiness is ethical action, which means subordinating the emotional desires, needs, and wants to the natural laws of moral action.

That leads us to the final issue regarding how we will formulate such moral laws—which are also *natural*. This requires a shift in thinking where emotion is acknowledged, but it is subordinated to morality. Acknowledging emotion implies adding a new kind of judgment—good and bad—to the current scientific judgments of true and false. Subordinating emotion to morality implies adding yet another type of judgment—of right and wrong—to the preexisting judgments of truth and good. We have seen how this shift is consistent with physical theories and life sciences, besides, of course, human psychology. But the more fundamental question now is: how will we *logically* and *mathematically* describe the world that involves three judgments—truth, right, and good? The final part of this chapter discusses this question highlighting how the twin ideas of *necessity* and *sufficiency* widely used in current logic[2] fall short when the world exists as a possibility rather than a reality, and *choice* has to be added to logic itself to achieve completeness.

This discussion on emotion is broad-based. It begins with the obvious fact that we read both emotive and cognitive content, and emotions change the cognition. It then leads to the question: If emotions change our cognition, then what is the ideal emotion to have the right cognition? Since emotions are involved in decision making, the questions of ideality lead us to the norms of ideal decision making in society, and then to the social system that manages society. Since this social system has to be based on natural laws, it leads us to the question of how nature itself is not just about *reality* but also *ideality*. The distinction between the real and the ideal forms a choice by which we can potentially select what is less than ideal—and it would still be real—although that choice entails a consequence, under a natural law of moral conduct. Given that this narrative involves complex turns, I briefly summarized it at the outset; hopefully, this will make the rest of the reading easier.

The Basic Plots of Storytelling

Fear is very common and it is overcome by its antidote—love. Every story involves an oscillation from fear to love, or love to fear, or love to fear to love, or fear to love to fear. Finding love and conquering fear are therefore the most basic positive stories and losing love or being overcome by fear are the typical negative stories. The stories that dominate in finding love are often called 'romance', 'fantasy', and 'family' dramas. Those describing the conquest of fear include the genres of 'war', 'sports', 'crime', and 'horror'. The mixture of finding love and conquering fear creates genres called 'thriller', 'adventure', 'action', and 'mystery'. Finally, the stories associated with loss of love or being overwhelmed by fear are called 'psychological', 'existential', etc. All these stories can be 'historical' or 'futuristic'; they can also pertain to different places. But we are not so bothered by the exact time and place context. We are primarily concerned with the essence of the story which makes it interesting—namely the conquest of fear and the discovery of love.

The stories which have stood the test of time, involve a good and honest person who leads a life of duty and diligence, but who falls into a tragic trap of deception or misfortune, loses the happy life and is sucked into sadness undergoing trials and tribulations in trying to reclaim the life of happiness. How he or she regains that life is the conquest of internal fear to fight an external battle. The story might seem to be about the external battles, but the sublime subtext of that story is the conquest of one's own fears to find that life of love and desire where one is now entitled to happiness again.

Everybody likes a winner, and the winners write the history. Nobody wants to listen to the stories of the losers—those who have lost love or have been overcome by fear. We want stories where we lose love and find it again. Or stories in which we are tested by situations that make us fearful, and we conquer that fear to regain happiness. This contributes to the 'happily ever after' theme. In rare cases, the protagonist dies or loses a significant contributor to his happiness, in the process of conquering fear and injustice. The story doesn't end in a 'happily ever after' but becomes an 'inspiration' for others to lead such fights, despite the cost—because conquering fear and injustice, even at the cost of one's own life or the lives of near and dear—is 'inspirational'. In such stories, death is a signifier of a better life after death. It may be a better life for those who have survived, a posthumous recognition by those who live or meeting again in the afterlife to be happily ever after.

Since fear is caused by 'evil', and love is 'good', the conquest of fear to regain love represents the victory of good over evil. The love can be directed to various objects—one's own life, the lives of family and friends, the love of one's nation, the pursuit of greater goods such as liberty and enlightenment, or the establishment of peace and prosperity. Everyone is seeking happiness and avoiding fear. Stories are written to describe the lives of those who have found love, lost it, and found it again. Or stories of one's life in the pursuit of the greater good. The circumstances of love and fear can vary—from being very narrow to being very broad—but the theme of victory and conquest is universal. People love the protagonists who win and ignore those who have lost. It is not because people are fundamentally cruel, but only because they fear the fear of loss. They want to focus on their winning, finding love, and being happy. The greater the hurdle, the sweeter is the taste of final victory. Everyone wants a winner because they see themselves in that act of winning. The stories of the 'heroes' and 'heroines' who conquer evil and find their love are very serious and they reach the core of one's emotional depths.

There are also stories that don't go so deep—we call them tales of humor. We laugh at stupidity, and to laugh at something, it must be portrayed as being stupid, ridiculous, unintelligent, or mismatched. You can laugh at things in a superficial way, or in a deep sense. Superficially, humor is enthralling because the problems are temporary and fixable. At a deep level, humor can be used to bring detachment because life is viewed as a succession of bumbling mistakes. But this humor makes sense only when we replace the life of bumbling mistakes with an ideal picture that may be humorous in a superficial sense—e.g. creating linguistic confusions by using words out of context—but not in a deep sense in which life is funny because it is meaningless.

When humor deepens without replacing the ridiculous with the ideal and sane, it becomes dark because we see life as a cruel joke in which there is no right or wrong, no evil or good, but only a succession of mistakes and mismatched expectations created through ignorance or misinformation. This portrays the meaninglessness of life, and that ultimately there is no way to be happy except to treat the pursuit of good vs. evil itself as being pointless and not to be taken seriously because evil is no more than mismatched expectations, but the match is relative to a person, who keeps changing, and hence there cannot be a definition of good and right. The struggle in life is no longer to fight evil and fear, knowing what is good. The struggle is also not transcending the conflict between good and bad into something that is devoid of this duality. The struggle is rather to just give life some sense of goodness. If we can't find goodness in life, we cannot fight the battle against evil. Humor at a deeper level becomes cynical about the possibility of good itself.

The existentialist and post-modern philosophical themes have adopted such a cynical view—there is humor in it, but it cuts at the roots of 'good vs. evil' themes, in which we are not laughing at others because they are foolish while we are intelligent. We are rather laughing at life itself because it is meaningless. Much of post-modern literature and movies have departed from the traditional good vs. bad themes. Now, you can see that the heroes and heroines have shades of gray, while the evil monsters are not entirely morally wrong. Often, the monsters are fighting for their right and justice—although seen from a different viewpoint—because they were originally denied justice by the very system that they fight. The evil monsters are also capable of love, and the good Samaritans are also filled with hate. Everything is relativized to a particular type of audience with a pre-decided winner or loser because the story would not sell unless portraying the classic good over evil battle, and it would not be 'critically acclaimed' unless the joke is on life itself.

The post-modern genre of storytelling moves from an absolutist sense of good vs. evil to a relativized world of struggle in which everyone thinks they are fighting the good fight, but the difference between them and their opposition keeps blurring. This is the outcome of mixing humor with the classic divide between love and fear. Humor can be cathartic when it is used to bring a sense of detachment by seeing both hope and fear as ultimately pointless. But humor is carcinogenic if it homogenizes the good and the evil. The modern world is drifting into the nebulous zone of indecision about the nature of good and evil. In this zone, there are no battles over right and wrong. There are only battles of survival and seeking whatever little can be eked out of life. You don't create heroes and heroines in this world; perhaps every survivor is a hero unto himself who writes his own stories and believes in them.

Fear, love, and humor are the basic emotions underlying all storytelling. When love wins, there is a good principle that defeats evil, and humor is used to mock the loser. When fear wins, love is mocked by humor, and life ends in destruction. When humor wins, both love and fear are mocked, and we transcend the duality between the two[3]. But when humor is mixed with love and fear, then the joke is on the pointlessness of love and fear. In the ultimate analysis, humor is the best emotion because it dissipates the anguish arising from fear and the false hopes arising from temporary successes. But to see the best of humor, the humor must be intelligent—i.e. recognize that hope is better than fear, and rejection of temporary hopes and fears is better than either of them. But detachment from futile hope is not the same as hopelessness. Nor is the rejection of hope the same as the acceptance of fear. Nor is one man's hope another man's fear—because hope and fear are not mutually defined by an opposition. Laughter that makes a person happy without making another person unhappy—i.e. the laughter is not at someone's expense—is the real humor. The distinction is very subtle, but without it, the rejection of hope doesn't bring detachment; it rather brings hopelessness.

There are infinite ways in which fear, love, and humor can be combined, making one the dominant, and the other two subordinate features of a story. As the story progresses, the dominant and subordinate features can also change; the story may primarily dominate in love, secondarily dominate in fear, and occasionally mock love or fear. There can be multiple layers of love, fear, and humor, which intonate and nuance the higher-level emotion. There can be fear with humor which intonates the fear with sarcasm—sometimes making the fear more terrifying, and at other times making it less frightening.

Expression of Emotion in Music

In Indian classical music, love, fear, and humor are associated with different times of the day. Mornings are cheerful, joyful, and sprightly; they are associated with happiness and detachment. One is neither hopeful of becoming successful nor fearful of failure. It is the mood of staying calm, peaceful, and positive, without craving or despair. The mornings are also associated with *sattva-guna* which is the mode of enlightenment, knowledge, and detachment from the world. There can be anger in *sattva-guna* as well, but it arises out of compassion for others, not due to hope for oneself, or fear due to imminent failure. Similarly, there can be envy due to competition—either in becoming more knowledgeable and renounced than others, or in excelling in compassion, kindness, and charity relative to the other compassionate and kind people. The mode of *sattva-guna* should therefore not be equated with 'peace' and 'seclusion' because anger, pride, envy, and greed can exist too. Greed and detachment are not contradictory when the greed is compassionate: you are greedy to make others happy, and you enjoy that effort.

Afternoons are governed by hope and craving; they are serious, determined, and purposeful. This time is governed by *rajo-guna*. In this mode, one works hard, is decisive and resolute, but also gets angry when goals are not achieved. That anger is not driven by fear of imminent failure, but to drive a change in one's situation. Anger, therefore, can be associated with any of the three modes: in *rajo-guna* anger is created by the hope of making a positive change, in the mode of *tamo-guna* it is driven by the fear of failure, and in the mode of *sattva-guna* by the compassion and urgency to bring happiness to others. The anger of *rajo-guna* is constructive while that of *tamo-guna* is destructive; in *rajo-guna* you compete to be better than others for your selfish desires. Under *tamo-guna* the anger tries to bring others down and destroy them. Under *sattva-guna*, anger pushes to improve others' condition.

During the night everything becomes somber and gloomy. In a positive sense, one uses this time to rest and relax, but it can also indicate depression, sadness, melancholy, and despair. There is happiness of sleep and relaxation—which relieve one of anxiety and fear. Similarly, there is anger and envy, which emerge if one's anxiety and fears go out of control and result in destruction. The fear of *tamo-guna* results in paralysis, inertia, and reduction. Thus, there can be happiness in *tamo-guna* if one gets to rest and sleep, but the same inertia and paralysis can be felt as unhappiness if one is unable to move due to confusion or anxiety of the unknown and the impossible.

All emotions exist in all modes, but their origin and hence the *purpose* underlying their creation can be different. The emotion itself is therefore not the criteria for distinguishing the time; however, purpose is. Morning is therefore not the only time of happiness, and afternoon or night are not necessarily times of distress. Rather, at all times one can feel happiness, anger, greed, pride, envy, confusion, desire, etc. Nevertheless, their *cause* is different because the time is supposed to be used for a different purpose. This has an effect on music too, which expresses a variety of emotions, but there is a qualitative difference in those emotions, and hence the music differs as well.

The Indian *raga* system[4] divides musical genres according to the time of the day, the month of the year, the nature of the occasion, etc. Thus, there are different *raga* for morning, afternoon, and night. There are different *raga* for seasons such as summer, rains, and winter. There are different *raga* for birth, marriage, and death. There is nothing equivalent to it in Western music, but if one were to compare, classical music would be in the morning, rock music would be in the afternoon, and jazz and blues would be for the night. This comparison is illustrative, not to be used for stereotyping. One should see the mode of nature—i.e. *sattva*, *rajas*, or *tamas*—to identify the type, besides remembering that each type has subtypes, produced by a relative domination of the three modes, and as a secondary mode Y becomes prominent under a primary mode X, it begins to resemble the situation where the primary mode was Y and the secondary mode was X. It is difficult to decode the emotion from the sensual observation, because the same observation has many likely explanations, although there is always only one true explanation.

That true explanation can be provided by the person creating that music, if the creator understands the tree of the sentiments he or she experiences, and the specific purposes for which those emotions are felt. Others may experience the emotions too, but those experiences are based on their *interpretation* of the sensation. The fact that interpretation is involved often means that many people cannot even decode the sensation into emotion; for example, one has to be trained to an extent in classical music to appreciate the emotional meaning. In many cases, the emotional interpretation is driven by the words employed in music, and in some cases—e.g. opera—the theme is set by the description of the performance that you will see. That contextualization through words and themes assists the mind to interpret the sounds into emotions. Similarly, one gradually listens to a particular genre of music he or she also develops *taste* for that kind of music because the mind acquires the ability to interpret the sound into emotional meaning through repetition.

We must note that music—like language—is contextual and the meaning depends on the mental capability to interpret the sound into emotion, and then judge—like or dislike—the emotion based on one's inherent tastes. Not everyone can therefore appreciate all kinds of music because the mind has to be trained to interpret, and the ego has to be trained to appreciate the interpretation. If the mind is not trained, then the musical performance is not understood, and if the ego is not trained then the performance is not enjoyed. Of course, you cannot enjoy if you cannot understand, therefore, interpreting is prior to enjoyment. Conversely, in musical creativity, one has to first appreciate and then interpret. The ego appreciates a type of emotion, the mind creates that emotion, and the senses then convert the emotion into a symbolic expression. The senses, the mind, and the ego are all involved in the musical appreciation, although in reverse paths for the listener and the performer.

Music is also contextual—like language—in an *objective* sense, namely, that when multiple instruments are played, the result of each is modified by the other. Similarly, the musical content builds up over time, and the meaning at any time is based on the meaning you obtained earlier, and some-times—once you have heard the song many times—the meaning is enhanced by the *anticipation* of what comes in the future because you can appreciate how this is a gradual build-up. Finally, there is contextuality in a genre built up by other songs or performances, and then contextuality created by an artist through their previous works. This is objective contextuality because everyone—in a third-person manner—can receive the context, quite differ-ent from the subjective context of the subjective interpretive and judgmental faculties.

The key reason for mapping emotions to time is that time is produced due to purpose, and that purpose creates emotions. Therefore, if we keep our purpose aligned with time—by being detached in the morning, active and purposeful during the day, and relaxed and restful during the night—then we will experience the emotions of that time appropriately. In effect, certain times of day are well suited for certain purposes, and we can best use that time of day for that goal. The body and the mind when aligned to the mood of the time also get support from the natural flow of time, and by that sup-port the mood is enhanced, while the body and mind relish that mood and activity far better than if it was performed out of sync with the property of time.

To understand the relationship between music and time we must see time as being *typed*—i.e. that morning, afternoon, night have different qualities, and time is not moving "uniformly". Instead, the parts of the day domi-nate in different modes—*sattva*, *rajas*, and *tamas*—which means that time is suited for different moods and purposes. You don't try to bring the emotions of one part of the day into the other parts; you rather adapt the musical genre to the time of day. Linear time has no types because if you tried to type linear time, you will end up with infinite types. Time gets typed when it is divided into *cycles*. Something must be closed and finite for the portions to be defined in relation to each other and therefore typed. In linear time, there is no beginning or end, there is no day and night, and there is no morning, afternoon, and evening because such types presuppose a closed cycle. Things begin and then they end; the start and end constitute a cycle because after the end there is a new beginning. Similarly, day is the end of the night, and the night is the end of the day. The musical scales are themselves cyclic—the end of one scale marks the beginning of the other. The key point is that material *change* has to be defined *cyclically* rather than *linearly* in order to create types.

Once this cycle has been constructed, there can be linear progress too, because these cycles are *hierarchical*. Thus, the fast repetition at a lower level in the hierarchy is a slower repetition at a higher level, and that slowness of the cyclic change creates our sense of linear progress. As we go bottom-up in the hierarchy, the cycles become slower and wider, which gives the impression of linear progress, even though it is still cyclic because at each level of this hierarchy, the types are defined mutually and not independently.

Our life, therefore, has a rhythm—given by the elapsing of day and night—and associated with it is a *frequency* of progressive changes. Atomic objects have a higher frequency, and the cosmos has a much smaller frequency. There is a linear progression in the frequency scale as we go from top to bottom in the hierarchy—the detailed picture changes faster but the abstract picture changes slowly. However, at each level of abstraction, we can employ words such as 'morning', 'afternoon', and 'night' as unique *types* in the cycle. They will indicate not the rising and setting of the sun, but a time that is fit for birth, growth, and decline. There is, hence, no *linear time*. Time is always cyclic. However, there is a linear *scale* on which we can measure these cycles either as bigger or smaller cycles, and faster or slower repetitions.

Space similarly must be typed and that is possible if space is hierarchically divided into closed regions. The linear and open notion of space is without types, and hence it cannot be given meanings. Without the types in space and time, music can have no types; it will only be described as frequencies but not *notes* which are associated with meanings and emotions. To even understand how music gives rise to meaning and emotion the notion of space and time has to be modified. In music the types appear after we define an *octave* which determines the bounds within which the frequencies become notes. Similarly, time is also typed by defining the beat and rhythm, as a result of which some notes are in the beginning of the cycle while others are at the cycle's end. The octave and the beat constitute the closure of space and time in music. Once the octave and the beat are defined, then the cognitive meaning can be associated with the types associated with spatial locations and the emotional feeling can be tied to the evolution of types over time.

There are historical debates in music regarding *cognitivism* and *emotivism*. Cognitivists claim that musical appreciation is cognitive, while emotivists suggest music is about emotional pleasure. Both positions are partially false because meaning derived by the mind involves a three-fold interpretation into cognition, emotion, and relation. The relation pertains to the person, thing, or situation being described; the cognition pertains to the concepts about that person, thing, or situation, and the emotion refers to the fact whether we like that person, thing, or situation. When music is without lyrics, the mind can conjure an object because the primary relation is to the listener and the performer has left the object of that composition up to the listener. However, when music includes words, then the possible interpretations of the composition are reduced, although not completely eliminated. There can be, for instance, many interpretations of a song's meaning. The listeners can still relate the song or composition to their life situation—e.g. imagine that a romantic song pertains to their lover—but the alternatives are fewer.

The key point is that aside from cognition and emotional feeling, there is also an object in musical experience, and if that object is absent in a musical performance, the listeners must still conjure that object in order to complete the interpretation and the performers too must conjure an object to even give that performance an appreciable quality. If the listener is unable to conjure that object then the musical perception is incomplete, and even the cognitive types and emotive feeling would not be experienced. This often happens in the case of classical music when it doesn't employ words, and most listeners are unable to conjure an object, which means that the interpretation is incomplete and unless this object is found, the judgment of true, good, and right cannot be performed. As a result, the music cannot be understood and enjoyed, and those who are unable to conjure such objects are also unable to enjoy the music. Classical music has therefore earned the reputation of generally being 'incomprehensible' by the lay person because comprehension, in this case, involves imagination coupled with contextualization so the listener must have far greater powers of understanding and creativity because the meaning of the composition is not apparent from the performance[5].

Music now becomes a symbolic expression of the composer's or the performer's mental state, however, the full meaning of these symbols—the relation to a target object, the conceptual description of those objects, and the purpose of describing those objects—is not completely apparent to the listener. This is no different than how mental states are expressed in the body where the third-person observation must interpret and derive the mental state from the bodily expression. The derivation is not just contextual upon the culture, tradition, and customs in which the event occurs, but also the dispositions of the person who interprets, and thereby brings their own culture, tradition, and customs to plug the gaps in meaning not immediately obvious from the sensations—i.e. musical sounds—themselves.

Emotional Expression in Art

The problem of interpretation has recently emerged in modern art as well because art has become more symbolic than literal: art depicts forms whose intended meaning is quite different from the literal objects being depicted. For example, people in an oppressive and subjugated society may be depicted by concrete buildings with thick dark clouds over them. The concrete buildings could indicate that the people are caught in their situation and the dark clouds over these buildings could denote that people see no light: there is little hope for them. Overtly, the picture is about a city landscape, but covertly the picture indicates life in an urban society, as the city landscape is used symbolically. To see what the picture means, we have to see the buildings and clouds as indicative of people and their lives rather than, naively, as a landscape by itself. Which object is a symbol of what then becomes subject to interpretation. For instance, the same picture could also be interpreted as ideas in a person's mind covered by the paralysis of depression which makes the ideas stagnant. The perceiver of the art has to use his or her imagination to interpret the picture beyond the sensations, judge whether it is true, right, and good—creating far greater room for human speculation.

The problem becomes harder when the forms used for symbolism are themselves unclear. For instance, the buildings and clouds may not be clear, and one might only see incomprehensible shapes, which makes form deriva-tion an even prior problem before the forms are given meanings. The issue is similar to that of reading text. Even if the alphabets and words are clear, the meaning could be ambiguous. But if the words themselves are ambig-uous—e.g. because they don't follow established dictionary usage, or don't conform to standard grammar usage—the task of interpreting might become even harder. Modern art takes liberties in the usage of symbolism or con-formance to established conventions. In a sense, art not only creates new meanings but also expresses the meanings through a different *language* of expression—called the *style* or *genre* of artistic expression. Art connoisseurs have to first master the language, understand the manner in which a partic-ular artist uses the language, and then interpret the specific meanings in his mind.

All this would not be problematic if we acknowledged that there is a language of artistic expression with a well-defined meaning which can be decoded once we understood the conventions. The problem deepens if we say that everyone is free to invent their language and grammar and that freely created language and grammar cannot be known by others because describ-ing it itself needs a language, which is, too, subject to peculiarities of sub-jective interpretation. If everyone spoke their own language there could be no communication, especially because we could not *teach* other people that same language. Meanings can be communicated only if there is at least one universal language using which we can explain the *rules* of subsequent lan-guages, using which we can find novel ways of expressing new meanings. In other words, to speak anything at all, we have to acknowledge a universal lan-guage that can be used to formulate the rules of subsequent languages. The idea of universal language is called *linguistic structuralism*[6] but it entails that there must have been a universal mind that created the universal language.

The existence of the universal mind would now imply the existence of purposes beyond individual existence—i.e. the universe would be meaning-ful and purposeful—even if humans did not exist, or 'evolved' much later. All these ideas uncannily and inadvertently lead to 'God' and anyone who wants to deny that prospect would have to retroactively deny a universal lan-guage, followed by the comprehensibility of *any* language. Such is the state of affairs in postmodernism[7] where meanings are in the human minds; no human can truly express their meaning—except by using their chosen rules of expression—which can never be truly understood by another mind. Every perception, therefore, involves a subjective interpretation such that you can never be certain about the true 'intended' meaning of a symbol. Ultimately, every meaning we gather is a subjective construct—you can't claim it is 'real'.

Modern art is deeply influenced by post-modernism in which there is no objective reality 'out there'. Rather, we construct that reality mentally from sensations, and that construction is subjective. Thus, we are suspended in the fleeting flurry of passing impressions—a 'dustbowl empiricism'—which is converted into a solid world by choosing social rules, cultural norms, and scientific theories. Two things fall out of the post-modernist ideology.

First, if objects are just human constructions, then what is the need to make these definite such that we *lose* our *freedom* to interpret their meanings according to our choices? Would it not be better if we had even greater freedom corresponding to lesser definition? The goal of art is now the resurrection of freedom from the oppression of the modernist society that tries to define, rule, and limit the individual through numerous axioms, laws, and theories. The dismantling of that oppression recovers our freedom and art is the vehicle to a 'spiritual emancipation' by which we are freed of social statutes.

Second, if all axioms, laws, and theories are viewed as oppressing the human choice, then art (as the vehicle to resurrect our freedom of interpreting the world) becomes anti-establishment—the establishment identified with that which creates the axioms, laws, and theories and forces us to think according to these handed-down norms. Opposition to the establishment now acquires an *activist* flavor. Most artists in the postmodern era have also therefore aligned with the left-wing, revolutionary, and socialist ideologies, aiming to overthrow all that the modernist, enlightenment, and renaissance periods had achieved in terms of social, scientific, and cultural order.

Leaving the world undefined to be interpreted by the human mind, and then judged by the intellect, ego, and moral sense creates more burden for the viewer and less contribution for the artist. How can a painting that provides less detail expect more remuneration than one that defines more? If we took this idea to its logical limit, a blank piece of paper would give everyone the perfect canvas to interpret whatever they want, and by virtue of enabling the greatest freedom, that paper should also be the most valuable painting! But who is going to pay for a blank sheet of paper—or an amorphous mass of clay—just because it gives them the ability to interpret whatever they like? People don't call a blank sheet of paper a 'painting', and don't consider a lump of clay 'art'. There is a reason for that—they are not looking to do the hard work of defining themselves while paying the artist for leaving the paper untouched. Value is proportional to the level of detail and complexity because you have offloaded the job of creating that intricacy to someone else.

Leaving the art underdetermined is a choice that allows others to exercise their freedom of interpretation. But the extent of their freedom is equal to the extent to which the artist has left things undefined. In other words, if the artist increases their definition, then the viewers have lesser freedom. Can an artist who defines things accurately be oppressing another man's freedom to interpret and judge things according to their choice?

The right answer to the issue of interpretation and judgment is for each artist to leave less to the imagination and use all the freedom they have to define as much detail as one is capable of, and then allow the viewers to decide if their portrayal is worthy of being seen. The artist's freedom is meant to be used in creating the work of art, and the viewer's freedom is meant to decide if that art is worthy of being on their wall. The artist reducing his freedom to give more interpretive freedom is a misunderstanding of the nature of their respective freedoms. The artist does not encroach upon the viewer's freedom by defining more; he or she rather exercises their freedom to the fullest. Similarly, the viewers don't gain more freedom if the artist leaves the world underdetermined; the viewer's freedom lies in choosing the art which they desire. We don't decide the freedom *after* choosing a work of art. We rather apply freedom in deciding what that work of art should be and if we want it.

The decision to create or purchase a work of art involves a judgment on whether the art is true, right, and good, but the judgments are mistaken most of the time because in postmodern thinking the true, right, and good are personal choices. It is here that most of the problem in judging a work of art emerges because we are unable to define the criteria by which to judge the nature of truth, right, and good. The criterion is that falsities are temporary, wrongs lead to bondage, and the bad results in suffering. The soul desires eternity, freedom, and happiness, but to judge the truth, right, and good, we must find that which produces eternity, freedom, and happiness. Most people don't know that eternity is created by truth, freedom by righteousness, and happiness by goodness. Under ignorance of the laws of nature, which produce temporary life, bonded situations, and unhappiness, we artificially talk about increasing freedom and spiritual emancipation, when this discussion is futile unless we first know the nature of truth, right, and good.

Truth, right, and good are not personal choices because eternity, freedom, and happiness are not choices—everyone desires an eternal life, the freedom to choose, and the attainment of happiness. The judgment of truth, right, and good is not optional, although there can be varieties of truths, rights, and goods. But not everything is true, right, and good. The truth is objective as it pertains to the reality outside the self, although this truth can be contextual—neither universal nor subjective. The right action is also contextual and given by the role in relation to other persons, which are outside the self. Again, right action is neither subjective nor universal. Only the judgment of good—i.e. what *I* want—is subjective, but I cannot get what reality doesn't permit, or my role doesn't allow. In that sense, my purpose is limited by situations. Thus, the truth and right are contextual, the desire for happiness is universal, and only the purpose that will make me happy is subjective. My choices are therefore not entirely free, nor am I fully determined. Rather, I have to subordinate my choices to what is true and wrong in the given situation. If I want to be happy in another way, I have to change my situation, presuming what I want is *theoretically possible* in some situation. Clearly, full freedom—without a sense of imminent responsibility—is impossible.

The postmodern idea that we have to recover our freedom through free choices is appropriate, but those choices are not entirely free. Every choice comes with a responsibility—the effects and consequences of choices—and the effect is causal, but the consequence is moral. The choice of what we want is the 'good', the causal effect is the 'truth', and the moral consequence is the 'right'. The truth, right, and good form a tripartite causal-effect-consequence model, in which the cause is a choice. Modern science removes the question of 'good' when it replaces the choice with a physical state. Once the choices are removed, responsibilities are not needed and therefore one doesn't need to speak of the right. Now, we are left only with the question of truth—from one physical state to another. Postmodernism rejects the determinism of the above picture, and while it recovers the choices, it doesn't go far enough to accept responsibility. There is hence, in a sense, a physically determined world, overlaid with a completely free choice, with nothing to connect them, and the artist who exemplifies this freedom has no responsibility for his choices. You cannot thus *demand* an artist to portray only that which will constitute responsible action because the natural causal model is broken.

An artist is responsible to portray the truth, right, and good. By seeing this perfection, the viewers can understand, desire, and act truthfully, righteously, and happily. The work of art can be inspirational, moral, and knowledgeable. Conversely, what can be an artist's contribution if their creation remains ambiguous, leaving the viewer to figure out the nature of truth, right, and good, because such dilemmas on judgment exist even without any work of art? What can be the value in portraying depressing experiences when everyone wants to avoid such an experience in their personal lives? Art has a purpose to symbolize the nature of truth, right, and good, when we cannot find that in other material objects. The value lies in the truth, right, and good, because they are uncommon, and art must facilitate them. But even if they were very common, they would still be valuable. After all, who gets tired of eternity, freedom, and happiness—even if they were pervasive?

Emotion in Economic Decisions

Emotions play an enormous role in economics, as the basis of the supply and demand theory[8] of pricing, the demand driven by emotions. The supply and demand theory contends that there is no innate value in a product or service; the value is what *we* perceive according to our needs and desires. Therefore, as we attribute a higher value to things—by making them more desirable or necessary—they also become valuable and hence pricy. The value of a commodity or service is, in this approach, entirely due to our perception; if we find something valuable, it is valuable; otherwise, it is not.

I will dispute this contention here and argue that there is indeed objective value in things—governed by how much effort it takes to produce them—which determines the lowest possible cost for producing the commodity. A price lower than the cost would not make economic sense, as nobody will produce a commodity that can only be sold below its price point. However, a commodity can be sold at prices much higher than its cost, which is when the demand-and-supply equation becomes important. The question, however, is: As the demand rises, why can't the supply match it?

The free market system is expected to keep prices of commodities in check by allowing the supply match the demand, and vice versa, keeping prices stable. Any time the prices rise significantly, someone can sell the same commodity at a lower price, and competition will drive down the prices. Similarly, if the prices fall too low due to competition, some supplier will exit the business, creating a shortfall in supply, and the prices will rise again to reasonable levels. The main principle underlying the free-market economics is price stability. Typically, the prices would be driven as low as possible due to competition, coming at just a notch above costs, and therefore prices should always be determined by the base costs and would be very close to it. If we include into the costs the compensation of those who contribute to the creation of the product, then competition entails that prices equal costs.

Costs and prices can differ significantly only if the market is not *free*. This is achieved by the monopolization of natural resources, the methods of production, or of the talented workers, etc. which enables a producer to prevent other producers from competing. Increasing the demand doesn't give the producer any advantage, because the demand can be met by other producers. The benefit is only when one can increase the demand and then stifle the supply by conditions in which the market is no longer freely competing. In such a situation, instead of stabilizing the prices, the monopolized supply leads to price rise, and the resulting profits create even further monopolies.

Free market is good, and monopolies are evil. But you can also see that if monopolies were disallowed competition would automatically drive down the prices, and hence the profits. Those who want to eke out undue profits, therefore, consider free economy a bane; they subvert the free market system by injecting loopholes by which monopolies can be created—these include laws that support intellectual property, which monopolizes the methods of production, access to capital which disallows a competitor to invest in their business and squatting on natural resources, which disables competitors from the market. As monopolies are created, the prices far exceed the costs, and the profits are then used to further monopolize methods of production, access to capital, and cornering the natural resources for the production. The free market system is presently subverted by numerous monopolies.

Meanwhile, the prices cannot rise if there is insufficient demand, and the consumers consider the products not worth spending on. Therefore, demand must be 'stimulated' through desires by which consumers are compelled to buy things because someone else is buying them. The producers win if they can create competition among the buyers through advertising a product to make it highly desirable. The free market system—originally meant to create competition between the suppliers—resorts to competition between the consumers, to raise the prices for commodities that can't be produced by others. The competition among the consumers rests on emotional manipulation—triggering either hope by buying something, or fear by not buying it.

The ability to invent new products constitutes the cognitive component of economics. The control of a product's supply by monopolizing the methods of production, access to capital, cornering the methods of production, or simply being able to reach the consumer, is the relational aspect of economics. Finally, the use of advertising to increase the desire[9] for the product is the emotional ingredient in economics. Like everything else, economics can be divided into demand (emotions), supply (relations), and production (cognition and conation). Since all three must combine to create a transaction, emotions alone don't create economics, although the economic system can be significantly changed by altering either demand, supply, or production.

The free market system includes the *currency* in terms of which value is benchmarked and exchanged. We can think of currency as a standard meter or clock in terms of which space and time are measured. You expect to measure long and short lengths and durations using a meter and a clock but you don't expect the meter and clock themselves to expand or contract, thereby creating longer and shorter lengths and durations. In short, you want to keep the *standard* of measuring stable in order to determine the value of the finished products relative to raw commodities. If, however, the standard shrinks by the time something is converted from a raw commodity to a finished product, it appears that we produced far more than we put into the commodity. For example, if a meter is used to measure the length of yarn and cloth, but the meter shrinks while the yarn is converted into cloth, then you may imagine that a lot more cloth was produced from a small quantity of yarn. The same principle applies when currency—as the standard of value—inflates or deflates in value. On inflation, you charge a price, but because the value of the currency has reduced, you may lose money although you sell your product. On deflation, your legitimate price appears to earn you far more profit, but now there is a shortfall in currency and you might not even sell the product.

Inflation or deflation of currency creates natural *risks* in the economy, and every business tries to offset these risks by building a higher margin than necessary—to beat the odds of the risk over a longer period. That entails a greater gap between costs and prices, which necessitate monopolies, advertising, and creativity. If the profit motive weren't causing cost-price gaps, then the natural risks—emerging from the inflation or deflation of currency—themselves are fully capable of generating a gap between cost and price.

The question is: why would we change the value of currency when we don't change the length and duration of a meter and a clock? Currencies themselves have become commodities in the economic system and by changing the supply and demand of currency, you can change its value— like expanding or contracting a meter or clock. Each currency is under the control of a different government, which manipulates the currency's value, which then forces all other governments to manipulate their currencies too. The situation is like adjusting the length of a meter because the length of a foot is changing—because someone wants more feet, you cut the size of the foot in order to give the appearance of more feet within the same given length.

The cost-price difference is furthered by increasing or decreasing the supply of currency, which creates a greater risk in the economy, which forces price rise. Those who have a lot of currency—e.g. the banks—are not affected by the changes in the currency supply because they maintain their stockpile of currency. But those who don't have a stockpile of money always pay an interest to those with the stockpile in order to get the currency. Controlling the interest rates controls the access to all other downstream resources and production—and constitutes a *currency monopoly*. Banks are thus able to manipulate the economy in two ways— (1) they monopolize the access to capital, and (2) they change the value of capital via currency trading.

All the above evils emerge from *greed*. Modern economics legitimizes this greed by allowing unlimited private ownership of property, resources, ideas, and people, which leads to monopolies. Once a monopoly is created, the price of a commodity is at the whims of whoever holds it. Typically, it is the rich who hold monopolies and use them to further their wealth. The net result of monopolies is that the rich get richer, and the poor, poorer. Eventually, the private owners start lending to the government, and the government now gives them tax breaks and adjusts the laws of the land favorably for the lender because it stands weak without the mercy of the lender. Most governments around the world have been weakened by the privatization of national property, but the alternative is not nationalization of the property to abolish fair market competition. The alternative is to prevent monopolies and foster fair market competition, which achieves two important things: (1) prevents currency inflation or deflation, and (2) keeps prices close to costs.

Every economist understands how monopolies destroy the free market, but they also help enact the laws to enable that monopoly. Intellectual property is one example, in which ideas and procedures are patented when the fact is that ideas—by definition—span across multiple objects (e.g. the idea of a car is instantiated in many cars) and we can only own individual objects, not the ideas that exist across objects. All ideas are always possibilities, and no idea is ever an *invention*. Mathematicians, for instance, recognize that numbers and their properties forever exist in a "Platonic world". We did not create or invent a theorem; we only discover the theorem. Similarly, physics and chemistry are not inventions; they are discoveries. When you are discovering something, it clearly existed before you discovered it. You can be credited for its discovery, and you are fully entitled to keep the discovery secret. But you have no right to claim ownership of ideas. Patent laws all over the world recognize 'traditional knowledge' as a category of ideas that cannot be patented. What they don't recognize is that all ideas are traditional—i.e. that they have always existed as possibilities, but they come in and go out of fashion with time. Everything that we see today has existed in the past because time is cyclic, it brings the world into existence and then takes it out.

Similarly, the ownership of property must also be restricted. But the restriction is not a legal mandate; it is a moral guidance. What we can own is due to *karma* but being in a position of power entails a moral responsibility of sharing the ownership. The power of ownership is not without the responsibilities of compassion toward those who lack that ownership. Dereliction of that responsibility entails a reduction in the power and ownership in the future. So, while everyone is entitled to exploit the ownership to their ends as much as they want—a country's law cannot prevent you from your choices—the moral imperative is also nature's law that one cannot escape from.

Our power, therefore, is not independent of moral responsibility. If we don't execute that moral imperative, then we won't have the power because we have demonstrated we cannot wield it appropriately. In fact, the consequence of such misuse is that we will ourselves be forced into a helpless situation to be exploited and controlled by others. Domination and monopolization are thus not our prerogatives, even though nature affords us that option due to our past good deeds of discharging our responsibilities admirably. Just because we acquired power due to previous good actions isn't an indicator of the future course, and that consequence is a *moral* law of nature.

As I said earlier, the sense that causes purpose, and hence emotion is called the *ego*; it leads to the judgment of good and bad: good being what we want and enjoy, bad being what we dislike and suffer about. The sense that helps us judge the nature of right or wrong is the moral sense (also called *mahat-tattva* in Vedic philosophy). The moral sense is higher than the ego, which means our sense of right and wrong *can* overpower our desire. When the sense of right and wrong is overwhelmed by the desire for pleasure, then emotions have conquered morality. With this understanding, we can trace economic problems to their root in monopolization, the problem of monopolies to greed, and then to the fact that greed overpowers the moral sense when the moral sense is actually higher and should dominate the desires.

Inherent in modern economics is the subordination of moral judgment to individual greed. While physical sciences study what is true and false, social sciences—e.g. sociology, economics, and psychology—study what makes us happy, or good and bad. There is literally no science that studies right and wrong, and the population is not educated in how morality is a natural law. At best, philosophy speaks about how ethical action could be the greatest good for the greatest number of people, or how each person is free to decide what is good rather than worrying about how something is good or bad for another person. The laws of the government evolve frequently making universal generalizations when the laws are unique to each context and situation.

In some cases, morality is associated with a transcendental God, not with a natural law, and if you happen to reject God, you consider yourself "free" of the moral obligations. When society is bred on the principle of individualism, it cannot be faulted with doing what is only in its best interest, because you can talk about desires and ambitions, but not the responsibilities attached to a role. To describe the world as roles and duties—in addition to desires and possibilities—we must attend to an even deeper level of reality (the moral sense) and study its nature, subordinate the judgment of good and bad to that morality, then control the experience of emotion (e.g., greed) by that judgment. The key point is this: what is immoral is not good for *us* because it causes suffering in the future. Even selfishly speaking, therefore, irresponsibility is not rewarding in the longer run, once we know the moral law.

The Role of Emotion in Politics

Our government is expected to instill the sense of right and wrong, based on scientific knowledge—i.e. true and false—which should be used to control unbridled desires. However, the converse happens: we subordinate the sense of right and wrong and even scientific knowledge of true and false to what we want. For example, modern science describes nature as something without a purpose, while governments create laws that give us purpose, allowing us to exploit nature, without consideration of a natural purpose in life.

Matter has a hierarchy in which the intellect judges the nature of true and false, although not everything is eternally true. A subset of the temporarily true things is then expected to be selected by the ego as what we desire, while other true things are neglected. Following this, a subset of things that we desire must be judged by the moral sense, and only those things that are right must be permitted. In this way, we are expected to obtain the combination of true, right, and good. But if we remove the consideration of right and wrong, then we are left with all the truths, and with all that we might desire, which allows us to choose from among the possibilities. Of course, even the combination of possibilities and desires presents a problem in modern science because this choice is not viewed as a purpose—which *refers* to the future—because of scientific biases that only the past is causally efficacious. But even if we overcame this hurdle, we would only have causes and effects, without consequences—i.e. choice without a sense of responsibility.

The sense of responsibility comes from the recognition that we are situated in a *role*—a relation to another role—and roles are different from objects. The material object enters and exits a role, like objects change their *position* in space. As a result, we require two kinds of positions— (1) that produces macroscopic objects by *connecting* atomic objects into a form, and (2) that relates macroscopic objects to each other through a role. The macroscopic forms constitute the *truth* judgment through the "has-a" relationship—e.g. the body has a hand, the hand has fingers, the fingers have nails, etc. The roles on the other hand constitute the judgment of *right* through the "is-a" relation—e.g. that a person is a soldier and is therefore required to protect the country. The relationship of roles can be violated because it doesn't involve the judgment of true or false; when it is violated it doesn't become false, and when it is followed it doesn't become true. Therefore, we have to induct a new kind of judgment—that of right and wrong—to describe roles.

A government's job is to enunciate the roles and their responsibilities. A noteworthy fact is that roles are also hierarchical which means that everyone doesn't have the same level of empowerment or responsibility. The role that owns a higher level of responsibility also has a higher level of empowerment.

Conversely, the roles that have lesser empowerment also have lesser responsibility. The point is that society cannot be *flat*. It must have tiers, and the laws of the land can define those tiers as long as they also define their expected behaviors in *accordance* with the moral laws of nature. We are not free to define our own laws, and therefore governments chosen by people's votes—in order to fulfill their desires—are as immoral as autocrats if they don't understand and follow nature's laws of right and wrong.

Just as science studies an object's properties and attributes its behaviors based on those properties, similarly, there is a science in which we can talk about the *position* of an object relative to other objects, which prescribe their expected behaviors, and actions in those roles produce consequences that change the object's state—i.e. the role. The difference is that this space of roles can be described without reference to objects because every object that enters this position is expected to abide by the rules of the role. In a sense, the space of roles can be 'empty'—i.e. it exists without objects—although objects occupy these positions and are then governed by the position.

The laws of action and consequence are not uniform across roles. Each position brings a set of expectations and hence laws. We cannot consider space as homogeneous and isotropic (as in modern science)[10]. We must rather describe space as roles, which means that the laws of nature cannot be uniform across all locations in space. The law of nature is relative to the *form* of the role or position in space. We can find a law that describes the expected behaviors and action consequences at different locations in space, but this law *constructs* the space by stipulating different expectations for each position. We can also say that each position has a different *type*—there are potentially infinite types of positions—but all positions may not always be occupied. As a result, space is 'empty' and it cannot be measured (although we can see it as a possibility) unless an object occupies the position.

Anyone can enter any position provided— (1) they are qualified, and they have the necessary *ability* to execute that role, (2) they want to occupy and execute the role, and (3) they have the necessary *karma* from the past to be permitted that role. Society can therefore be organized as a *class-system*[11] or as a *caste-system*[12]. In a caste system, a person doesn't satisfy all the conditions above; for instance, he might have the requisite *karma* and a strong desire, but not the necessary qualification. Or, he might be qualified and have the necessary *karma* but may be reluctant to play the role. When a person is pushed into a role without qualification or desire or both, a caste system is produced. Typically, such castes manifest as generational inheritance of roles and responsibilities—e.g. a president's son becomes a president, simply because of their family connection. The *class-system* is on the other hand based on satisfying the three criteria above: the person must have the *karma*, must be qualified, and willing. Many times, we find qualified and willing people who don't get to play a position in society—we tend to call them 'unlucky'—but that 'luck' is their *karma*. No one can take a position without the requisite *karma*, and no one can avoid a position when the *karma* manifests. However, as we have seen earlier, *karma* manifests relative to *guna* or desires. Therefore, one is expected to choose the type of role they are qualified to play and which they desire, and *karma* will create experiences *within* that role.

When a person enters a role they are unqualified to play, they create bad *karma* for themselves as the role's expectations are unchanged whether or not one is qualified. Incapability is thus not an excuse for the non-performance of duties. One is expected to perform duties admirably or relinquish the position for someone else, even though one might have the requisite *karma* to continue in that role for more time. If an unqualified person relinquishes their powerful role and takes a lower position more suited to their capacities, they will conserve their good *karma* (by relinquishing their position of power) and not create bad *karma* (by taking a role where they can perform their role). They may not enjoy the previous position of power, but they will enjoy the lower position much longer, and they wouldn't have produced adverse consequences, which means that their future is also better.

The class system is *meritorious* without being *meritocratic*. That is, the meritorious will have a higher position, provided they desire and have the requisite *karma*. This is not meritocracy where merit is sufficient to occupy a position, because factually this does not happen. All qualified people cannot occupy powerful positions, but every person occupying the position should be qualified. We might say that merit is necessary but not sufficient for a person taking a position; one's *karma* and desires are also important conditions, and eventually their combination produces the sufficient condition. We often find that due to past *karma* the sufficient condition is satisfied, but the necessary condition of being suitably qualified for the role is not.

The Role of Emotion in Science

Modern science has failed to delve into the motivations of life—i.e. the quest for eternity, freedom, and happiness. It decrees that all material objects are temporary, that there is no freedom because laws of nature predetermine all reality, and happiness is an epiphenomenon of chemical reactions. Consequently, we have lost the ability to judge the nature of truth, right, and good, because we tend to believe that the quest for truth, right, and good is flawed. How can the soul ever be happy when its fundamental needs are denied? How can life be fulfilled if our innate cravings are constantly scoffed at?

The essence of scientific quests should be to establish three facts—that only those things that are eternal are true, only those actions that create freedom are right, and only those choices that produce happiness are good. This requires the understanding of the natural laws in which the illusion appears temporarily—entirely due to scientific laws—but we must call that illusion *phenomena* rather than *reality*. The study of temporary phenomena is useful only to the extent that we can determine why those phenomena are temporary—i.e. why they evolve. The laws of evolution of material reality, therefore, inform us that matter evolves because it is *false*—the truth never evolves. To distinguish between true and false, we have to see matter as a symbol of meaning, where some symbols exist but are false, whereas other symbols exist and are true. If a symbol is evolving, then it is false. The faster it changes, the lesser it is true. Conversely, the things that are longer-lived have greater truth in them. The longevity of phenomena is indicative of their truth. By measuring that longevity, we can progress from less to more true.

The world is organized hierarchically, in which things close to the root are eternal, the stems and branches are longer lived but not eternal, while the leaves and fruits are short-lived. Accordingly, going from the leaves to the fruits—signified by greater unity in the diversified phenomena—is not only the quest for the truth but also the search for eternity. The true and the eternal are identical because the root of the tree is eternal, it grows and sustains longer-lived branches, but the fruits and leaves grow and die rapidly. The fruits and leaves too can be observed temporarily but they are not the reality. For instance, short-lived atomic objects are less real as compared to the longer-lived particles. The short-lived phenomena are only indicators that we haven't yet found the unity in this short-lived diversity that will unify them—and would be longer lived. Reality is therefore connected to time—the real is free of death. This should be the first conclusion of scientific knowledge.

The second conclusion is that we are not just material bodies; these bodies are related to other bodies through a *role*. The role produces *expectations*—of right and wrong—and accords us a position of superiority or inferiority by which we are either controlled or have the power to control others. Our roles are hierarchical—those lower in the hierarchy are controlled by those higher in the hierarchy. Clearly, those who want more freedom would desire to *rise* in this hierarchy and become the controllers with power over others. But as you rise higher in this hierarchy, you also have a greater responsibility. If one uses their currently available position of power correctly, then their freedom is increased because they demonstrate their proclivity to use their power responsibly. Conversely, those who misuse their current position of power demonstrate they are not fit to continue in the current position, let alone rise in higher positions; they must hence lose their power.

The rise and fall in this hierarchy are governed by the appropriate use of one's power and one's freedom is a consequence of one's previous actions—i.e. whether they used their freedom responsibly or irresponsibly. To maintain one's position, or to rise in that position, one must continue to behave responsibly because irresponsible behavior will eventually subjugate a person to others who behave responsibly. Moral action is therefore the cause of greater freedom but immoral action results in lesser freedom. Since nobody wants to lose their freedom, they must act morally—and to act morally they must know the demands of their role. The role-based *consequence* of an action is different from the object-based *effect* of that action. Modern science only studies the effects and not the consequences. Furthermore, it describes the effects as being caused by the properties of the objects, when the objects are only possibilities. By eliminating the role of choice, science eliminates freedom, and this manifests in the idea that every object interacts with all other objects simultaneously. Role-based interactions are necessitated when objects only act pair-wise. In that case, the *abilities* of a person are not the sole arbiter of causality; their *role* is also an important determinant.

The third conclusion must be that the selection of an ability, to be enacted in a role, is a function of choice, governed by our *purpose*. These purposes are different from the role and the possible object states. If the purpose is bad (e.g. to hurt others), then the resulting action would also be contrary to the demands of the role and result in lesser freedom in the future—including the choice of our own happiness. But even if the purpose is good (e.g. to enjoy one's life), and if the morality is weak, the person might act irresponsibly thereby taking away the opportunities to enjoy. The freedom accorded to a person is relative to their purposes. For example, if you enjoy X and the freedom only affords you X, lesser freedom has no meaning because you can always obtain what you desire. Lesser freedom would be meaningful if it acts contrary to what you desire. Therefore, the notion of 'freedom' is not *quantitative*—i.e. it doesn't indicate the total number of alternatives one has to choose from. It is rather *qualitative*—i.e. relative to what we *desire* to enjoy.

Freedom means that we can enjoy, although we may not do so. Bondage similarly means that we don't have the opportunity to obtain what we desire. Effectively, we can define the role and expectation by the present role, but the consequence of the action—resulting in greater or lesser freedom—will act *relative* to our desires at that time. If our desires change, but we have acted responsibly in the past, then the consequences of previous actions will afford those situations where we can fulfill what we desire at the present.

Modern science is very far from this understanding of natural causality, although it has moved closer to it with the advent of atomic theory where material objects are described as possibilities, and the causal relation between objects is quantized—indicating that objects don't interact simultaneously—which then prepares us for the idea of a *role*. However, these are not adequate because there is a need for the idea that a role brings expectations of behavior, that actions in accordance or opposition to these expectations change our freedom, and that freedom is effected relative to our purposes.

While atomic theory tells us that there are many possible actions and relations, it doesn't tell us which of these are *right*. As a result, it cannot explain why the possible states and relations increase or decrease as the actions themselves are changed; in modern atomic theory the states spread after each 'collapse' and the spread is not different based on the choice; that is, all choices are equally 'right' because the freedom of choice returns after each choice. A moral law will stipulate that after a choice, the states don't spread uniformly; some choices lead to greater freedom while others lead to lesser freedom—i.e. the possible states depending on the chosen alternative. Furthermore, even though the alternatives increase, the 'right' choice doesn't increase. The increase in alternatives acts as a *temptation* to make the wrong choice and cause a 'fall' from greater freedom. As one chooses the right action, the temptations grow, which means that it gets harder and harder to make the right choice, and the likelihood of a further increase in freedom is smaller. Conversely, as one's freedom reduces, one is forced to do the right thing and the likelihood of performing the right action under the given circumstances increases. As the right action is performed, the freedom grows.

The result of this dynamics is that if one acts immorally, one would fall but reach a point at which they have nowhere to go but upwards. Similarly, if one acts morally, one would rise but reach a point at which they have nowhere to go but downwards. The moral law produces a cycle in which one goes up and down. At each level in this hierarchy, one can enjoy different desires *legitimately* and to relish that pleasure one would be situated in a different role. By the desire for pleasure, one can choose the role. If a role is chosen, there are strictures of behavior, and consequences of actions.

The critical step in the evolution of science is the induction of morality as a natural law in which matter exists as a possibility and we have the choice to select an alternative, but all choices are not equal, regardless of their *probability*. The probability only indicates *our* disposition—i.e. what we are likely to do—but it doesn't mean that the action is *right*. The likelihood of action must be complemented by its *righteousness*, coupled with the law that predicts the consequences. Since science has historically rejected choices, it has also neglected responsibilities. Atomic theory recognizes the need for choices, but just adding a choice to possibility—without *moral responsibility*—doesn't solve the problem. Such a choice is no different than randomness because all choices are essentially equivalent—whether they are more or less likely. The room for choices in atomic theory is inadequate without a moral law, and the induction of such a natural law is the key next step in science.

Emotion in Logic and Mathematics

Karma is sufficient to determine if something will happen. But *karma* is insufficient to decide *when* and *where* it will happen. The material possibilities are the answer to the *where* question, while a person's intentions are the response to the *when* problem. For something to happen, there must be capable actors involved in the action, therefore, capability is essential for the event, and ability is the necessary condition. But since ability by itself exists only as a possibility, a choice driven by a purpose also must be applied.

Modern logic employs necessity and sufficiency to decide outcomes. Something is necessary when things could not happen unless that condition is satisfied. Of course, they may not happen even when the necessary condition is satisfied, because there may be other necessary conditions that are not yet satisfied. Necessity by itself is therefore incomplete in determining the outcome because we don't know if there are other conditions that must be satisfied, and that leaves room for other factors to play in the decision even when a necessary condition is present. As we noted above, material ability is a necessity for something to occur; if this ability is absent the event will not occur. However, even if the ability is present, it may be unused, and therefore the existence of that ability doesn't guarantee the outcome itself. For example, I may be capable of eating food, and that ability is the necessary condition for eating, but I still have the choice of whether I eat or not.

Similarly, something is sufficient if it will definitely cause an effect, although there could be other causes that might also create the effect. This presents us with the scenario that a single cause may be *individually* sufficient to create an effect, but since the effect can equally well be produced by other causes we cannot deduce the presence of a particular cause from the observation of the effect. For instance, receiving a large inheritance is a sufficient condition for you to be rich. But inheritance is not the only possible cause of richness—there can be other potential causes such as you being rich because of your own effort. Therefore, we cannot infer the existence of richness into the conclusion of inheritance, although an inheritance would be sufficient to explain the effect. As we noted above, *karma* is a sufficient condition to determine an effect, but given an effect, we cannot deduce the *karma*. For example, just because a person wears ragged clothes or eats simple food, we cannot conclude that he has bad *karma*; the person may have chosen to lead a simple and austere life and renounced the opportunities *karma* affords.

The inadequacy of both necessary and sufficient conditions points to *choice*. Ability is necessary but it doesn't become an action without a choice. Similarly, *karma* is sufficient but because of choice the effects of *karma* may not be obvious. The effects of *karma* can be warded off in two ways— (1) we have good *karma,* but we choose not to use it, and (2) we have bad *karma,* but we can balance it against good *karma*, nullifying one cause with another, or overcompensating the bad with the good. When the effect has been nullified, it appears that *karma* is not acting although good and bad *karma* have canceled each other. Similarly, any desirable outcome may be because there is more good *karma* and less bad *karma* acting simultaneously, although we may not know the exact proportions. Finally, even in an undesirable outcome more bad *karma* may be acting with a smaller amount of good *karma*, producing a mixed result. There is room for choice which decides to just accept the good or bad *karma*, or decides to cancel them adequately, or compensates one by another—e.g. making a bad situation worse by voluntarily accepting more austerity and renunciation than the *karmic* situation demands.

Therefore, both necessity (ability) and sufficiency (*karma*) are inadequate to decide the outcome, which is why emotion and purpose must be added to logic. *Karma* and material possibilities are also not necessary and sufficient conditions for happiness. One can be happy even in adverse conditions—caused either by inability to enjoy the available opportunities or having the ability frustrated due to lack of opportunity. This is because happiness is produced by one's intentions and purposes. If one can control one's desires, and practice detachment, then the shortfall in ability or opportunity doesn't make one unhappy. The process is difficult, but its possibility means that ability and opportunity are not the sole determinants of our happiness. Coupled with the fact that ability needs to be converted into an action by a choice, and that opportunity must be exploited to obtain a result by choice, we can see a clear role for choice beyond necessity and sufficiency.

This conclusion rests on an understanding of necessity and sufficiency as *ability* and *opportunity*, which depends on seeing the world not as fixed things but as possibilities—(1) each object is the ability of many alternative states, and (2) each object has the opportunity to potentially interact with other objects. Only when we fix the state of the object and then fix the interactions with other objects do we arrive at the idea that material states and material relationships are adequate to determine an outcome. Modern logic operates under these assumptions of classical physics—it assumes that each object is in a certain state and that each object has fixed interactions with other objects. When these two conditions are taken away—due to atomic theory—classical logic must also fail to adequately describe the outcome.

The problem of choice runs deep—all the way into logic—even to determine the physical outcomes. When we consider the fact that choice plays a role in deciding our purposes and our happiness (based on abilities and opportunities) then we can see why logic must be fundamentally revised in order to explain the physical world and why we sometimes become happy and at other times unhappy in it. The subjective motivation to think about choice is our happiness, but there is also an objective motivation to even explain the effects because ability and opportunity are inadequate causes.

To necessity and sufficiency therefore we must add *choice*. The distinction between these is common. For instance, we distinguish between needs and wants—e.g. food is a necessity to survive, but I want tasty food. We also distinguish between sufficiency and wants—a certain amount of food is sufficient to survive but I want to eat beyond sufficiency. We have seen how necessity and sufficiency are different: it is necessary to wake up in order to go to work but waking up is not sufficient to reach the workplace (as you might wake up and go to other places). Finally, if you are in the workplace, it is not necessary that you have woken up in the morning to reach there; you could have also worked through the night, never gone home and slept, and your presence, therefore, cannot be inferred to mean sleep, waking, and travel.

In modern logic, necessity and sufficiency are studied as implicational rules, but intention is not. Since intentions create time, logical conclusions are time-independent—true at all times. Similarly, because possibilities—as ability and opportunity—create our sense of space, by removing possibility logical conclusions become independent of space. In effect, logical inferences produce things that must be true in all space and time—and we construe all such conclusions as *laws* of nature, which apply at all places and times in nature. This view of logic is obtained when space is not a domain of possibilities but of fixed *things*, and time is not the choice among alternatives but determinism in which the successive states of nature are produced from previous states. How deeper could classical thinking have penetrated logic itself?

The key problem in logical stance is how we use logic to explain the real world of events that change with space and time when logic only provides us the truths that must prevail across all space and time? The short answer is that logic itself is insufficient to make these predictions, and a famous distinction between *reason* and *experience* was instituted in philosophy to overcome this shortcoming. The distinction claimed that logic and mathematics only give us the universal truths but only some of these truths become real in the present world. Therefore, only some mathematical theories will apply to the real world, only some of the possibilities described by those theories will be observed. To fill the gap between the universal truth and the contingent truth, one had to limit the universal truth by some *initial conditions*—e.g. fixing the states of all particles in space, by which the universal truth (i.e. the laws of nature) could deterministically predict the future states.

Science has been a mixture of reason and experience because each is inadequate without the other. Given an observed fact, you can't be sure which theory is the best explanation, because there are other theories that will explain equally well the same facts. Conversely, given a theory, you can't be sure that it adequately explains the facts because you just might not have fed the appropriate initial conditions into the universal truths—laws of nature. Philosophy of science—as the act of trying to justify science as the ultimate method of knowledge—has therefore suffered from numerous conceptual problems because of the way nature was conceived without possibility and choice, and then logic and mathematics were defined to fit that ideology.

We are now faced with a new type of ideology based on possibility and choice, under which there is necessity and sufficiency, but they are individually and collectively inadequate to produce an outcome without a choice. This is a new way of looking at logic as something that is both necessary and sufficient still doesn't produce an effect, unless a choice is made. The possibilities themselves are not equal, and when a choice is made, a consequence of that choice must be created depending on whether the possibility was right or wrong. That consequence then changes the sufficient condition of opportunities—restricting or increasing our choices—which change the necessary conditions of our ability to bring a change. Our choices alter the opportunities, which then change the abilities, which then modify our choices. This is the unceasing cycle of nature in which choice gradually ripples through the material necessary and sufficient conditions and comes back to effect choice itself. And yet, you can change the entire cyclic process by choice itself.

When choice is studied without consideration of responsibility—i.e. what should happen (because I desire it) but without what should not happen (because it is immoral) it remains incomplete in describing the real world. Choice has therefore to be viewed as having both assertion and negation: the assertion pertains to what we want, and negation describes what is immoral. Possibility by itself is incomplete, but simply adding choice to it, without seeing that choice has two facets, is also incomplete.

8

Emotion and Religion

Knowledge, Relationship, and Devotion

Religion, like everything else, requires three things fundamentally. To begin with, we must know the nature of reality—i.e. that which is eternal. All that exists temporarily is a fact, but not reality because we distinguish between *phenomena* (which exist temporarily) and *reality* (which exists eternally). In Western philosophy, the phenomena-reality distinction has been twisted to accommodate a contorted idea about reality. The contortion is that reality is all that *exists* (even though temporarily) and phenomena is how that reality *appears* to us. Once the definition of phenomena and reality are twisted in this way, then all phenomena become illusions, and the observer who experiences these phenomena must always be under an illusion because, fundamentally, reality is always different from the phenomena. That not only creates an epistemological problem—How do we know reality by observing the phenomena if the phenomena are always illusions? —but also undermines the reality of the observer who knows. Why should I care about knowing anything "out there" when "I" is only an extravagant illusion?

There is a fix to this problem—namely, that reality is not that which exists temporarily, and phenomena is not how that reality appears to us. Reality is instead only that which exists eternally, and phenomena is that which exists temporarily. Sometimes we experience reality (when we contact that which exists eternally) and at other times we experience phenomena (when we contact that which is temporary). The phenomena exist, although temporarily, and the experience of that phenomena is based on our encounter with those facts, just as the experience of reality is based on our contact with reality. To be religious is to know the difference between reality and phenomena—i.e. what is eternal and thus different from all that exists temporarily.

An outcome of this revision is that the world that exists "outside" the observer (and which the observer contacts during an experience) exists just as the observer experiences it. As a result, the material world is to be described using the same words as the phenomenal experience—i.e. as color, taste, smell, sound, touch, concepts, judgments, intentions, and morals—not as particles, waves, and forces. The above revision also entails that the eternal reality will also be described using the same phenomenal constructs—i.e. as color, taste, smell, sound, touch, concepts, judgments, intentions, and morals—although this experience would be eternal, and hence reality.

In other words, some color, taste, smell, sound, touch, concepts, judgments, intentions, and morals are eternal while others are temporary. Knowing reality doesn't mean giving up experience—i.e. color, taste, smell, sound, touch, concepts, judgments, intentions, and morals; it means changing the experience from temporary to eternal. Religion means moving from temporary to eternal, not from experience to lack of experience. All "religion" which talks about discarding experience to attain 'salvation' from phenomenal existence is mistaken because it carries the Western philosophical distinction of reality being the background and phenomena being its "impression" on our consciousness[1]. That ideology about reality and phenomena is a nonstarter because we can never know reality through phenomena, so discarding phenomena only means that we stop even trying to know reality.

We might assume that we are eternal—and hence reality—but it is only an incomplete conclusion because if we were the only reality then I must be the cause of the phenomenal world, and if I am the real cause then I must be able to fully control the phenomena. If I was fully in control of my life and the rest of the world, then why would I be unhappy? Why would I *seek* the knowledge of this reality if this reality is ultimately my creation?

First, the self is eternal, but it is only one of the many eternal things. Knowing the self to be eternal is a good start (because the materialists consider the self to be a phantasm), but it does not constitute complete knowledge. Knowledge is complete when I know my eternity and the eternity of other things which I encounter and experience—eternally. In order to obtain that eternal experience, I must contact things other than myself.

Second, the need to contact things other than I requires us to define a relationship to those things—i.e. the roles in which the self and the other are mutually defined for an interaction. Knowledge also involves an exchange of knowledge between the knower and the known; we normally call that exchange an *action* because it is the prerogative of the known to reveal itself through an action, just as it is the privilege of the knower to absorb that revelation as knowledge. Knowledge and action are therefore two sides of an exchange—action from the perspective of the known, and knowledge from the perspective of the knower. What we know is not necessarily all that can be known, because the known must unveil itself to knowledge, and that depends on the relation between knower and known. Therefore, the same thing can be known to different extents through different relations. We might say that each relation reveals a different *aspect* of the known—like looking at one of the six faces of a dice only reveals to us knowledge of one of the faces.

To see the other faces, we must establish new relationships, and the problem of knowing the known becomes a problem of establishing the appropriate relationships. In different relations we can know different aspects, and we can organize these hierarchically—at the lowermost level we will know mutually exclusive facets, but at higher levels knowledge attains more unity; at the highest level, we can know the object of knowledge in full.

Third, the possibility to know different aspects through different relations brings the question: Which aspect do we *want* to know? What aspect of reality excites and motivates us the most? If we know what we desire, then we will determine the relationship we need to establish to know the specific aspects of reality, and through that relationship we will then know the chosen facets of the known. In Western empiricism it is widely supposed that there is no "choice" in knowing reality because reality is that one thing which exists independent of us, and since it is independent of us, we can't enforce our choices on what exists independently. This idea is wrong if reality has many facets which are organized hierarchically. The six faces of the dice are, for instance, mutually exclusive aspects if we want to measure the dice sensually. If, however, we want to describe the dice conceptually then we can say that it is a six-faced object with numbers imprinted on the different sides.

The sensual knowledge can only be complete if the object has no faces, and this is possible only if the object is a *dimensionless* particle. The concept of a particle in classical physics is not an accident; it is the claim that sensual knowledge can be complete—i.e. we can know the full system through measurement—as reality doesn't have *facets*. If the world was not comprised of point particles, then to measure it, we would have to choose a relationship and knowledge would be the outcome of those choices. The idea of dimensionless particles helped physicists conclude the completeness of sensual knowledge, thereby eliminating the need for choices—evidenced in the determinism of classical physics. But, then, the key problem is: to claim determinism you must always be able to reach dimensionless particles in nature, because the moment things are dimensioned, you must employ choice.

We now know that there are no dimensionless points, and fundamental particles—like the electron—are dimensioned. Quantum physics means that matter and energy are not infinitesimal. But if they are discrete, then we cannot know all facets of an object simultaneously, although we can know them in different relations. Niels Bohr[2] called this problem *complementarity*[3] because the classical properties of matter—e.g. position and momentum—could be measured in a single relation, but they can only be measured through different relations. What was previously a point particle, has now become a multifaceted dice, which led Einstein to complain that "God does not play dice". Einstein did not recognize that if we cannot see all the faces of the dice it doesn't mean that reality is not objective. However, it does mean that it is not any of the observations: the reality can be *conceived* (as a dice) but not *perceived* (as one of the six complementary faces of the dice).

Atomic theory also teaches us that these particles have *aspects*, which cannot be known simultaneously. So, we are no longer looking at a dimensionless point, but a coin that has two faces, or a dice that has six faces, and only one of the faces can be completely measured at any time. That, in turn, gives rise to a choice—heads or tails—of which all of us are familiar.

Despite this sensual choice, we can speak of a *coin* with two sides, but we cannot *see* the coin. The coin is a concept associated with an object that has mutually exclusive facets. By using that concept, we arrive at a conceptual unity about the object when sensually we cannot know the coin at once. In other words, our knowledge is no longer sensually complete—because it has opposite facets—but it could be conceptually complete because the opposite facets *belong* to the same object, which can never be sensually perceived. Therefore, any time we encounter dimensioned objects, sensual knowledge must always be complemented by the mental conception in order to obtain completeness. Of course, a given object may also be described by mutually exclusive concepts—e.g. the same thing can be called a table and chair—and then to unify the irreconcilable concepts we would need to look even deeper at the *intention* for which something was designed. In this way, we construct a hierarchy of mutually exclusive alternatives—i.e. the inverted tree.

A person is similarly known at many levels—from the body to their sensations, thoughts, judgments, intentions, and morals. We can only see one side of the body at any time, and no instrument can measure the whole body at once. If you have multiple measurements, you must ask: Why should these measurements pertain to the *same thing*? Even if we took at pictures of the different parts of body—e.g. a picture of the front and another one of the back—who is to say that these two pictures pertain to the same *person*?

To unify the sensations, we must construe the idea of a *body*—i.e. a single thing—which is a concept. Thus, we must walk up the inverted tree of concepts to complete our knowledge which is never complete unless we reach the soul of the body, who is the ultimate *person* that unifies all the mutually exclusive parts into a whole. To recognize the deeper levels of reality that unify the disparate and irreconcilable aspects of sensual experience we require deeper forms of perception to form a more and more complete picture of the person in our understanding. Completing our knowledge thus means deepening our perception. But we don't necessarily have to complete our knowledge. Even if we superficially know reality—which is eternal—our superficial and incomplete knowledge would also be eternal. This gives us a choice—how deeply and how completely do we *want* to know reality?

To practice religion, we must first know the distinction between reality and phenomena, then determine how complete or fragmented our knowledge is, and then establish a relation in order to complete it. These three things are called *sambandha* (relation), *abhidheya* (knowledge and action), and *prayojana* (our desire that excites and motivates us to know something superficially or completely). We also call them *sat* (relationship), *chit* (knowledge and action), and *ananda* (pleasure). There is no fundamental difference between religion and science because both involve an identical process in the creation of experience. The difference lies only in the phenomenal vs. real objects. Spiritual experience can be demystified by understanding material experience because both are built out of the same three components. The difference is only that science studies temporary objects and religion wants to experience the eternal objects. To understand their difference, we need to delve into why some things are temporary while others are eternal.

Temporariness vs. Eternity

In the temporary phenomena there is time, but the eternal reality is without time. Now, we might think that if there is no time, then there must be no change either: we would be fixed in experience, seeing and knowing the same thing eternally. This is a wrong conception of time, drawn from the temporary phenomena because the phenomena involve two kinds of changes—the objects of our knowledge are changing, and our relations to those objects are changing as well. Eternity means our relationships can change but the objects are not changing. For example, if the present world were eternal, then I could see my family in the morning, my colleagues during the day, and my friends during the evening, but the family, colleagues, and friends would be eternal: nobody would ever be born, grow old, or die. In the phenomenal world, change means that the objects of our knowledge are themselves created and destroyed, and our relations to those objects also change, due to which we experience different objects at different times, and if we encountered the same object again it would have also changed. In the eternal world, change means that we can know different things at different times, but those things themselves don't change. In the phenomenal world change means changing objects and changing relations, but in the eternal world change only means changing relationships—i.e. encountering different objects.

Eternity doesn't entail a lack of variety by which I am forced to see only one thing—which denies free will. Eternity only means that whatever I see exists forever, although I have the choice to see those eternal things one after another. I also have the choice to know those eternal objects at various levels of unity or diversity. My free will pertains to the *encounter* with different realities and different levels of knowing the same reality at different times, but the change in that encounter doesn't mean birth, old age, disease, or death. As the relationship to the object changes, the knowledge may be altered, but the object never loses its capacity to recreate the earlier experiences.

Vedic philosophy distinguishes between *material* and *efficient* causes. The material cause is the capacity to be known and the ability to act—it always exists as a possibility; we call this *chit*. The efficient cause is our desire to enjoy the world in a certain way, and the relation which is established to that reality in order to enjoy; we call this *ananda* and *sat*, respectively. As we have seen, the *ananda* and *sat* also manifest in the *guna* and *karma* of the person, and these are the efficient causes. In the phenomenal world, both material and efficient causes change, which means that the known objects are changing as are our desires and relations to those objects. In the world of reality, the material cause never changes but the efficient causes can change. We can thus know the same thing in new ways, or repeat the same knowledge over and over because the known object never disappears materially. There is hence eternal reality and changing experience—caused by the soul's free will—and time is experienced as the evolving free will (which causes changing relations to reality and the concomitant shift in pleasure) but that time does not cause material change—i.e. birth and death.

Why is the phenomenal world temporary? Why does the material cause when pertaining to phenomena undergo change when the material cause pertaining to reality is eternal? The short answer to that quandary is *conservation laws*[4]. When you see a material object, some energy from that object must be transferred from the known to the knower and the known object is *different* after the knowing because it changed by transferring energy to the knower. To bring the known object back to its original state, the lost energy must be replenished through absorption from some other energy source.

The reality can be eternal if either this cycle of absorption and emission is eternal, or if the conservation of laws doesn't hold. If the eternity were caused by the perpetuity of the cycle of absorption and emission, the known object would change during an interaction—i.e. *lose* some energy. This energy may be gained back through another exchange, but the loss itself entails that the reality has been 'disturbed' in the process of observation because some energy was transferred from the known to the knower. If, however, the conservation laws don't hold, then our knowledge of an object would not change the known object even though knowledge is transferred from the known to the knower. Now you can have your cake and eat it too!

The experience of eternity means that conservation laws don't hold. When you know the reality, it is not because of energy transfer from the known to the knower. Rather, you must be able to know without changing the object of knowledge. Effectively, we are talking about continuously increasing or expanding energy because the source of knowledge is not diminished by what the knower has gained. The knowledge you absorb also cannot be lost in the eternal reality, which means that if you have experienced something once, you never *forget* it. For instance, if you have tasted some food once, the memory of that taste is eternal and can never be forgotten. You still want to taste food again and again, and each such tasting creates an eternal impression. Once acquired, the knowledge is eternal and never diminishes.

A world of eternity entails an *expanding* space in which new knowledge is added as additional branches of the tree of your knowledge, and the tree grows perpetually because the previously acquired knowledge is never destroyed. Of course, your *awareness* of that knowledge—created by a relation to that knowledge—may change and therefore you might not always be aware of your previously acquired experiences. But that knowledge is materially eternal—i.e. it exists as *memory* which may be recalled later[5].

We can conclude that the material cause indeed changes over time, but that change is continual *increase*. There is no loss or diminution and therefore eternity doesn't mean a fixed reality; it means an ever-expanding reality. Everyone is therefore becoming wiser and more knowledgeable over time because everything experienced is eternally remembered. Knowledge is not a destination; it is an eternal process because the tree of knowledge is infinite and keeps expanding forever. As you become wiser and more enlightened, your encounter with other knowers brings something new to the table—they can now see that you know something new, and that novelty makes the previously known person even more interesting: you want to know what new things were recently learned. There is no limit to this learning. The more you learn, the more you can transmit your knowledge to others, which makes the receivers even more knowledgeable (about you having the knowledge and the object of that knowledge) as you can hear their perspective on reality. The ever-expanding reality is a place of continuous talking and listening; as more knowledge is gained, it nuances all the previous knowledge.

Energy conservation means that the number of nodes in the tree is constant, although they can be rearranged in the tree. If the tree collapses, then energy is lost; if the tree grows, the energy is created. The phenomenal tree is created, maintained, and destroyed. But the tree of reality is ever-expanding such that you can never find the origin when nobody knew anything. In that sense, the tree is eternal. And yet, we can still imagine a time when there was only the root of the tree—the original knowledge—from which the tree grew. The key question to understand this reality is therefore not why time acts differently in reality (than in phenomena). The key question is why the knowledge of reality is not conserved, or why it is always expanding, when the knowledge of phenomena involves conservation, and thus everything acquired during our present experiences must eventually be lost.

Origins of Phenomenal Conservation

The conservation laws are a property of the phenomenal world because of the *logic* employed here. The phenomenal logic has three components—identity, mutual-exclusion[6], and non-contradiction[7]. The identity can say that there is a 'cake'. Non-contradiction says that the cake is either chocolate or vanilla, not both. And mutual-exclusion says you can either have your cake or eat the cake, not neither. Both non-contradiction and mutual-exclusion use the term 'either', but they are used in different ways: non-contradiction is the *denial* of *both* (the cake cannot be *both* vanilla and chocolate) and mutual-exclusion is the denial of *neither* (the cake must either be present or eaten).

Often, contradiction is only apparent as we rise in the knowledge tree because the tree is diversified in the leaves and convergent in the root. The leaves appear contradictory, but the root is devoid of contradiction. Therefore, rising up the tree means going from diversity to unity, and hence from contradictions to consistency. For example, you can say that nothing can be both heads and tails, but the 'coin' is both heads and tails, although the 'coin' is a higher-level concept than the heads and tails. Unification in knowledge is achieved as we traverse from the leaves to the root and what appeared to be contradictory is gradually unified. Thus, non-contradiction is a fact about the phenomenal world, but it is also a *driver* toward complete knowledge because if you see a contradiction between facts then you seek a theory that explains contradicting facts. The facts are superficial, and the theory is deeper, which can explain contradicting superficial cases as special instances of the same thing. Contradictions mean that a deeper theory that unifies the knowledge and resolves the conflict is waiting to be found. Contradiction only means that we haven't gone deep enough—from leaves toward the root. We can conclude that even the phenomenal world is non-contradictory, and therefore we can do science—i.e. know without contradictions.

The conservation laws in the phenomenal world are due to mutual-exclusion because if energy is transferred from one object to another, then the cake has been eaten and you can't have it. Violating conservation laws means that the world is governed by a logic without mutual-exclusion. In the real world, you can know reality without changing it; your growth in knowledge doesn't entail a reduction in the known object. Since knowledge is organized as an inverted tree, the branches of the tree appear contradictory and the world may indeed be known in contradictory ways—e.g. heads vs. tails—but there is also a unifier (the 'coin') that reconciles the contradiction. The conflict is therefore apparent and never real. The mutual-exclusion is, however, real in the phenomenal reality and unreal in the eternal reality.

The reality of non-contradiction means the world is always created through opposites—e.g. heads and tails—and when you see the head, you don't see the tail, and you don't see the contradiction. But when you see the 'coin' you see opposites, but they are reconciled. Non-contradiction means that even if you are seeing heads, you can know that there must be a tail without seeing it, because concepts are defined through oppositions. Thus, 'hot' cannot be defined without 'cold', and if there is heat somewhere then there must be cold somewhere else. In the world of mutual-exclusion, this is easily understood because you transfer the energy and create the cold at the source and hot at the destination. This is not easily seen without mutual-exclusion because you are creating knowledge without *transferring* energy.

How can you know something without transferring knowledge? This is possible if your knowledge of hot is *correlated* with someone else's knowledge of cold, and both instances of knowledge are created simultaneously—although they pertain to the same object. Effectively, one person sees the head, while the other person sees the tail, at the same time. The experience of hot and cold is created at once, without a contradiction (because the known object is both hot and cold) and without mutual exclusion (because two opposites are created simultaneously). Therefore, *I* may eat the cake, but someone else can still see the cake. The cake, therefore, existed as one thing before this experience, but it has now forked into two experiences— of eating and of observing it. Since both experiences are created simultaneously, the cake is not *transferred* into my mouth. And yet I can still have the experience of eating it. From the standpoint of conservation, the total energy—comprising of opposites—is still constant because the opposites cancel each other. The unified has now split into opposites, thereby creating new experiences. This is a semantic expansion—like dividing the number 0 into two opposites +1 and -1. The total remains the same after the division, so conservation is not violated. And yet, a branch has now forked into two twigs.

The paradox in the knowledge of reality (as opposed to phenomena) is that the same thing must be *simultaneously* known through opposites; the known thing is both opposites and yet neither of them, and the knowledge is obtained without reducing the known. In the phenomenal knowledge, there is only a need for correlation between the knower and the known—when the known reduces, the knower gains; this correlation is only pair-wise. But in the knowledge of reality, even the different knowers must be correlated, which means that for every person who sees the head of a coin, there must be simultaneously a person who will see the tail of the same coin. This would mean that as the coin flips, there are always two observers flipping along with the coin—one always seeing the head and the other always seeing the tail. The flipping coin constitutes the dance of reality, and there are always observers dancing with that flip. If one observer flips over from head to tail, the second observer will also flip over from tail to head, such that both observers see both head and tail (at different times via different relations) but everything is always known (by someone or another). That coordinated change means that no two observers see the reality from the same perspective at any time, but everyone can see the reality in the same way at different times.

This difference between phenomenal and real worlds is because the real world is *synchronized* in the sense that nobody is competing for the same perspective at the same time, and everyone is prepared to vacate their perspective for someone else to see the reality from that perspective. In fact, they are competing to give up their perspective to someone else, and take another position in a role swap. In the phenomenal world, we compete to have the same thing, and we are not prepared to relinquish what we have to someone else. As a result, I see only what I can get—through competition—but I can't see what others see. Competition here means remaining attached to what you have and fear that you might lose it. Cooperation there means wanting to give up your pleasure to someone else, and that change is itself the pleasure. As a result, each person sees much less variety in the phenomenal world (because they are afraid to lose what they have), and far greater variety in the real world (because they enjoy the very act of generosity).

The key point is that the phenomenal world is with mutual-exclusion and the real world is without it. Both worlds are non-contradictory due to which both can be known and described rationally through language. But to maintain the rationality in the real world (without mutual-exclusion) we must replace selfishness with generosity. Under selfishness, each person's free will is *independent,* but under generosity, free will is *coordinated*— "I will do what you want me to do". The selfish free will is competitive, but the generous free will is cooperative. Cooperation removes mutual-exclusion, which means that you can have your cake and eat it too and the world never deteriorates even though it is continuously consumed. Since the world is never destroyed, and because it keeps expanding, we call it the eternal world.

Materialism vs. Religiosity

This idea can be described logically, although it requires a logic without the mutual-exclusion principle. The principle can be restated as one of cooperation instead of competition, or as the place where free will is used generously rather than selfishly. In every religion, eternity, cooperation, and generosity are emphasized, while competition, selfishness, and temporariness are denounced. Conversely, materialism emphasizes competition and selfishness to obtain temporary happiness. From materialism, we cannot understand religion, and materialism and religiosity are incompatible. But materialism is also a philosophy of fear (of losing) and hope (of gaining), while religiosity is the philosophy of freedom from both fear and hope to practice the ideology of compassion, cooperation, charity, and generosity. When religions are mixed with ideologies of fear (e.g., that other people must be punished if they don't follow my ideology) or hope (e.g., that I will go to heaven by giving things to others) they are nothing but variations on materialism.

True religion is misunderstood today because (1) the theoretical basis on which eternity is achieved is unknown, (2) the fact that the eternal must be described using a different logic is not obvious, and (3) religions are mixed with selfishness and fear. The hope in most religions is one of selfish endeavor, and the fear propagated by religion is one of competing and destroying others. When mixed with materialism in this way, religiosity is perverted.

As we noted, nobody can be happy with the ideology of fear and hope. One needs the ideology of compassion and cooperation, keeping the nature of truth and righteousness in mind. Thus, you don't cooperate and empathize with what is false and evil, but you also don't disagree with opposite sides of the same truth. True religion, therefore, depends first on the development of knowledge about the nature of eternal reality—which is eternally true. Then you also adopt a perspective on that reality, because that perspective appeals to you, and makes you happy. However, you are also compassionate and generous in giving up your perspective and adopting another person's perspective if they are willing to exchange their position with yours. There is one reality, but diverse perspectives on that reality. We have the choice to pick a perspective but not without the generosity of exchanging it with the other's viewpoint. Any religion that either doesn't understand that there is one reality, or that there are diverse perspectives, or just sticks to their perspective remaining ungenerous to others, mixes materialism with religion.

There is emotion in religion, it is not founded on hope and fear; it is founded on the clarity of knowledge, the humility of diverse perspectives, and the charity of exchanging our views. The diversity of perspectives and the generosity of changing our perspective only *follow* the true understanding of a single reality. Modern notions of perspectival generosity—where everyone's viewpoint is equally good—actually don't result in eternity because we see the different things, but don't recognize that they are *perspectives* on the same *reality*. It is important to know reality and then hold a perspective. Just having a perspective without knowing reality is no different than experiencing the phenomena, which will remain temporary as one keeps changing their perspective and keeps seeing contradictions between viewpoints.

Reality is the root of the knowledge tree, from which different branches emanate. We have the free will to choose a branch and obtain a perspective. We need the generosity to relinquish our branch and let others have the same perspective. But before we use our free will and practice generosity, we must know how the branches emanate from the root. Without it, we cannot know which branch is real or illusion, and unless we know the distinction between reality and illusion, we cannot know whether to be generous and cooperative. Therefore, religion cannot be practiced without knowledge as we will cooperate and be generous to the illusion while remaining competitive and selfish to reality. The emotional happiness derived from cooperation and generosity is pointless without knowing what is eternally true and righteous.

Conversely, just knowing the truth and right doesn't make us happy unless we are prepared to cooperate and act generously because we will be stuck to our view, which must differ from the views of others—the different branches of the knowledge tree. If we are unprepared to see reality from different perspectives, then others will be unprepared to change their thinking as well. While everyone knows the truth and right, they remain isolated individually stuck to their views. They have the pleasure of knowing the truth and right from a perspective, but they don't have the happiness of compassion and generosity by which one sees things from the other's perspective.

Three Forms of Religion

Vedic philosophy thus distinguishes between three forms of religion, which are all true and right, and yet they are very different in nature. These forms are respectively called the *Brahman*, *Paramātma*, and *Bhagavān* realizations of the same reality. In the *Brahman* realization, one is able to distinguish the eternal from the temporary and discards the temporary to exit the phenomenal world. He sees that the self is eternal but has no idea that there is a world—i.e. other people and things—which are also eternal. The person only sees the self as being real, and in the process of rejecting the phenomena, he also rejects the reality that causes the phenomena. *Brahman* means "I am real" because I am eternal, but there is nothing else real and eternal.

In the *Paramātma* realization, one can see that there are other eternal living beings, which means that there are not just phenomenal experiences but also a reality outside the self. This reality is understood as being comprised of the same three parts as the self, but there are other individuals of the same *type*—i.e. *sat*, *chit*, and *ananda*. These individuals have ideological bodies, different roles, and methods of enjoyment, who derive their happiness from knowing the truth from a chosen perspective; they know that there are other perspectives, but they don't experience those perspectives.

In the *Bhagavān* realization, one sees that beyond the other individuals there is also a Supreme Individual in relation to Whom there are many individuals with their own ideological bodies, roles, and methods of enjoyment. There is not just a good understanding about the self, a recognition of the difference with the others, but a profound insight into the perspectives of the other viewpoints. One also realizes that all these perspectives are not equal because they have been created from an original perspective—God knowing His self from His perspective—which is the highest viewpoint. All other viewpoints are defined relative to that viewpoint, in terms of the object they know, the manner in which they know it, and whether they enjoy the knowledge. The *Bhagavān* realization is highest because a person is generous and humble enough to exchange their perspective with those of others.

In each of the successive steps, there is a dramatic increase in knowledge and happiness. In the *Brahman* realization, there is happiness based on the soul's eternity and distinctness from matter. Therefore, the person is neither fearful of dying or losing things, nor enthusiastically pursuing that which will eventually perish and give him grief. This freedom from fear and (false) hope, however, only produces the knowledge and happiness from knowing the self—not knowing the others. In the *Paramātma* realization, one knows that there are others, and besides knowing the self, he also knows the reality outside himself, although situated on a viewpoint. This happiness is greater because you know yourself and you know something else, realizing that yours is one of the many perspectives, although that perspective remains unchanged. In the *Bhagavān* realization, you know the reality from many perspectives, and your knowledge and happiness concomitantly increases.

This progressive realization and happiness requires an increasing departure from the focus on the self. In the *Brahman* realization, one gives up the pursuit of pleasure through others, but remains selfishly focused on the self as the primary goal of life. In the *Paramātma* realization, one progresses to the knowledge of reality other than the self, and which becomes the primary purpose of life. The person is, however, still attached to a specific perspective as the only way of knowing the truth, and will not relinquish it for other viewpoints; there is still selfishness in the belief that my perspective is the best perspective and I cannot renounce the perspective because I'm enjoying this view and nobody else can deprive me of this happiness derived from my perspective. In the *Bhagavān* realization, one discards this form of selfishness and concludes that even though I can enjoy a view, there are other perspectives more important and much better than mine. Thus, my pleasure is not as important as that of the others, and I would be happy to renounce it.

Each of these forms of religiosity is increasingly difficult but their associated happiness is also increasingly greater. The happiness derived from knowing oneself is lesser than the happiness derived from knowing reality from a chosen perspective. And the happiness derived from a chosen perspective is lesser than the happiness from many perspectives. To move forward in religious practice, one must progressively become less selfish about their happiness, and the emotional satisfaction comes from making others happier. For this reason, religion is often described as 'unselfish love' where one's happiness is increased not by focusing on self-happiness, but by preferring other's happiness. There is increasing cooperation and compassion in the successive forms of religion, which is completely contrary to materialism where happiness means the selfish pursuit of one's pleasure even at the cost of others' pleasure. The key point is that this material pleasure of selfishness is insignificant in comparison to the pleasure of truth from generosity.

The pleasure of self-realization or *Brahman* is pursued by the impersonalists who recognize the temporary nature of the phenomenal world and see themselves as eternal. But they are unable to see that there are other eternal individuals besides themselves. Hence, they reject the variety of the material world and the individuality of the different souls; they just consider themselves as eternal and claim that all other selves must also be identical to this one self. That latter claim is false because there are indeed innumerable individual souls, but if each one is focused on their self-realization, then their consciousness is focused upon their own selves and they cannot see others.

The impersonalist rejects the phenomenal manifestation of the *chit* and focuses on the consciousness (*sat*) on the self as the only object of knowledge. But even self-knowledge requires *śakti*; in this case, one needs *bhūti-śakti* at the least to focus on the self. Since this *śakti* is ultimately the power of God, one cannot know oneself without God's grace: the *śakti* must be available to a person for self-knowledge. *Brahman* by itself is all the individual souls devoid of the *śakti*. They exist, but they don't even know that they exist. It is possible to reach this situation by focusing the attention on the self, and withdrawing it from other things, but ultimately if you want to be just by yourself—i.e. without recognizing the existence of God and His *śakti*—then you would also be unconscious. *Brahman* is that state of deep sleep and unconsciousness which is perfectly restful because it is devoid of any kind of experience.

Although this state is superior to phenomenal experiences, the soul gets tired of existing and not knowing and not enjoying anything. His search for experience, relation, and pleasure causes the soul to 'fall down' from *Brahman* into the material world. Therefore, even though the soul is eternal, and hence *Brahman* is eternal, the soul's stay in *Brahman* state is temporary.

The impersonalist talks about the self as the only reality. They think that desires are material, and when this desire arises, a material body to fulfill the desires is created. So, if we get rid of desires then we can also get rid of the material body. This is not a false idea, although it is ignorant of the fact that the happiness derived from knowing oneself is lesser than that derived from knowing the reality of other living entities from a chosen viewpoint, or letting others see your perspective on reality. The impersonalist is also ignorant of the fact that even one's self-awareness is enabled by the *bhūti-śakti* and this *śakti* is available only through God's grace, which means that even to free oneself from material attachments one needs God's assistance to focus the consciousness away from matter and toward the self before one discards this awareness and decides to rest as an eternal existence unaware of one's own existence. In that sense, there can be no *Brahman* realization without acknowledging a personal God by Whose energy everything else is produced.

Emotion vs. Knowledge

Since time immemorial there has existed a contention between the theoretical and practical aspects of religion. In the Vedic tradition, they are sometimes contrasted as *jnana* and *bhakti*. The contention is that emotions lead us to material desires, anger, frustration, envy, pride, and greed, so overcoming emotions—through knowledge—must be the purpose of religion. The contention is also that if one only absorbs oneself in theoretical knowledge but has no emotions then there can be no happiness, and one's life becomes 'dry' through 'speculation'. Factually, both these positions are right and wrong. They are right because knowledge is indeed necessary to conquer one's material emotions, but just knowledge is inadequate to bring happiness and fulfillment. They are both wrong because knowledge and emotion are *necessary* but insufficient conditions for true religion. Devotion without knowledge is blind faith, and knowledge without devotion is dry mental speculation. They have to be combined because the soul is *sat*, *chit*, and *ananda*, and it needs *chit* or knowledge just as it needs the *ananda* or happiness of emotion.

Indeed, knowledge must pertain to something to which our awareness has to be directed and happiness must come from knowing the other. There is no contradiction between knowledge and emotion in religion, although there can be differences of emphasis. The emphasis can choose a type of relation to obtain a particular perspective out of the knowledge of the whole reality. The knowledge, therefore, pertains to the whole, the relation pertains to a part of the whole, chosen by the need for a particular type of pleasure.

Knowledge and emotion are reconciled when reality is known from a chosen perspective. To allow for this reconciliation, reality must have many aspects or perspectives, enabling a choice of a perspective. The conflict between knowledge and emotion emerges if one posits that there is only one view of reality—as the impersonalist does—and hence there is no choice in picking that reality, and hence there can be a role for emotion to make that choice. Effectively, the conflict between knowledge and emotion is an outcome of the impersonalist view that reality is devoid of diversity.

The personalist view, instead, says that there is a reality with many aspects; that the soul has the free will to choose an aspect. You must have both—i.e. a single original reality, and many individual perspectives on that reality—to avoid the pitfalls of impersonal universalism and individual relativism. The individual knows a chosen part of the whole and enjoys the choice of a perspective as well as the truth of the fact that the knowledge pertains to reality. There is universalism because there is a reality, but there is also individualism because there is a choice about which part of reality is experienced. The debate between individualism and universalism emerges only when we see many parts but not the whole, or the whole without any part.

Materialism sees the parts but doesn't see the whole. The impersonalist sees the whole but doesn't see any part. As a result, the choice of parts is attributed by the impersonalist to be a material desire, and the view of the whole without the parts is seen by the materialist as devoid of individuality. The debate between emotion and knowledge is therefore a flawed one, although the debate can only be dissolved by going to the whole-part view of reality. The problem in adopting this view of reality is that we want two contradictory things: (1) we want the self and the reality to be separate and independent things because without that separation there is no free will, and (2) we know that if there is a reality then we must also be parts of that reality. So, how can the self be part of reality and separate from that reality?

God and Reality

This problem can be resolved when reality is described as an inverted tree. The root of the tree is the whole, and the branches, twigs, and leaves are parts of the reality. In one sense, they are parts of the whole, but in another sense the branches, twigs, and leaves are separate from the root. This idea presents a paradox in the physical view of part and whole, where the whole is physically bigger than the parts. But this idea becomes very easy if both the whole and the part are treated semantically as concepts, in which the whole is the abstract concept and the parts are detailed concepts. Consider the idea of a 'universe'. What does this idea comprise? Does it only denote a *collection* of things, such that the universe is reducible to the collection? Or does it denote something that exists independent of the things that comprise it?

In the physical treatment, the universe is the collection of things, because we see the world as things. But in the semantic approach, even the things we see are ideas, and the smaller things we see are produced by dividing the universe into parts. This division is produced by *adding* details to the outline, where the outline is the root, and the details and the branches. The outline can exist when the details don't, and in that sense, the outline is independent of the details. However, the details cannot exist if the outline doesn't exist, and in that sense the details depend on the outline, although they are distinct from the outline. Thus, we arrive at a new understanding of the whole-part relationship in which the part depends on the whole but is separate from the whole. The whole however is separate from the parts and doesn't depend on it. From the perspective of the part, the part is separate from the whole and yet dependent on it. From the perspective of the whole, the part is still separate and the whole doesn't depend on the part. So, in both cases we can say that the whole and part are separate, and yet, the part cannot exist without the whole, so the part is actually tied to the whole.

The whole and the part are always distinct individuals, but they are also *joined* by the whole-part relation, just as a branch grows from the root. The root is a more abstract concept—e.g. a table—and the branch is the detailed concept—e.g. the leg, back or seat of a table. Both exist as ideas, and the idea of a table can exist even when no table exists. Similarly, when the table exists and has a leg, the leg is created from the detailing of the idea of a table.

There are three distinct trees and the root of all three is God. The souls are the branches from one of the trunks of this tree, and their material bodies are branches from a separate trunk. When they combine, the soul considers himself to be the root and the body to be the branches of itself. This identification with the body is considered an illusion, because even the body we inhabit is a property of God, rather than the property of the soul.

God is the origin of all that exists, but God is independent of the branches (souls) but the branches (souls) are not independent of the root (God). This relation between soul and God, between soul and matter, and between God and matter, is the subject of *Vedanta philosophy* and the whole-part relationship has been explained by many terms such as *Advaita* (the soul and God are not separate), *Viśiṣṭādvaita* (the soul and God are part and whole, but the part is dependent on the whole), *Dvaitādvaita* (the soul and God are separate and inseparable), *Śuddhādvaita* (that they are one because they have the same three qualities—*sat*, *chit*, and *ananda*), *Dvaita* (that soul and God are separate individuals who have their respective free wills), and *Acintyabhedābheda* (that soul and God are simultaneously different and non-different).

All these descriptions can be reconciled in the understanding that God is the root of the tree, the souls are branches of trunk called the *tatastha śakti* or marginal energy, and their bodies are branches of another trunk called the *bahiranga śakti* or the external energy. Each of these trunks also divides into three parts rooted in the *sat-chit-ananda* of God. Each soul is, therefore, *sat-chit-ananda*, and the material reality is also comprised of relations, possibilities, and purposes. The entire universe can be grasped by *sat-chit-ananda* that develops into a tree of pleasure, knowledge, and relationships. God, as the original truth, right, and good is the original *identity*. From this root new branches grow through the principle of *non-contradiction*. At this point, there are many things, but they are all consistent, and they are continuously growing. At some point in this development, the principle of *mutual-exclusion* is added and we obtain the material world that is created and destroyed.

The addition of mutual-exclusion to a diversified non-contradictory reality is the 'covering' of the soul by the material illusion which leads to the false idea that the living entities are unrelated and hence independent. The soul also thinks—due to the principles of mutual-exclusion—that he is independent of God. This results in competition and denial of other's individuality and choice. However, since mutual-exclusion is only added on non-contradiction, there is always a spiritual reality underlying the material conflicts, and in that sense the material world is not the only type of existence possible.

In the material world, we can see all three principles of identity, non-contradiction, and mutual-exclusion. As we rise above this material reality, we can see a world of non-contradiction with a modified understanding that we are parts of a whole. Beyond these worlds is the original identity from which everything is expanded. The world of non-contradiction is also divided into three parts based on the level of happiness derived in each part (called *Brahman*, *Paramātma*, and *Bhagavān*) and the entire existence has four parts of which three are eternal and one part (the material world) is temporary.

God is the original capacity for relationship (awareness), knowledge (concepts and activity), and purpose (pleasure). He is the root of the eternal and temporary branches of the tree. He is the original reality from which many eternal and temporary parts are created. The soul is an eternal individual, while the material reality is temporary. God's *ananda* or pleasure is the origin of time; it manifests in changing relations by which the soul enjoys pleasure in the eternal world, and in the changing relations and objects by which the soul enjoys and suffers in the phenomenal world. God's *chit* is the origin of all eternal and phenomenal bodies which exist as the abilities to know and act; the senses of knowledge and action are the separated forms of *chit*, but at the level of mind, intellect, ego, and morality, these abilities are unified. God's *sat* is the ability to relate to other things and become aware of them; *sat* is the cause of our consciousness and relationship to things.

The *sat*, *chit*, and *ananda* are always combined to create experience. Thus, in the material world, the possibilities, purposes, and relations combine to produce a phenomenal event. Similarly, in the real world, the body is utilized by a purpose to interact with other bodies. The understanding of God is non-different from the knowledge of the soul, and of the eternal and phenomenal worlds in the sense that once we grasp the three features called *sat*, *chit*, and *ananda*, and how they expand in a tree—from root to leaf—we can understand everything in this world and beyond. The study of the phenomenal world can enlighten us about the nature of God, not because the material world is itself God, but because the principles of *sat*, *chit*, and *ananda* exist both in this world and in God. The goal of this knowledge is happiness, and as we climb up the tree of experience, the happiness grows commensurately.

Epilogue

We all seek explanations of why things happen, but there are three kinds of explanations one can offer. First, you can describe the material state of an object, and attribute the causality to that state. This works well for material objects but not so well for humans where we do things because we are socially expected and morally bound to do them in a certain way depending on our role in society. Thus, you cannot say that you pulled the trigger on a gun because the gun was capable of firing; you must also rationalize that action based on your role and responsibility in society. Finally, we have the choice to pick roles and decide whether to fulfill the expected behaviors of the roles and responsibilities and therefore we can explain our action based on goals and purposes—namely that we want to be in a certain future state.

The state of an object is what the object is by itself—i.e. a possibility of being many things. The role of a person selects some states out of the many possible states, and you can attribute the selection to the role. Finally, we also *want* to be in a chosen state, and you can explain your action by attributing it to the goal. We can distinguish these explanations as *causes*, *reasons*, and *justifications*. The material state is the cause, but it exists as an ability to do things. The role is the reason why we are expected and morally obliged to do certain things, and it selects an ability out of the possibilities. Finally, our goals are the justifications for why we even take up a role—namely, that we perform a role because we have some ulterior motives that we would like to fulfill.

Each of these explanations is real, although in different ways. The material state constitutes what an object is by itself. The role is produced by the relation between objects. And the purpose is defined by the direction and destination to which we are headed. The problem is that in modern science we don't attribute causality to the role and the goal; we attempt to explain everything by the material state. Thus, questions of responsibility (toward others) and the moral questions of choice (for oneself) are outside scientific explanations. When the world exists as a possibility, then keeping the ethical and moral questions outside science makes science itself incomplete, because the world exists only in the state of possibility and cannot become anything definite. The incompleteness manifests in all areas of science from mathematics, to physics, biology, sociology, economics, and psychology itself.

In this book, I argued that emotion is tied to the moral question because based on emotion we make choices, based on what we consider good for ourselves. Ideally, these choices must be compatible with what is right—based on our roles and responsibilities toward others—because what seems good to us but is wrong according to our role, entails an ethical violation. Finally, what is moral and ethical must also be true—i.e. practically feasible, theoretically sound, and conceptually valid. The world affords us many possibilities. Some of these states are desirable, and of the desirables, a few are morally acceptable. We must choose that subset that is true, good, and right, which means removing many alternatives that are false, bad, and wrong.

We cannot study emotion in isolation. We can study it as the pursuit of happiness or the good, but after we have understood what is true and right. Pleasure that violates the conditions of our roles brings retribution. And happiness which stands on falsities is temporary. The good that is not right and true, therefore, will bring suffering or at best temporary happiness. The question of good cannot be answered without a profound understanding of the true and the right. In that sense, we cannot disentangle the study of emotion from the nature of possibility, and how this possibility is constrained by our roles and responsibilities. Goodness is that choice of alternative after we have eliminated the false or impossible, and the wrong or unethical. Since the good comes after this elimination, our choices are constrained by truth and rightness, and our pursuit of happiness must be limited by these restrictions.

In Vedic philosophy, the triad of truth, right, and good is called *satyam*, *shivam*, and *sundaram*, and it indicates the absolute and eternal reality. From this reality manifests the material world of falsities, wrongs, and sufferings. When science studies the truth, it will include even those truths which are not right, or not good or both. The study of all that exists or all that is possible should not be the goal of science. The goal must be to find all that is true, right, and good. The ethical and moral questions—i.e. separating right from wrong and good from bad—are fundamental for two reasons: (1) without a separation science remains incomplete, and (2) our life remains unhappy. Happiness in life and the incompleteness of science are intricately connected and constitute the problem to be solved. We cannot complete knowledge and then seek happiness. We must rather find how we can become happy to even know what it means to complete scientific knowledge.

Most people falsely consider emotion to be a subfield of psychology, which is a subfield of neurology, which is a subfield of biology, which is a subfield of chemistry, which is a subfield of physics, which is a subfield of mathematics, which is a subfield of logic, and because logic only deals with questions of truth, the questions of right and good are left out of science.

The surprise is that logic only deals with concepts, and all concepts are always possible. They don't become real unless combined with a choice based on the sense of good, which must be right for the good to persist. In that sense, the logic of truth is incomplete and everything else that follows from it is incomplete too. We need to complement the study of truth with that of right and good. But that study cannot emerge from conceptual analysis. We have to look deeper inside and see why emotions are different from concepts, and then deeper outside to uncover why relations are different from both concepts and emotions. There is a logic—waiting to be uncovered—that combines truth, right, and good. From that logic will emerge a new mathematics, a new physics, a new chemistry, a new biology, and a new psychology, that will tell us why all that exists is not necessarily right and good.

Of course, that may not be surprising because the world contains evil and ugliness. But, we will now be able to distinguish right from wrong, and good from bad, just as we today distinguish truth from lies. By that distinction will come right action, and with such action will come happiness.

Notes and References

PREFACE

1 Vedic texts are very extensive, and I don't expect anyone to have an in-depth knowledge of these texts. This book relies on a minimal core set of concepts from the Vedic texts, including—(a) the nature of the soul comprised of three parts called , , and , (b) the three qualities of matter called , , and , and (c) the consequences of actions called which too have three types called (good action), (bad action) and (no action). These concepts are described in many Vedic texts such as the Bhagavad Gita.

2 I use the terms 'pleasure' and 'happiness' interchangeably throughout the book. This is not to say that there isn't a difference between the two. The term 'pleasure' is generally used in relation to our senses—e.g. eating, smelling, seeing, sex, etc. The term 'happiness' is instead used for deeper feelings such as satisfaction, peace, contentment, fulfillment, etc. I use the terms interchangeably because they are both feelings, and as I describe throughout the book, they are organized in a hierarchy. The term 'happiness' therefore can be viewed as subtle or deeper feelings while the term 'pleasure' would indicate gross or superficial feelings.

1: EMOTION AND MATERIALISM

1 This idea was first propounded by John von Neumann in the attempt to explain the indeterminism of quantum theory. The interpretation postulated that consciousness is involved as a causal agent in "collapsing" the quantum wavefunction possibilities into a certainty. The reduction of the possibility to a reality was therefore caused by a conscious choice. The interpretation, however, suffers from classical mind-body dualistic theories unless we provide an explanation of how choice interacts with possibility. This has never been done so far, but it can be

achieved if—as I have noted—we acknowledged as a new kind of material reality that exists in the present materially but to something in the future. The so-called "collapse" would now be caused not by a non-material "choice" but by a material "purpose"—a new material category.

2   Neumann, John von (1932). "Mathematical Foundations of Quantum Mechanics". Princeton: Princeton University Press.

Wigner, Eugene; Henry Margenau (1967). "Remarks on the Mind Body Question, in Symmetries and Reflections, Scientific Essays". American Journal of Physics. 35 (12): 1169–1170.

3   Bell, John (1987). "Speakable and Unspeakable in Quantum Mechanics". Cambridge: Cambridge University Press.

4   This follows from Bell's Theorem where current quantum theory is "complete" in the sense that there are no additional "hidden variables" that can be conceptually described or empirically measured; addition of any such variables leads to contradictions in the quantum theory. Quantum theory is therefore complete, and yet it is incomplete. This problem can be addressed if the prediction involved in addition to .

5   Schrödinger, Erwin (1926). "An Undulatory Theory of the Mechanics of Atoms and Molecules". Physical Review. 28 (6): 1049–1070.

6   Barile, Margherita. "Orthogonal." MathWorld website. Retrieved from http://mathworld.wolfram.com/Orthogonal.html

7   Born, Irene (translator) (1971). "The Born-Einstein Letters, 1926". Letter to Max Born. New York: Walker and Company.

8   Einstein, Albert (1916). "Relativity: The Special and General Theory" (Translation 1920). New York: H. Holt and Company.

9   Dalarsson, Mirjana; Dalarsson, Nils (2015). "Tensors, Relativity, and Cosmology" (2nd ed.). Academic Press. p. 106-108.

10   Rovelli, Carlo (2008). "Quantum gravity". Scholarpedia website. 3(5):7117. Retrieved from: http://www.scholarpedia.org/article/Quantum_gravity

11   Miller, David (1997). "Popper Selections". Princeton: Princeton University Press.

12   Popper, K. R. (1994). „Zwei Bedeutungen von Falsifizierbarkeit [Two meanings of falsifiability]". In Seiffert, H.; Radnitzky, G. Handlexikon der Wissenschaftstheorie (in German). München: Deutscher Taschenbuch Verlag. pp. 82–85.

13   Dalela, Ashish (2014). "Quantum Meaning". Shabda Press.

14   Dalela, Ashish (2015). "Moral Materialism". Shabda Press.

15   Ideally, we are required to keep the name and the concept separate. But in classical physics, each particle was uniquely identifiable by its properties—position and momentum. In ordinary description, we continued to use the term 'particle'—as something that 'joined' its properties together—but this joining was not mathematically relevant if expressed the properties as a tuple—e.g. { , }. The particle corresponds to the braces that bind and together, but the braces are only human conveniences, not mathematically relevant. In ordinary language, however, we continue to use to identify quite separate from their properties because our awareness establishes a relation to the object in addition to its properties. We don't have to necessarily call the object by a proper noun; we also use pronouns such as "this" and "that" to refer to objects. This reference is necessary before we attribute the object properties (e.g. color). The reason that classical physics was able to discard the idea of a 'particle' separate from its properties is that the particle was now equated to the —the particle continued through a succession of states—and if you could establish that succession clearly (through mathematical laws such as the law of gravitation) then the state sufficed. The succession required determinism, so if determinism collapses, then the trajectory is not definite, which means that now you need to reinstate the idea of an separate from its properties. In an everyday sense, for example, the child grows into a man, and the properties change—e.g. the small body becomes a big body—but we say that the is unchanged because we want to the child's body into the adult body via a trajectory. If our life is not deterministic, then a is separate from the observed properties.

16 Goals are typically used for short-term targets while purpose is used for longer-term (sometimes lifelong) intentions. The longer-term intentions are deeper while the short-term targets are shallower. Nevertheless, we can talk about both of them in the same breath because they are both intentions for the future.

17 Rindler, Wolfgang (2011). Special relativity: kinematics. Scholarpedia website. 6(2):8520. Retrieved from http://www.scholarpedia.org/article/Special_relativity:_kinematics

18 The full quote, credited to Einstein, is as follows: "Though religion may be that which determines the goal, it has, nevertheless, learned from science, in the broadest sense, what means will contribute to the attainment of the goals it has set up. But science can only be created by those who are thoroughly imbued with the aspiration toward truth and understanding. This source of feeling, however, springs from the sphere of religion. To this there also belongs the faith in the possibility that the regulations valid for the world of existence are rational, that is, comprehensible to reason. I cannot conceive of a genuine scientist without that profound faith. The situation may be expressed by an image: science without religion is lame, religion without science is blind".

See Einstein, Albert (1949). "The World as I See It". New York: Philosophical Library.

2: THEORIES OF EMOTION

1 Pajares, Frank (2002). "Biography, Chronology, and Photographs of William James". Retrieved from: https://www.uky.edu/~eushe2/Pajares/jphotos.html

2 Snorrason, E (1973). "Carl Lange". Dictionary of Scientific Biography. 8: 7–8.

3 Cannon, Walter (1927). "The James-Lange Theory of Emotions: A Critical Examination and an Alternative Theory". The American Journal of Psychology. 39 (1/4): 106–124.

4 Gardner, L. (ed.) (1989.) "A history of Psychology in Autobiography (vol. VIII)". Stanford University Press.

5   Gruneberg E. Neil (2010). "In Appreciation: Jerome E. Singer". Observer. Association for Psychological Science. 23 (7).

6   Schachter, S.; Singer, J. (1962). "Cognitive, Social, and Physiological Determinants of Emotional State". Psychological Review. 69: 379–399.

7   Benison, Saul; Barger, Clifford A.; Wolfe, Elin L. (1987). "Walter B. Cannon: the Life and Times of a Young Scientist". Belknap Press.

8   Mader, S. S. (2000). "Human biology". McGraw-Hill.

9   Cannon, Walter Bradford (1915). "Bodily Changes in Pain, Hunger, Fear, and Rage". New York.

10   Chahine, Lama; Kanazi, Ghassan (2007). "Phantom limb syndrome: A review". MEJ Anesth. 19 (2): 345–55

11   Scherer, K. R., & Shorr, A., & Johnstone, T. (Ed.). (2001). "Appraisal processes in emotion: theory, methods, research". Canary, NC: Oxford University Press.

12   James, William. (1890). "The Principles of Psychology". Psychlassics. Retrieved from: http://psychclassics.yorku.ca/James/Principles/prin25.htm

13   This issue is called in philosophy of science.

3: EMOTION AND PERSONALITY

1   A physical space is one in which objects are identified purely by their physical properties. A semantic space is one in which objects are identified by their meaning. Accordingly, "distance" in a physical space is physical and position is a physical properties. However, in a semantic space, "distance" indicates the difference in meaning, while location indicates the meaning. A location in space is therefore a physical entity but only like a symbol, which also has a meaning. I have extensively discussed the nature of semantic space in my earlier work. The reader can refer to books listed at the end to see a further discussion of this topic.

2   Galton, Francis (1884). "Measurement of Character". Fortnightly Review. 36: 179–185.

3   Gardner, Howard (1993). "Multiple Intelligences". New York: Basic Books.

4   Gardner, Howard (2017). "Biography of Howard Gardner". Howard Gardner website. Retrieved from: https://howardgardner.com/biography/

5   Goleman, Daniel (2017). "About Daniel Goleman". Daniel Goleman website. Retrieved from: http://www.danielgoleman.info/biography/

4: EMOTION AND BIOLOGY

1   "Hilbert space". Encyclopedia of Mathematics website.

Retrieved from https://encyclopediaofmath.org/index.php?title=Hilbert_space

2   My book *Moral Materialism* discusses this topic at greater length.

3   Erhart, Jacqueline; Sponar, Stephan; Sulyok, Georg; Badurek, Gerald; Ozawa, Masanao & Hasegawa, Yuji (2012). "Experimental demonstration of a universally valid error-disturbance uncertainty relation in spin measurements". Nature Physics. 8, 185–189

4   Griffiths, David J. (2004). "Introduction to Quantum Mechanics (2nd ed.)". Prentice Hall.

5   "Autoimmune disorders". MedlinePlus website. Retrieved from https://medlineplus.gov/ency/article/000816.htm

6   Aguirre-Ghiso, Julio A. (2007). "Models, mechanisms and clinical evidence for cancer dormancy". Nature. 7, 834 – 846.

7   Everson, Tilden ; Cole, Warren (1968). "Spontaneous Regression of Cancer Philadelphia". Philadephia: JB Saunder & Co.

8   Schrödinger E (1935). "Discussion of probability relations between separated

systems". Mathematical Proceedings of the Cambridge Philosophical Society. 31 (4)

9 Carroll, Sean (2007). "Guidebook. Dark Matter, Dark Energy: The dark side of the universe". The Teaching Company.

10 Morii, T.; Lim, C. S.; Mukherjee, S. N. (2004). "The Physics of the Standard Model and Beyond". World Scientific.

11 Low, Phillip (2017). "Overview of the Autonomic Nervous System". Merck Manual Consumer Version. Merck Manuals website. Retrieved from http://www.merckmanuals.com/home/brain-spinal-cord-and-nerve-disorders/autonomic-nervous-system-disorders/overview-of-the-autonomic-nervous-system

12 Araiba, Sho (2019). "Current diversification of behaviorism". Perspectives on Behavior Science. 43 (1): 157–175

13 Fuchs, Eberhard; Flügge, Gabriele (2014). "Adult Neuroplasticity: More Than 40 Years of Research". Neural Plasticity.

14 Lashley, K. S. (1929). "Brain Mechanisms and Intelligence". Chicago University Press.

15 Dembski, William; Behe, Michael (1999). „Intelligent Design". Downers Grove, IL: IVPress Academic.

Meyer, Stephen (2009). "Signature in the Cell: DNA and the Evidence for Intelligent Design". New York: HarperCollins

16 Perakh, Mark (2003). "Unintelligent Design". New York: Prometheus Books.

17 Tolman, R. C. (1938). "The Principles of Statistical Mechanics". Dover Publications.

18 Plesch, Martin et al (2014). "Maxwell's Daemon: Information Versus Particle Statistics". Scientific reports vol. 4.

19 Zeh, Heinz-Dieter (1970). "On the Interpretation of Measurement in Quantum Theory". Foundation of Physics. Vol. 1, pp. 69-76.

20 Kellert, Stephen H. (1993). "In the Wake of Chaos: Unpredictable Order in Dynamical Systems". University of Chicago Press.

21 Such changes are sometimes called "phase transitions".

22, 23   Gladwell, Malcolm (2008). "Outliers". Boston: Little, Brown and Company.

24 Jaffe, R.L.; Taylor, W. (2018). "The Physics of Energy". Cambridge University Press.

25 "Universe 101: Big Band Theory". NASA website. Retrieved from https://map.gsfc.nasa.gov/universe/uni_fate.html

26 Stevenson, Ian (2000). "Children Who Remember Previous Lives: A Question of Reincarnation". Jefferson, NC: McFarland & Co Inc.

27 "Shiva Samhita". Chapter 3, verse 57.

28 Dawkins, Richard (1978). "Replicator Selection and the Extended Phenotype". Ethology.

29 Burkhardt, Richard W. "Jean-Baptiste Lamarck". Encyclopedia Britannica website. Retrieved from https://www.britannica.com/biography/Jean-Baptiste-Lamarck.

30 Richter F. C. (2015). "Remembering Johann Gregor Mendel: a human, a Catholic priest, an Augustinian monk, and abbot". Molecular genetics & genomic medicine, 3(6), 483–485.

31 Dupont, Cathérine; Armant, D. Randall & Brenner, Carol (2009). "Epigenetics: definition, mechanisms and clinical perspective". Seminars in Reproductive Medicine. 27 (5): 351–357.

32 Turner, Kelly A. (2014) . "Radical Remission". New York: HarperOne.

5: THE EMOTIONAL BASIS OF SOCIETY

1 "Uncle Ben (Cliff Robertson)". Spider-Man Films Wiki website. Retrieved from: http://spiderman-films.wikia.com/wiki/Uncle_Ben_(Cliff_Robertson)

2 "Spider-Man (film)". Spider-Man Films Wiki website. Retrieved from: http://spiderman-films.wikia.com/wiki/Spider-Man_(film)

3 Wightman, A.S. (1995). "Eugene Paul Wigner 1902–1995". Notices of the American Mathematical Society. 42 (7).

4 Wigner, Eugene (1960). "The unreasonable effectiveness of mathematics in the natural sciences. Richard Courant lecture in mathematical sciences". Communications on Pure and Applied Mathematics. 13: 1–14.

5 Isham, Chris J (1995). "Lectures on Quantum Theory: Mathematical and Structural Foundations". Imperial College Press.

6 Schrödinger, Erwin (1926). "An Undulatory Theory of the Mechanics of Atoms and Molecules". Physical Review. 28 (6): 1049–1070.

7 Popper, Karl (1994). "The Open Society and Its Enemies". Routledge Classics.

8 Foster, Richard; Kaplan, Sarah (2001). "Creative Destruction", New York: Doubleday.

9 The therefore opens with the statement which means "Now, therefore, we must inquire into the nature of reality". The meaning of "now" is the human form of life. The word "therefore" means that only in the human form of life this inquiry can be carried out. There is hence a finality and urgency because in other forms of life one could not perform this inquiry, and since the human form is one of the many forms, the inquiry is urgent.

6: EMOTION AND RELATIONSHIPS

1. Johns, Oliver Davis (2005). "Analytical Mechanics for Relativity and Quantum Mechanics". Oxford University Press.

2 The term 'narcissistic' generally has negative connotations because a person loves himself or herself, not anyone else. However, such a person cannot live without the other, because we still need to eat, live, work, learn, and play—which involve something other than the self. Narcissism in such cases is merely exploitation of the others for selfish ends, and it is not true narcissism in which a person is completely self-absorbed without needing or depending on anyone else. 's narcissism is different because He is independent of everyone else and doesn't need to use anyone for His pleasure. The term 'narcissistic' should therefore be viewed in this context, not in the conventional context of exploitation.

3 This dynamic between men and women archetypes means that polygamy is a natural outcome of the fact that a woman wants to take a man who is already loved by other women, but polyandry is unlikely because men don't want to take the same woman who has already been taken by other men. This is also reflected in the fact that women like an 'experienced' man—namely that he should have had the experience of being with other women. However, the men want a 'virgin'—a woman who has never been with another man. The fact that a man is liked by another woman excites a woman, but that prospect disappoints a man.

4 "Gaudiya Vaishnavism". Wikipedia website. Retrieved from: https://en.wikipedia.org/wiki/Gaudiya_Vaishnavism

7: THE SYMBOLS OF EMOTION

1 The multiple interpretability of words into meanings is one of the causes of incompleteness in modern science. I have previously discussed this issue in the book Gödel's Mistake, highlighting how logical contradictions emerge when a word is used to indicate a name and a concept (this is called Gödel's Incompleteness Theorem) or a concept and a program (this is called Turing's Halting Problem). By implication we can also create paradoxes when a word is alternately used to indicate a concept and a program. Similarly, there is potential for paradoxes between names and goals, goals and concepts, goals and programs, etc. or a chosen combination of these. The total number of such paradoxes is literally infinite, but

their root cause and fix is very similar—we must contextually determine whether a word is used to indicate a name (proper noun), a concept (common nouns and adjectives which denote the noun's properties), a program (verb), or a goal (something that lies in future or past). The use of such contextuality requires changes to logic—the logics employed currently are context-free, and they prove (or disprove) claims universally rather than contextually.

2   Bloch, Ethan D. (2011). "Proofs and Fundamentals: A First Course in Abstract Mathematics". Springer. pp. 8–9.

3   Cartoon movies, for instance, mock both love and fear. The character under love is shown to act stupidly by chasing the object of love and believing that someday that love will come to fruition. Similarly, the fearful character is depicted to overreact to all situations, foreseeing problems where none might exist.

4   Titon, Jeff Todd; Cooley; Locke; McAllester; Rasmussen (2008). "Worlds of Music: An Introduction to the Music of the World's Peoples". Cengage.

5   For instance in Vivaldi's Four Seasons concert, the composer has given a hint about the objects being transmitted by the music. Thus, if one knows this information before hearing the concert they may be able to correctly interpret the sounds as symbols of spring flowers growing, summer storms, autumn leaves falling or winter blizzards. But most classical music pieces do not offer such direct hints in their titles, and hence the listener finds them harder to interpret.

6   de Saussure, Ferdinand (1986). "Course in General Linguistics". Chicago: Open Court.

7   Nuyen, A.T., 1992. "The Role of Rhetorical Devices in Postmodernist Discourse". Philosophy & Rhetoric.

8   Akadeniz, Can (2019)."Law of Supply and Demand". Introbooks.

9   For a detailed story of the rise of 'demand engineering' through advertising techniques in the past century see Wu, Tim (2016). "The Attention Merchants". New York: Alfred.A. Knopf.

10 The homogeneity and isotropicity of space is responsible for the conservation of physical properties called momentum and angular momentum. Similarly, the homogeneity of time is responsible for the conservation of energy. A quantity that is conserved becomes real in science—we can say that it really "exists" because it is preserved. Conversely, if a property is not conserved it is also unreal. However, if the conserved properties of modern science are based on postulates about the nature of space and time—namely that the universe is uniform in all places, and time is uniform in the past, present, and future—then the notion of reality based on the conservation of physical quantities is also subject to the truth of the uniformity. If this uniformity is false, then all conservation laws are false, and that would imply that those physical properties are not real facts of nature.

11 Penney, Robert (2003). "Class, social". In Christensen, Karen; Levinson, David (eds.). "Encyclopedia of Community: From the Village to the Virtual world, Volume 1". SAGE.

12 de Zwart, Frank (2000). "The Logic of Affirmative Action: Caste, Class and Quotas in India". Acta Sociologica, 43 (3): 235–249.

8: EMOTION AND RELIGION

1 Most of the New Age "religions" fall into this category because they recognize the temporary nature of experience, but they also equate the eternity with freedom from experience. The origins of this New Age thought lies in Buddhism and its response via . In both these cases, the individuality of experience is rejected, which means the soul—if at all it exists—is not a , doesn't have an eternal body and mind, and has no innate personality. The personhood is therefore only an illusion of the present material embodiment. This caricature of the religion carries the same assumptions about the nature of phenomena and reality, as far as the present experiences go—i.e. that reality may be objective, but at least our experience of that reality is an illusion. Some even go further to say that there isn't an objective external reality, or at least even if it existed there would be no way to know its nature. Ultimately, they are victims of the "outside-in" picture of nature in which reality—if it exists—is 'outside' the observer. In the more nuanced "inside-out" picture, the body and mind are coverings of the soul, but the body is projected from the mind, the mind is created from desires, and the desires are founded on a moral worldview—i.e. what is right and wrong. This moral viewpoint is called or

"religion" but everyone carries their person notion of in themselves. Real religion is one in which these personal notions of right and wrong are although not . That is, a person in the same role would have the same , so that is not just our choice, although the choice indeed pertains to fixing our role in the hierarchy.

2   Pais, Abraham (1991). "Niels Bohr's Times, In Physics, Philosophy, and Polity". Oxford: Clarendon Press.

3   Wheeler, John A. (1963). "No Fugitive and Cloistered Virtue—A tribute to Niels Bohr". Physics Today. Vol. 16 no. 1. p. 30.

4   Godlewski, E. and P.A. Raviart, P.A. (1991). "Hyperbolic Systems of Conservation Laws". Ellipses.

5   In contrast, the material memory is temporary and is created and destroyed; if you do render service to another person, he or she will eventually forget.

6   Miller, Scott; Childers, Donald (2012). "Probability and Random Processes (Second ed.)". Academic Press.

7 Varzi, Achille (2014). "Logic, Ontological Neutrality, and the Law of Non-Contradiction". De Gruyter.

Index

www.ingramcontent.com/pod-product-compliance
Lightning Source LLC
Chambersburg PA
CBHW032102280326
41933CB00009B/734